Public Finance and Economic Development of Natal

Public Finance and Economic Development of Natal, 1893-1910

Zbigniew A. Konczacki

Duke University Press
Durham, N. C.   1967

To my wife

The economic history of Natal has so far been largely neglected. The choice of the topic of this work, therefore, is influenced not only by my deep interest in the field, but also by the desire to fill one of the numerous gaps which still exist in the writings on the history of the economic development of Southern Africa.

To achieve the desired depth I have had to cover a fairly short span of time: 1893-1910, which coincides with the period of responsible government. During these years the impact upon Natal of the 1886 discovery of gold on the Witwatersrand was gaining in strength. It was largely this event which was responsible for the extension of Natal's government-built railway system and furthered various other developments.

A new era was initiated in the Colony by the granting of responsible government. By a strange coincidence, this event took place in the jubilee year: fifty years earlier Natal had come under British rule. Seventeen years later the Union of South Africa would be formed, with Natal as one of its four provinces.

As things are, the position of economic history is not too clearly defined vis-à-vis its close neighbors—that is, history and economics. But, if it is true that historians are interested in the relationships among particular collections of facts, then it should be profitable for an economic historian to make use of economic theory to test the hypotheses concerning such relationships. The ideal approach to economic history should be based on a judicious balance between the historical narrative and the use of what economics can offer in the way of analysis and the interpretation of facts. In following such a procedure, it should be possible to pay adequate attention to historical reality and to eliminate a bias toward concepts devoid of empirical content.

Of course, research work has its problems. In my case they were mostly created by the scarcity of statistical material. But in many instances the difficulty of submitting some facts to quantitative treatment did not mean that they could not be analyzed and explained.

I have hoped that the study of Natal's public finance would contribute to a better understanding of the nature of her colonial system as it evolved toward the end of the nineteenth century. The economic development of the Colony was primarily the concern of the white settlers. But the impact on the non-whites went much further than the mere consequences of the developmental activities would suggest. First of all, the web of the relationship between the whites and the tribal Africans must be seen in the context of the cultural and racial hierarchy peculiar to the imperial era. Economic policy based on these premises tended to secure the benefits of development to the privileged layer of the society. For such benefits to be produced, the non-whites had to pay a price in terms of their share in the national product, but above all in terms of the disruption of their tribal and family life: things which can hardly be measured in material terms.

Of necessity, I had to limit myself to those aspects of interracial relationship which could be handled with the tools of an economist and which remained within the scope of my study. My efforts were in the direction of putting in the right perspective the changes which affected over nine-tenths of the population of the Colony.

It has also been my intention to contribute to the knowledge of the methods used to stimulate economic development in that part of Africa during the late nineteenth and early twentieth centuries. The merit of such a record of past achievements lies in that it brings out the similarities and the differences between the old and the new.

Finally, as a result of my attempts to discover the basic attitudes influencing economic activity, I have suggested in my concluding remarks a rationale of the Natal type of colonialism. It has been presented in a form which combines economic, social, and political factors.

The subject matter of this book is arranged in four parts. The aim of Part I is mainly to remedy the paucity of the systematic work on the economic history of Natal. The first chapter provides a concise description of the Colony's economic structure and outlines its growth. It serves as a background for the remaining parts of this work. The second chapter gives a short history of Natal's public finance prior to 1893. It was necessary to fill that gap in order to acquire a better understanding of the subsequent period. I felt that a summary of my findings would serve a useful purpose. The legal basis of the government's financial decisions and the question of the participation of the various races in the running of the Colony required a few words of explanation. This has been done in the following chapter entitled "The Legislative Framework."

Part II deals with the variations in government revenue and expenditure. An attempt is made there to explain these variations in terms of the causative factors of both economic and non-economic nature. A separate chapter discusses the problems of the public debt, and the final chapter in Part II reviews and analyzes the various aspects of the administration and the efficiency of the fiscal system.

Part III deals with the main theme of this work—the impact of public finance upon the economic development of Natal. I am indebted for part of the framework used in the chapter on the impact of taxes on economic development to a study on *Public Finance and Economic Development in Guatemala* by J. H. Adler, E. R. Schlesinger, and E. C. Olson, which, in the absence of similar studies on Africa, served as a useful model. Of course one has to allow for differences in emphasis. A chapter analyzing the gross public capital investment in Natal concludes this part.

Part IV of the book embodies the conclusions.

The pleasant duty remains of thanking those persons who have helped me with their advice and criticism. It is hardly possible to acknowledge all the help I have received, but I should especially like to thank Professor S. Swianiewicz who provided valuable comments on an earlier draft of my work. I am mindful of the privilege of receiving the benefit of his knowledge and experience in the field of economic development.

I am grateful to Professor E. H. Brookes, Professor N. Hurwitz, and Professor G. J. Trotter, who gave me many stimulating ideas. Moreover, I am intellectually indebted to Mr. C. E. Axelson whose unpublished work, "The History of Taxation in Natal prior to Union," I was able to consult while engaged in my research in South Africa. Of course, none of the above persons is in any way responsible for any of the opinions I have expressed in this book.

I must also thank the staffs of the following libraries for their unstinting assistance: the Government Archives, the University of

Natal Library, the Natal Society Public Library at Pietermaritzburg, and the Public Library and Killie Campbell Collection at Durban.

I would also like to express my gratitude to the University of Natal for covering the traveling expenses between Durban and Pietermaritzburg necessitated by my research and to the institutions which contributed financially to the costs of publication. This work has been published with the help of a grant from the Social Science Research Council, using funds provided by the Canada Council.

Very special thanks are due to my wife, who typed the final copy and without whose encouragement this work would never have been completed.

Zbigniew A. Konczacki

London, July 1966

Contents

Tables

Part I

Part I

Chapter 1. The Growth of the Economy of Natal

Introduction

The germs of growth of the economy of which Natal's public finance later on formed an integral part date roughly from 1843, when the territory, after the short-lived Boer Republic of Natalia, was annexed by the British Crown. In 1856 it was granted colonial status with a limited form of representative government.

The initial development of Natal began in the coastal area, which enjoyed two important natural advantages. First, it had a rainfall of between thirty and fifty inches, very much higher than that in the midlands and the northern districts of the Colony. Second, it had one of the best harbor sites on the eastern coast of Africa. Thus the favorable climate attracted both the African pastoralist and the European farmer; the easy access from the sea fostered commercial activities with the outside world. Originally the economic development of the Colony was the result of the European immigration and the capital and skill brought by the new settlers. The discovery of diamonds in 1870 in Kimberley in the Cape Colony and the development of gold on the Witwatersrand in the Transvaal from 1886 provided powerful stimuli to the growth of the Colony.

Territory and Population

At first the territory of the Colony was not clearly defined. It was roughly bounded by the Umzimkulu River in the south, the Drakensberg Mountains in the west, and the Buffalo and Tugela rivers in the north. In 1865 a district south of the Lower Umzimkulu River was annexed and named Alfred County.[1] Prior to the territorial changes which took place toward the close of the century, the total area amounted to 20,460 square miles. The territory of the Colony increased to 35,370 square miles, or by 73 per cent, with the annexation of Zululand in 1897, and with the addition of the districts of Vryheid, Utrecht, and part of Wakkerstroom, as a result of the Treaty of Vereeniging in 1902.

The population of Natal consisted of the indigenous Bantu, the immigrant Europeans, a small group of persons of mixed race, called

1. Sir Charles Lucas, *A Historical Geography of the British Colonies* (Oxford: The Clarendon Press, 1918), IV, Part I, 252.

Coloureds, and the Indians, who were first brought from India in the 1860's as indentured workers to increase the Colony's labor force.

The early population data cannot claim any degree of accuracy. Even the two colonial censuses taken in 1891 and 1904, respectively, were confined to Europeans, Coloureds, and Indians, providing only estimated numbers for Africans.

Table 1.1. Population of Natal, 1852-1909

Year	Europeans		Coloureds		Indians		Africans		Total
	Per-sons 1000	Per cent	Per-sons 1000	Per cent	Per-sons 1000	Per cent	Per-sons 1000	Per cent	Per-sons 1000
1852	7.6	6.3	..	..	—	—	113.0	93.7	120.6
1859	11.6	7.2	..	..	—	—	148.6	92.8	160.2
1870	17.7	6.3	..	..	4.9	1.7	257.8	92.0	280.4
1880	25.3	6.2	..	..	18.9	4.6	362.5	89.2	406.7
1891	46.8	8.6	..	..	41.1	7.6	456.0	83.8	543.9
1904	97.1	8.8	6.7	.6	100.9	9.1	904.0	81.5	1108.7
1909	92.6	7.4	7.1	.6	118.7	9.5	1030.1	82.5	1248.5

Note: In this and the subsequent tables, a dash (—) is used where the item involved does not appear or is not significant and hence excluded; two dots (..) are used where the item exists but the data are not known.
Source: Natal, *Blue Books, Statistical Year Books,* and *Census Reports* of 1891 and 1904.

The 1891 census disclosed a population of 543,913, giving an average density of 27 persons per square mile. By 1904 the total population had increased to 1,108,754, with an average density of 31 persons per square mile. During the period under review the population increased by more than tenfold.[2] Between 1870 and 1909 the proportion of Africans fell from 92 per cent to 82.5 per cent, whereas, during the same period, the Indian population increased from 1.7 per cent to 9.5 per cent.

According to the 1891 census only 43 per cent of the total number of Europeans and Indians were born in Natal. African population growth was due to natural increase, the influx of pastoral tribes, and the return of Zululand refugees who had fled from Chaka,

2. This increase was, of course, partly due to the extension of the territory.

whose wars had greatly depopulated Natal prior to the coming of the Boers.

In the early fifties one-third of the small European population of Natal lived in the two urban centers of Pietermaritzburg and Durban. By 1891 54 per cent of the Europeans and 22 per cent of the Indians lived in towns; by 1904 their proportions had risen to 67 and 24 per cent respectively. Urbanized Africans in 1904 were estimated at 4 per cent of the African population of the Colony. In 1904 a little over one-tenth of Natal's total population were town dwellers.[3]

Table 2.1. Occupational Distribution of Europeans and Indians, 1891 and 1904 (*as percentages of total European and total Indian population*)

	1891		1904	
	Europeans	Indians	Europeans	Indians
Occupation				
Agriculture	7.1	33.5	7.6	30.5
Manufacturing and mining	14.2	14.9	15.5	12.5
Commerce and transport	6.5	.8	11.6	5.2
Public service and professions	7.6	.3	11.2	.5
Domestic services	1.6	3.6	1.9	3.7
Gainfully employed	37.0	53.1	47.8	52.4
Not gainfully employed	55.9	41.9	50.7	47.3
Unspecified and not adequately described	7.1	5.0	1.5	.3
	100.0	100.0	100.0	100.0
Total number	46,788	41,142	97,109	107,604

Note: In 1891 the 4,000 Coloureds were included with the Europeans. In 1904 the 6,686 Coloureds were included under the heading of Indians.
Source: Natal, *Census Reports*, 1891 and 1904.

Occupational distribution of Europeans for the given years is shown in Table 2.1. The occupational distribution in 1891 is somewhat marred by the large percentage of people enumerated under

3. *Blue Books* and *Census Reports*, 1891 and 1904.

unspecified and not adequately described occupations. However, it can be seen that the European occupational pattern was influenced by urbanization. Indian employment, on the other hand, was markedly rural. In the intercensal years Europeans engaged in manufacturing and mining increased by 1.3 per cent, while the number of Indians declined by 2.4 per cent. Employment of both races in commerce and transport was considerable. But again, a shift away from agriculture toward the tertiary industries was more noticeable in the case of Europeans than of Indians.

African occupations are not given in the 1891 census and those of 1904 were merely estimates: thus, of the 904,000 Africans in Natal in 1904, 56 per cent were employed in agriculture and mining, 4.5 per cent as domestic servants, and 2 per cent in manufacturing, commerce, and transport. The large number of Africans listed as employed is accounted for by the inclusion of peasant farmers.

Whereas the Europeans were pioneers in the economic field, the Indians came as immigrants to satisfy the labor requirements of the developing sugar cane plantations. Thus, in addition to the primitive Bantu civilization, two other dominant social and cultural groups emerged. The existence of these groups influenced the structure of Natal's economy and contributed to its complexity. The arrival of the Europeans laid the foundation for the new market economy which was superimposed upon the subsistence economy of the Bantu. Gradually increasing numbers of Indian immigrants and of wage-earning Africans were absorbed in the European sector.

In the sections which follow, a short outline of the development of the exchange sector of the Colony's economy is given.

Agriculture

During the early years of the Colony economic activity was, in the main, limited to agriculture. Africans practiced subsistence farming and were largely concentrated in the reserves set aside for them. It soon appeared, however, that the principal problem of the reserves was the shortage of land, which became more and more acute with increase of population.[4] The shortcomings of the reserve

4. E. H. Brookes and N. Hurwitz, *The Native Reserves of Natal* (*Natal Regional*

system gave rise to the problems of migratory labor, detribalization of a landless class of urbanized Africans, and the gradual spoliation of the reserves themselves. Some Natives acquired freehold land outside the reserved zones or Crown lands under long terms of payment, or leased European land on a quitrent basis. At the beginning of the twentieth century over 400,000 Natives lived as tenants on land belonging to private and often absentee European owners.[5]

African agriculture consisted of cattle breeding and the cultivation of staple crops for home consumption. Cash crops, which could have been produced within this framework of Native agriculture, were absent. Cash was necessary for the payment of taxes and rentals. In the districts where the Africans could depend on regular and plentiful crops, they could dispose of surpluses; in the remoter parts of the country proceeds were often insufficient to provide the necessary funds. Thus the main source of cash was labor. Already during the seventies a significant proportion of the African adult males worked for the Europeans for at least a part of the year.[6]

The transition of the European agriculture from an almost subsistence level to commercialized farming was made possible by opportunities for the export of international staples and the development of the internal market. The colonists utilized the coastal belt for the production of subtropical products, and the midlands for the production of maize, sheep rearing, and later for wattle and dairy products.[7] An internal market was created by an expanding population which was becoming increasingly urbanized.

Total area under cultivation was subject to wide year-to-year fluctuations, partly because of biological and climatic factors, and partly because of variations in export prices of staple products. Certain factors determining long-run trends were, however, discernible. Acreages cultivated were also influenced by population growth and changes in the profitability of certain export crops.

Survey, Vol. VII) (Capetown, London, and New York: Oxford University Press, 1957), chap. i.

5. The South African Natives: Their Progress and Present Condition, ed. the South African Native Races Committee (London: John Murray, 1908), p. 75.

6. C. W. de Kiewiet, The Imperial Factor in South Africa: A Study in Politics and Economics (Cambridge: Cambridge University Press, 1937), pp. 199-206.

7. N. Hurwitz, Agriculture in Natal 1860 to 1950 (Natal Regional Survey, Vol. XII) (Capetown, London, and New York: Oxford University Press, 1957), p. 9.

The total area under cultivation increased more than fivefold between 1870 and 1909. During the same period there was a marked increase in the acreages cultivated per capita by Europeans: from 2.08 to 4.88 acres. At the same time there was a slight fall from 0.56 to 0.48 acres cultivated per capita by the African population. The intensification of land utilization by Europeans reflected their interest in the large-scale cultivation of staple export crops. Too, animal husbandry played a prominent part in the development of Natal's agriculture. The African was per se a pastoralist: he was averse to restricting cattle numbers because of the high social value he placed on the size of his herds. The per capita decrease in African cultivation was the result of increased population which was not offset by increases of land utilization.

In the European sector wool production, which had its beginnings in the fifties, was superseded in value in the nineties by extensive beef production and the growth of dairying. Nevertheless, between 1870 and 1895 the number of cattle increased from 121,700 to only 229,500, whereas the number of sheep rose from 299,800 to nearly 952,000. The history of cattle farming was marked by heavy losses due to lung-disease in 1855, red water in 1875, and, most serious of all, the rinderpest of 1897. The latter was the cause of

Table 3.1. Land Cultivation in Natal, 1870-1909

Year	Europeans		Indians		Africans		Total
	1,000 acres	Per cent	1,000 acres	Per cent	1,000 acres	Per cent	1,000 acres
1870	36.8	20.1	..	..	145.9	79.9	182.7
1875	35.8	18.7	..	..	156.0	81.3	191.8
1880	81.0	27.2	..	..	217.1	72.8	298.1
1885	88.4	22.8	..	..	299.8	77.2	388.2
1891	85.8	21.9	..	..	305.4	78.1	391.2
1895	115.6	25.5	..	..	337.2	74.5	452.8
1900	176.7	27.8	38.3	6.0	421.4	66.2	636.4
1905	395.9	43.2	40.4	4.4	479.6	52.4	915.9
1908/9	451.6	45.5	42.0	4.2	500.0	50.3	993.6

Source: Natal, *Blue Books* and *Statistical Year Books.*
Note: The acreages cultivated by Asiatics and Africans were in the nature of estimates.

the sharp fall in cattle numbers, especially those owned by Natives. In Sir John Robinson's words, agriculture was hindered by many causes: "Plagues, locusts, drought, fire, storms, failing markets and a capricious labour supply—such are or have been some of the difficulties and drawbacks against which the settlers of Natal have had to contend."[8] To this one might add the policy which allowed large speculation in land. This tended to create an artificial scarcity of land for agricultural use. Prospective farmers with small capital resources were handicapped and immigration was also discouraged.[9] Agricultural progress was affected by the discovery of diamonds in Kimberley in 1870 and the exploitation of gold on the Witwatersrand in 1886. These mineral discoveries gave rise to the lucrative "overberg" trade, which induced many farmers to take up transport-riding. Consequently agriculture in Natal suffered, but in the long run it benefited by the expansion of inland markets for farm products.[10]

8. Sir John Robinson, A Lifetime in South Africa (London: Smith, Elder and Co., 1900), p. 92.

9. Hurwitz, op. cit., p. 20.

10. D. A. Farnie, "The Mineral Revolution in South Africa," The South African Journal of Economics, XXIV (June, 1956), 131.

Table 4.1. Livestock, 1870-1909 *(thousands)*

Year	Owned by				Total	
	Europeans		Non-Europeans			
	Cattle	Sheep	Cattle	Sheep	Cattle	Sheep
1870	121.7	299.8	378.5	46.3	500.2	346.1
1875	123.6	336.2	326.0	49.4	449.6	385.6
1880	149.9	377.6	324.3	23.6	474.2	401.2
1885	160.6	500.3	440.4	35.2	601.0	535.5
1890/1	169.8	804.9	516.8	22.6	686.6	827.5
1894/5	229.5	951.9	508.9	19.3	738.4	971.2
1900	202.6	530.8	147.0	55.7	349.6	586.5
1905	273.4	587.2	510.5	182.4	783.9	769.6
1909	210.4	917.0	282.8	152.0	493.2	1,069.0

Source: Natal, *Blue Books* and *Statistical Year Books*.

Mining

Prior to 1890 the growth of mining in Natal was slow and its output insignificant. Prospectors were mainly interested in gold and coal. Gold diggings were, however, of minor importance: between 1884 and 1907, they produced only 4,770 ounces of gold.[11]

Coal, on the other hand, played a major role in the closing years of the Colony's existence. Although coal deposits had been known since the early years of the European settlement, they were not commercially exploited until the late eighties. An early obstacle to coal mining was the high cost of transport. Durban was its main market, but Natal coalfields were distantly situated in the districts of Klip River and Newcastle. The outcrops on the seacoast were of little commercial value. Ox-wagon transport was costly and highly seasonal, because of the state of the veld. In the early eighties coal which sold for 10s. per ton at the pit's mouth at Dundee, fetched 70s. in Pietermaritzburg.[12] Large-scale coal mining in Natal was made possible by the extension of the railway line in 1890 to the Newcastle coalfields. This development proved to be of mutual benefit. The railways could now purchase local coal at 10s. at the pit's mouth, instead of imported coal at more than four times that price.[13] Moreover, trains carrying goods up country could now carry coal on their return to the coast.

Coal output, estimated at 8,000 tons in 1888,[14] showed a tenfold increase by 1890, and fifteen years later it exceeded one million tons. With the exception of the two war years (1899 and 1900), when mining was seriously affected, output increased steadily. It is interesting to observe that from 1901 until 1909 output increased threefold as against a twofold increase in the labor force. This enhanced productivity was largely due to mechanical power, which rose from 3,306 HP in 1904 to 7,042 HP in 1908.[15] Despite the economic depressions of 1904 and 1909 the labor force continued to expand. It should, however, be remembered that a downward adjustment in coal railway rates, after the Anglo-Boer war, improved the

11. *Official Year Book of the Union of South Africa*, No. 29, 1956-7, p. 614.
12. L. C. A. and C. M. Knowles, *The Economic Development of the British Overseas Empire* (London: Routledge, 1936), III, 216.
13. *Ibid.*, p. 219.
14. *Sessional Papers* of the Legislative Assembly, 1898, p. 6.
15. *Statistical Year Book*, 1908.

competitiveness of the Natal coal.[16] The demand for coal, which was seemingly price-elastic, contributed to the maintained prosperity of coal mining. A significant proportion of output was consumed locally by the railways, and increasing quantities were absorbed by the bunker and export trade.

Manufacturing, Building, and Construction

The manufacturing industry was originally devoted to the processing of the agricultural products of Natal's economy. During the

16. Knowles and Knowles, op. cit., p. 220.

Table 5.1. Coal Mining, 1889-1909

Year	Output tons (1,000)	Value at pit's mouth (£1,000)	Coal-bunkered tons (1,000)	Coal-exported tons (1,000)	Number of workers employed	
					Euro-peans	Non-Europ.
1889	26	13	—	—	..	..
1890	82	41	—	—	..	..
1891	88	44	—	—	..	..
1892	142	71	—	—	..	..
1893	130	65	—	—	..	..
1894	141	76	—	—	..	..
1895	160	80	—	—	..	..
1896	216	108	—	—	..	..
1897	244	122	—	—	..	..
1898	388	175	195	—	..	..
1899	329	140	164	—	140	2,656
1900	241	241	136	—	160	3,017
1901	569	549	247	58	193	3,557
1902	593	513	227	13	228	3,904
1903	714	419	276	23	275	4,788
1904	858	457	384	112	283	5,627
1905	1,129	467	561	210	306	5,985
1906	1,239	524	487	362	327	6,264
1907	1,530	690	667	458	461	7,266
1908	1,670	737	711	553	483	7,879
1909	1,787	634	836	556	431	8,109

Note: The operations in 1899 were limited to nine months and in 1900 to seven months owing to the war.
Source: Natal, *Blue Books* and *Statistical Year Books.*

last three decades of the nineteenth century most of the manufacturing establishments were still those needed for the processing of the raw materials supplied by agriculture. Flour, corn, and sugar mills were numerically most important and were becoming increasingly mechanized. There were also beverage and drink manufacturers, coffee-processing plants, soap and candle factories, tanneries, wool-washing works, cotton gins, and mills for crushing wattle bark. Next in importance were plants supplying building materials. They included brick and tileyards, sawmills, etc.[17] Builders and contractors, first enumerated in 1904, accounted for 9 per cent of the workers of all races, and for over 21 per cent of Europeans employed in industry.[18] This also indicates that building activities must have been of significance. There were also several iron foundries and general engineering workshops and a number of coppersmiths and plumbers. Of particular importance were wagon-builders and blacksmiths, whose numbers rapidly increased when gold discoveries in the Transvaal made wagon transport a flourishing occupation.

Available statistics on the secondary industry prior to 1900 are limited to the enumeration of industrial establishments. No information concerning their size is provided. Between 1865 and 1900 the number of manufacturers rose from 200 to over 600.[19] Industry was growing, but its rate of growth cannot be accurately measured. From 1900 the colonial authorities attempted to provide more details on manufacturing. Unfortunately, a change in the definition of the minimum size of the firm in 1904 makes comparisons difficult.

As regards employment and the value of output, 1902 and 1903 were the peak years of war and postwar boom. The year 1904 marked the beginning of a slump which lasted until 1908. There was a decline in employment, which particularly affected the Europeans. Employment and output of the manufacturing industry reached their lowest point during 1907-8. The increase in horsepower and the value of machinery and plant indicated the growth of mechanization of manufacturing industry during 1904-6. A glance at Table 6.1 shows that in 1909 a revival took place, as indicated by the

17. *Statistical Year Books*, 1893/4-1909.
18. *Census Report*, 1904.
19. *Blue Books* and *Statistical Year Books*, 1865-1900.

increase in employment, horsepower, value of output, and value
of plant and machinery.

On the whole the manufacturing industry made little headway
during the nineteenth century and the early part of the twentieth.
Progress was hampered by the smallness of the market, shortage
of skilled and efficient labor, and lack of capital and cheap power.
Although gold mining in the Transvaal helped to enlarge the South
African market, it attracted skilled labor from other industries and
absorbed most of the country's capital. The only important source
of power in Natal, coal, became available in large quantities and
at reasonable prices at a fairly late stage in the history of the Colony.
Thus the increased demand for manufactured goods primarily increased imports from overseas. Although the Anglo-Boer war and
the period of reconstruction which followed gave a temporary
impetus to Natal's manufacturing, this was soon dampened by the
ensuing depression.

Table 6.1. Manufacturing Industry: Employment, Power, Value of Output, Land and Buildings, Machinery and Plant, 1900-1909

| Year | Number of estab-lishments | Employment | | HP of machine-ry 1,000 | Value of output £000 | Value of land & buildings £000 | Value of machine-ry & plant £000 |
		Euro-peans 1,000	Non-Euro-peans 1,000				
1900	615	4.9	17.1	. .	2,282	1,612	935
1901	658	5.4	20.6	. .	2,267	1,832	1,282
1902	644	7.4	21.5	. .	5,304	2,507	1,584
1903	625	7.1	21.0	. .	5,259	2,511	1,519
1904	770	4.6	18.7	13.5	3,744	3,138	1,376
1905	811	4.9	19.3	15.1	3,444	3,292	1,411
1906	828	4.6	18.7	15.2	3,444	3,523	1,485
1907	757	3.7	16.5	14.3	3,002	3,189	1,359
1908	838	3.6	17.5	14.7	2,985	3,145	1,299
1909	922	4.1	20.4	15.3	4,347	3,118	1,386

Note: Between 1900 and 1904 the returns included establishments where four or more persons
had been employed at any time during the year, or where an engine driven by steam, water, gas, or
electricity had been used irrespective of the number of persons employed. After 1904 the returns
included all establishments at which goods to the total value of £100 and upwards were manufactured
during the year under review.
Source: Natal, *Statistical Year Books.*

Natal was more interested in promoting the transit trade of the Transvaal and other inland territories than in developing its own secondary industry. Customs duties were kept low in order to encourage the overberg trade; protection of its own industries was not envisaged. Sporadic protection was afforded to some home manufactured goods through customs duties supplemented by insurance, freight, and other import charges.[20] Somewhat higher customs duties were introduced with the conclusion of the Customs Union with the Cape in 1898. The general customs duties were raised from 7.5 to 10 per cent with the extension of the Customs Union to the rest of South Africa in 1903, and in 1906 these were further increased to 15 per cent. This was claimed as a victory by the protectionists. These changes in the customs duties became a bone of contention between the manufacturing interests, which were not satisfied with the new level of duties, and the commercial and mining interests, which objected to them as being too high and hampering trade.

To assess the measure of protection enjoyed by industry, two more factors must be taken into account. First, the impact of tariffs was mitigated by Imperial Preference in the case of British goods. These enjoyed from 1903 a reduction of one-quarter of the actual duty, and after 1906 a flat rate of 3 per cent. Second, protection was strengthened by Natal's preferential railway rates, which favored local manufacturers. Railway rates favored finished articles and not raw materials. This, however, handicapped inland manufacturers using imported raw materials.[21]

Protagonists of secondary industry founded the Manufacturers Association of Natal in 1905.[22] They furthermore received encouragement from the report of the Industries and Tariff Revision Commission of 1906. This Commission aimed at encouraging the establishment of secondary industries. Also the report of the Customs Tariff Enquiry Commission of 1908 was unequivocally in favor of protective duties.[23] Not until the formation of the Union of South

20. A. J. Bruwer, *Protection in South Africa* (Stellenbosch: Ecclesia Printing Works, 1923), p. 75.

21. Knowles and Knowles, *op. cit.*, pp. 303-304.

22. *Fifty Years of Progress: The Development of Industry in Natal 1905-1955* (published by the Natal Chamber of Industries, 1956), p. 17.

23. A more detailed treatment of these issues can be found in Chapter 9.

Africa, however, was substantial progress in the field of secondary industry made in Natal.

Trade Relations

Natal was far from being self-sufficient in the production of some of the vital foodstuffs and of manufactured goods. The neighboring territories suffered from similar disadvantages. On the other hand Natal benefited from the harbor facilities of the Port of Durban. The Colony could, therefore, engage in the entrepôt trade with its neighbors and derive from it certain advantages. Thus the Port of Natal owed part of its prosperity to the trade with the Transvaal, the Orange Free State, Zululand, Pondoland, and Griqualand.

Complete records of the overberg trade are unfortunately lacking.[24] This was not remedied by the Customs Union of 1903, or by the establishment in 1905 of a customs statistical bureau whose duty it was to keep accurate records of trade statistics.[25] It is impossible to separate from the existing statistics the quantities and the values of goods imported for Natal and those for the neighboring territories.

24. In 1898 the collector of customs complained with respect to overberg trade that there was no legal power to require traders to supply the information necessary for the compilation of statistics (*Report of the Collector of Customs*, 1898, p. D. 3).

25. D. M. Goodfellow, *A Modern Economic History of South Africa* (London: Routledge, 1931), p. 20.

Table 7.1. Average Merchandise Imports and Exports of Natal, 1850-1889*

Five-year period	Average imports £000	Average exports £000
1850-54	112.6	27.1
1855-59	149.3	80.4
1860-64	454.4	153.0
1865-69	337.2	254.9
1870-74	777.5	594.1
1875-79	1,471.0	674.3
1880-84	1,978.2	816.5
1885-89	2,506.2	936.7

*Excluding bullion, specie, and raw gold.
Source: Natal, *Blue Books.*

Export figures were distorted by the inclusion of re-exports, some of which were produced in other South African territories, but were not statistically distinguishable from Natal's own products. Export figures are also incomplete because they exclude overland exports of Natal-produced goods which were not accounted for by the customs authorities. Until 1899 only goods subject to "transit dues" were recorded. With the implementation of the South African Customs Union in that year, other categories of goods such as goods exported under the Convention, and goods from open stocks which were free from Natal duty, were included in the records. This partly explains the increase in total exports (Table 8.1). Customs returns were accurate only with respect to the goods exported by sea because of the stringent control exercised by the controller of customs at the port.[26]

Another weakness of the foreign trade data arose from the change in the method of calculation after 1899. Thus the values before and after that year are not strictly comparable. Prior to 1899 imports were recorded at CIF prices, and afterwards at FOB prices.[27] The import and export data used in this study are the same as those given in the *Blue Books* and *Statistical Year Books*. It was considered inadvisable to recalculate the values of imports after 1899 at CIF prices because of the lack of reliable data.

The average values of merchandise imports and exports shown in Table 7.1 reveal two major trends. In the first place imports and exports were growing. A comparison of the first and the last quinquennium shows that during the forty years under consideration imports increased by over 2,100 per cent and exports by 3,350 per cent. In the second place, there was a tendency for imports to exceed exports, sometimes by a considerable amount. The most important factors for the growth of imports were the rapid population growth and rising standards of living in Natal and in the inland territories. Capital goods requirements of the Colony and those of the gold mining industry in the Transvaal accounted for much of the imports. Increased exports reflected the growing productive capacity of the Colony and the adjoining territories. In order to pay for the badly needed imports the Colony concentrated on the

26. *Report of the Controller of Customs, Blue Book,* 1890/1, p. D. 12.
27. *Report of the Collector of Customs, Departmental Reports,* 1899, p. D. 2.

exports of such staples as sugar, wool, and later, coal. Despite the gradual rise of manufacturing industries, the Colony's prosperity was strongly tied to the export of primary products.

It is probable that Natal suffered from deficits in its balance of trade[28] during the whole period of its colonial history. Capital imports of immigrants and private enterprise, government borrowing overseas, Imperial military expenditure, as well as the income from the heavy railway transport of goods to the Transvaal, helped to narrow the gaps in the balance of payments.

Briefly, fluctuations in the volume of trade were in part due to business fluctuations; additional factors from the 1880's were the

28. Excluding the trade of other territories passing through the Colony.

Table 8.1. Natal's Merchandise Imports and Exports, 1890/1-1909*

Year	Imports £000	Exports £000
1890/1	3,620.8	1,142.3†
1891/2	3,690.7	1,136.2
1892/3	2,456.6	1,104.0
1893/4	2,171.3	973.5
1894/5	2,370.0	990.7
1896	5,437.9	1,682.8
1897	5,983.6	1,603.7
1898	5,323.2	2,144.0
1899	5,359.3	2,625.0
1900	6,016.6	1,134.2
1901	9,723.0	4,140.0
1902	13,529.3	7,218.9
1903	15,274.1	9,315.5
1904	10,991.3	8,093.2
1905	10,968.5	9,152.5
1906	9,705.3	8,595.6
1907	8,704.2	8,218.0
1908	7,903.4	7,831.4
1909	9,251.5	9,273.4

*Excluding bullion, specie, and raw gold.

†This figure includes goods valued at £97,212 sent overland under the transit system during the period between January 1 and June 30, 1891. No record for the previous six months exists. In subsequent years the full annual value of this item was included.

Note: Data for the first five years were taken for a twelve-month period beginning July 1 and ending June 30 of the following year. From 1896 onward data were collected for the year beginning January 1.

Source: Natal, *Blue Books* and *Statistical Year Books.*

differing railway and tariff policies of the neighboring territories.[29] Thus the completion of the railroad between Capetown and Johannesburg in 1892 caused a diversion of Natal traffic with the Transvaal. The decline of trade lasted until Natal's railway reached the Witwatersrand toward the end of 1895. Again, Natal's accession to the South African Customs Convention in 1898 led to a marked improvement in the Colony's exports. This was largely due to the extension of the free trade in South African products over the Colony's territory.

The Anglo-Boer War, which broke out in 1899 and lasted until 1902, curtailed Natal's overland exports, but enhanced imports of goods required by the Imperial troops and the large numbers of refugees. During the postwar period large quantities of goods were needed by the Transvaal for reconstruction purposes. During the years of depression, which began in the second half of 1903, imports declined markedly. On the one hand, this was due to the deficiency of demand, and on the other, to the increase in the internal supply of commodities which previously had to be imported.

A detailed analysis of the geographical pattern of Natal's foreign trade can be found in Tables 9.1 and 10.1. During this period Great Britain was the principal source of imports. Politically and financially the Colony was largely dependent on the Mother Country. Until the middle nineties Natal's exports depended considerably on the British market, especially such products as wool, hides and skins, wattle, etc. From 1890, however, Britain's share of the total imports declined rapidly, whereas imports from other overseas countries increased in importance.

During the first decade of the twentieth century South African markets provided a rapidly expanding outlet for Natal goods and re-exports. Thus, between 1865 and 1909 the proportion of exports to Great Britain declined from 76.2 to 10.6 per cent, whereas exports of Natal goods and re-exports to South African territories rose from 19.4 to 69.7 per cent of the total value of exports. Imports reflect goods imported for Natal's own needs and also the re-exports to the adjacent territories.

Except for the year 1865, when the values of imported manufactured goods were unusually low and imported raw materials

29. See Chapter 5, pp. 65-70.

and semi-manufactures exceptionally high, the proportions between the different imports did not materially change. The dislocation of agriculture in Natal and the Transvaal in the war and postwar years accounted for the large imports of foodstuffs.[30] The outstanding feature of Natal's imports was the relatively high proportion of finished manufactures.

It must be borne in mind that exports tended to seem unduly low because of incomplete records. This was particularly the case prior to 1900.[31] The development of the gold mining industry in the Transvaal after 1885 resulted in a striking change in the proportion of the Colony's own exports and re-exports.

Table 12.1 not only reveals the dependence of Natal on a small number of staples, but also shows the changing nature of the economy. Originally, owing to the absence of other products, the young settlement had to turn its attention to the export of such commodities as ivory, ostrich feathers, and skins of wild animals; but already by 1865 sugar and wool were of major importance. Prior to 1900

30. Imperial government stores were not included in the total value of imports.
31. See Table 8.1.

Table 9.1. Geographical Pattern of Natal's Imports, 1865-1909 (*as percentages of value of total imports*)

| Year | Total | | Imports from | | |
	£000	%	Great Britain	South African territories	Other countries
1865	455.2	100.0	81.3	2.1	16.6
1870	429.5	100.0	84.6	5.0	10.4
1875	1,268.8	100.0	84.8	5.4	9.8
1880	2,336.6	100.0	84.8	5.5	9.7
1885	1,518.6	100.0	81.1	9.8	9.1
1890/1	3,620.8	100.0	79.7	6.2	14.1
1894/5	2,370.0	100.0	69.1	8.3	22.6
1900	6,016.6	100.0	61.9	15.7	22.4
1904	10,991.3	100.0	57.1	14.6	28.3
1909	9,251.4	100.0	51.4	11.5	37.1

Note: Total imports include imports for re-export to other South African territories.
Source: Natal, *Blue Books* and *Statistical Year Books.*

Table 10.1. Geographical Pattern of Natal's Exports, 1865-1909 *(as percentages of value of total exports)*

| Year | Total £000 | Exports to | | | Bunker coal & ships' stores |
		Great Britain	South African territories	Other countries	
1865	210.2	76.2	19.4	4.4	—
1870	382.7	68.0	26.6	5.4	—
1875	807.2	75.6	20.2	4.2	—
1880	890.8	72.0	22.7	5.3	—
1885	825.3	78.1	14.9	7.0	—
1890/1	1,142.3	75.1	11.6	13.3	—
1894/5	990.7	44.4	26.0	29.6	—
1900	1,134.2	14.4	57.4	15.3	12.9
1904	8,093.2	3.9	87.3	3.9	4.9
1909	9,273.4	10.6	69.7	12.9	6.8

Note: The above figures include re-exports. The commodity pattern of Natal's imports and exports is shown in Tables 11.1 and 12.1.
Source: Natal, *Blue Books* and *Statistical Year Books.*

Table 11.1. The Commodity Pattern of Natal's Imports, 1865-1909 *(as percentages of value of total imports)*

Year	Total £000	Food & drink	Finished manufactures	Raw materials & semi-manuf.	Other
1865	455.2	24.7	15.4	59.5	.4
1870	429.5	17.4	66.7	15.7	.2
1875	1,268.8	18.5	60.1	20.7	.7
1880	2,336.5	22.0	61.6	16.0	.4
1885	1,518.6	22.0	55.3	22.1	.6
1890/1	3,620.8	17.5	45.4	36.0	1.1
1894/5	2,370.0	19.1	50.7	28.6	1.6
1900	5,911.5	33.5	40.9	23.1	2.5
1904	10,991.3	32.1	38.6	27.6	1.7
1909	9,251.4	21.0	55.0	21.1	2.9

Note: Total imports include imports for re-export to other South African territories.
Source: Natal, *Blue Books* and *Statistical Year Books;* South African Customs Statistical Bureau, *Fourth Annual Statement of the Trade and Shipping of the Colonies and Territories Forming the South African Customs Union,* 1909.

Table 12.1. The Commodity Pattern of Natal's Exports, 1865-1909 *(as percentages of exports of South African products)*

Commodity		1865	1870	1875	1880	1885	1890/1	1894/5	1900	1904	1909
Sugar		38.0	31.0	23.1	25.7	18.6	1.6	9.5	27.4	15.4	16.0
Maize		.3	.3	—	.5	1.7	1.1	.1	10.4	5.0	9.4
Ostrich feathers		5.6	1.8	.5	1.1	1.0	.1	—	.2	—	—
Ivory		9.5	3.4	1.1	.8	.5	—	.1	—	—	—
Hides and skins		3.9	19.5	20.0	6.1	13.5	6.8	6.6	5.3	1.7	5.3
Wool		33.1	33.6	53.2	63.1	60.8	81.8	58.7	10.7	15.0	18.6
Wattle bark		—	—	—	—	—	.6	2.5	8.1	4.8	4.0
Coal		—	—	—	—	—	2.4	9.0	20.5	24.2	5.9
Other foodstuffs		4.5	8.0	1.6	1.0	1.5	1.4	3.6	9.2	19.5	12.9
Other commodities		5.1	2.4	.5	1.7	2.4	4.2	9.9	8.2	14.4	27.9
S. Afr. products*	%	100.0	100.0	100.0	100.0	100.0	100.0	100.0	100.0	100.0	100.0
	£000	201.5	359.1	733.6	839.5	777.6	899.0	698.4	571.4	1,931.3	4,890.0
Other (†)	£000	8.8	23.6	73.6	51.4	47.7	243.3	292.3	562.8	6,161.9	4,383.4
Total exports	£000	210.3	382.7	807.2	890.9	825.3	1,142.3	990.7	1,134.2	8,093.2	9,273.4

*Exports produced in Natal and exports from adjacent territories through the Port of Durban.

†Non-South African products re-exported from Natal to adjacent territories.

Source: Natal, *Blue Books* and *Statistical Year Books*; South African Customs Statistical Bureau, *Fourth Annual Statement of the Trade and Shipping of the Colonies and Territories Forming the South African Customs Union*, 1909.

they accounted for more than two-thirds of the exports. During the first decade of the twentieth century their proportion fell to one-third. During the nineties wattle bark and coal made their appearance; in 1904 coal contributed one-quarter of the value of exports. The twentieth century witnessed an increase of exports of maize and miscellaneous foodstuffs.

Table 13.1. The Development of Natal's Railways, 1875-1909

Year	Total mileage at end of year	Capital invested in open lines (£000)	Tonnage conveyed (000 tons)
1875	6	..	..
1880	82	..	..
1885	116	..	193
1890	285	3,651	302
1895	401	6,117	343
1900	567	7,808	1,092
1905	783	12,958	2,277
1909	987	14,161	3,005

Source: Natal, *Blue Books* and *Statistical Year Books.*

The Railways

In 1872 there were no railways south of the Sahara, with the exception of 150 miles in the Cape and two miles in Natal.[32] The year 1875 marked a turning point in Natal's history, for then a policy of railway construction and harbor development was decided upon.[33] Originally, railway building was stimulated by the opening up of the diamond fields and was oriented toward the Orange Free State. Prior to the discovery of gold in the Witwatersrand, railway expansion in Natal had been slow, and by 1885 only 116 miles of tracks had been laid down. Railway building was stimulated by the desire to share more effectively in the increasing Transvaal traffic and to exploit coal deposits in the districts of Dundee and Newcastle. By April, 1891, the line extended to Charlestown on the

32. S. H. Frankel, *Capital Investment in Africa* (London: Oxford University Press, 1938), p. 375.
33. Law No. 4 of 1875.

Transvaal border. When the negotiations with the South African Republic were successfully concluded in February, 1894, Natal railways were allowed to join the Transvaal railway system; this provided a direct connection with Johannesburg by 1895.[34] In the nineteenth century Natal railways were built mainly with a view to providing the shortest routes to the north. However, insofar as the main line touched agriculturally important areas, farming became more intensive and diversified. The wattle and the dairy industries in particular benefited from rapid and cheap transport.[35] During the first years of the twentieth century agricultural development became a conscious aim of railway policy. In order to serve agricultural areas flanking the main rail route, costly branch lines were undertaken. In 1909 the total mileage of the Natal railways was 987 miles, and the capital invested in open lines amounted to £ 14,161,000.[36] The tonnage of goods carried by the railway system rose from 192,500 tons in 1885 to over 3,000,000 tons in 1909.[37]

The construction of railways was financed by the government. In this respect Natal was no exception, as the Cape Colony in the south and Egypt in the far north of Africa built their railroads in a similar manner. The railways were regarded by the government as imperative for economic development. They enabled the Colony to compete with the Cape and Delagoa Bay in the inland trade. Being state-owned, they also served as a source of colonial revenue. After 1886 the net revenue of the railways grew steadily and by 1909 it reached £ 837,619. The railways created a new demand for land, labor, and capital. By ousting the ox-wagon, the symbol of the old way of life, they helped in the expansion of the internal and foreign trade of the Colony.

Banking

At the time when subsistence farming was in vogue, the scope of credit institutions was naturally limited. In 1850 British coin

34. J. Van der Poel, *Railway and Customs Policies in South Africa 1885-1910* (*Royal Empire Society Imperial Studies*, No. 8) (London: Longmans, Green and Co., 1933), p. 76.
35. Hurwitz, *op. cit.*, p. 12.
36. *Statistical Year Book*, 1909.
37. *Ibid.*

amounting to an estimated £25,000 was the circulating medium.[38] The Natal Fire Assurance and Trust Company, founded in 1849, carried out the first banking operations.[39] Five years later the Natal Bank was established. At that time the colonial authorities made a rough estimate of the coin hoarded by Europeans and Natives living considerable distance from towns. Hoardings apparently exceeded £50,000, whereas the coin in actual circulation amounted to some £15,000. Inland bills of exchange averaging £10,000 to £15,000 were also in use.[40] Because the Colony suffered from the absence of an organized market for credit, loanable funds were scarce and interest rates high.[41]

During the early sixties three local banks and two branches of expatriate banks were established. They were the Commercial and Agricultural Bank of Natal, the Colonial Bank of Natal, and the Durban Bank. Branches were opened by the Standard Bank of British South Africa and the London and South African Bank. Some of these financial institutions did not survive the severe economic depression of 1865-9. Others had to amalgamate, e.g., the London and South African Bank, which was merged with the Standard Bank. After 1877 Natal was left with the Natal Bank and the Standard Bank, which were soon joined by the Bank of Africa. Later on two other banks commenced business in Natal: the African Banking Corporation in 1892, and the National Bank of the South African Republic in 1895.[42]

By 1885 the amount of coin circulating in the Colony was estimated at £700,000, and the total note issue of the three then active banks amounted to some £28,500. Bank deposits, including time deposits, stood at £1,050,000. Changes in the note issue strongly reflected business fluctuations. During the postwar boom of 1902 the note issue rose to its highest level—£357,283; within four years

38. *Blue Book*, 1850.
39. E. H. D. Arndt, *Banking and Currency Development in South Africa (1652-1927)* (Cape Town: Juta & Co., Ltd., 1928), p. 296.
40. *Blue Book*, 1855.
41. In 1874 Mr. William Campbell (Davis's *Almanack*) wrote: "This was a poor country, and without credit . . . . The little money there was was under the control of a few, who gave or withheld as seemed to suit themselves; 12 per cent to 14 per cent per annum was the rate of discount at the banks 7½ per cent per annum to the merchant for his name to discountable paper . . . ."
42. The National Bank of the South African Republic subsequently changed its name to the National Bank of South Africa.

it fell to £93,283, the lowest figure recorded in Natal during the first nine years of the twentieth century.

The rapid growth of banking in Natal during the last fifteen years of colonial rule is indicated by the rise of the commercial banks' deposits from £2,481,020 to £3,823,157 between 1895 and 1909. During the same period the five banks operating in the Colony increased the number of their branches from eleven to thirty-five, thereby markedly improving the diffusion of banking facilities in the more distant parts of the country.[43]

The early currency and banking arrangements in Natal were characterized by two features which deserve particular attention. The first was the relatively low proportion of banknotes to coin in circulation.[44] The popularity of coins was due to the monetary habits of the public and the legislative measures which prohibited the issue of notes for less than £1. Moreover, total note issue of any bank could not exceed its paid-up capital, and a specie reserve of at least one-third of the issue was required.[45] Another interesting feature was the high cash-to-deposits ratio, which fluctuated between 38 per cent in 1895 and 24 per cent in 1908. This phenomenon is not uncommon in underdeveloped countries: in the absence of a lender of last resort and a short-term money market, the liquidity of the banking system can be secured only by the existence of considerable cash reserves kept by individual commercial banks.

On the whole the economic progress of Natal was in no small measure due to the activities of commercial banks. At times the banks, by expanding credit too freely, precipitated financial crises and also aggravated their intensity. But this was a common feature of the nineteenth-century banking systems.

A different type of credit institution was represented in Natal by building societies. The oldest and also the most important was the Natal Permanent Building Society, which began operations in the Colony in 1882. Between 1901 and 1909 the total assets of the building societies rose from £345,381 to £600,728.[46]

43. *Statistical Year Books.*
44. *Blue Books.*
45. Arndt, *op. cit.*, p. 451.
46. *Statistical Year Books.*

The Gross Geographical Product of Natal, 1903/4

At the beginning of the twentieth century the economy of Natal comprised four major groups of activities:

1. Food and raw-material production for local consumption.
2. The export of staples such as sugar, maize, wattle bark, hides and skins, wool, etc., as well as coal, which was Natal's only important mineral export.
3. Manufacturing, which was originally devoted mainly to food processing; later on it included such activities as the manufacture of construction materials, carriage and wagon building, manufacture of leather goods, etc.
4. Commerce, transport, banking, and other allied services, which developed rapidly toward the close of the nineteenth century and became a vital part of the whole system.

From the above the gross geographical product of Natal for the year ended June 30, 1904, can be estimated. The national product cannot be calculated from existing data. On the other hand, the concept of the geographical product provides a useful understanding of the structure of a given economy. The gross geographical product was calculated in order to add quantitative information to the descriptive matter thus far used. The choice of 1904 was due to the publication of a comprehensive census; it was also influenced by the fact that 1903/4 was a year of normal economic activity. It was followed by a depression which lasted until 1909. The gross geographical product for 1903/4 therefore provides a measure of the productive capacity of Natal's economy before it became an integral part of the Union of South Africa in 1910.

The output of the private sector of the economy amounted to £14.7 millions, or 83 per cent of the GGP. Agriculture, which employed four-fifths of the Colony's labor force, contributed only 20.8 per cent to the GGP. This extremely low average agricultural productivity was a distinctive mark of economic backwardness. "Manufacturing" and "other services" contributed 16.5 and 14.2 per cent respectively. The latter included financial and banking services, professions, and the earnings of domestic servants. Income derived from the ownership of private dwellings (11.4 per cent) was followed by "distribution," which contributed 9.6 per cent to the total. The importance of the entrepôt trade in the Colony's economy explains the large contribution of the distributive services. The importance of transport is, on the other hand, obscured in that the railway services are included under "government."

The value of the distributive and transport services depended largely on the volume of imports destined for adjacent territories. Of particular importance is the proportion of the GGP accruing to the European and non-European populations. On the basis of the detailed estimates[47] the Europeans' share amounted to £12.1 millions and that of the non-Europeans to £5.6 millions. In terms of per capita income Europeans earned £124.9.10 per annum. This contrasts sharply with the per capita income of £3.18.6 per annum for Africans, and £20.1.0 per annum for Indians.[48]

47. *Ibid.*

48. It must be remembered that the Europeans owned most of the factors of production other than labor, whereas the non-European earnings were largely limited to wages and the output of the subsistence sector. A comparison is made between the 1904 and 1936 per capita income of Africans and Indians. The figures for 1936 are given in the *Handbook on Race Relations in Southern Africa* (London: Oxford University Press, 1949, p. 347). The income figures for 1936 are re-valued at 1910 prices, since earlier price indices are not available. The modified figure for African per capita income in 1936 is thus £7.18.0 as compared with £3.18.6 in 1904. The latter figure was based on the concept of the GGP, and therefore excluded the wages of migrant laborers earned beyond the borders of Natal. The 1936 figure, on the other hand,

Table 14.1. **Estimate of Gross Geographical Product of Natal, 1903/4**

Source	£000	Per cent of total
Agriculture, forestry and fishing*	3,651.1	20.8
Mining	332.0	1.9
Manufacturing*	2,919.4	16.5
Building and construction	975.5	5.5
Distribution	1,685.9	9.6
Transport	586.8	3.3
Ownership of houses	2,018.4	11.4
Government*	2,973.8	16.8
Other services*	2,516.5	14.2
Total gross geographical product at factor cost	17,659.4	100.0

*See Appendix A, Table 5.

Thus a quantitative measure is obtained for the distinctive economies of the European and the non-European. The basic difference lies in the partial participation of the bulk of the non-European population in the market economy. The majority of Africans depended on a subsistence economy supplemented by seasonal employment in the European sector. Indians worked on plantations where money wages were supplemented by payments in kind, or in industry. Some cultivated land as small landholders, primarily to satisfy their own food requirements; any surplus was sold on the local market. A small proportion were shopkeepers or engaged in other occupations. The substantial difference between the per capita income and hence in the standard of living of the ethnic groups was initially due to wide differences in culture and economic background. In particular there was little contact between the groups; Africans were incapable of participating in commercial enterprises. They were also hampered by their primitive methods of farming.

Natal, after a half-century of development, still had a dual economy. Alongside a modern thriving exchange economy was ranged a subsistence economy burdened by traditional tribal life. A limited contact between the two economies was brought about by the imposition of taxes on Africans by the politically dominant European group.

---

was an average for the total African population of South Africa, and therefore included the relatively high wages earned by African workers in the Transvaal and in the Cape province. The difference can also be partly explained by the rise in real incomes between 1904 and 1936.

The 1936 per capita income for Indians, at 1910 prices, was £22.2.4, i.e., only £2.1.4 higher than in 1904. This small disparity can largely be attributed to the fact that the bulk of the Indian population lived and worked in Natal; thus the two figures are more comparable than in the case of Africans.

Chapter 2. Public Finance in Natal Prior to 1893

The Native Rule

The idea that government can hardly exist without revenue was not alien to the Bantu before the arrival of the Europeans. It was generally recognized by them that a tribal chief was entitled to payments in kind and to the personal services of his subjects. The former were derived from fines, confiscations of property, and presents. The latter consisted of the labor required to cultivate the chief's fields. He could even order that his subjects render services to others for which charges were made. A considerable portion of such earnings would accrue to the chief. In some of the tribes the ruler was considered to be the owner of everything. In such a case he did not raise his revenue by a levy; he simply collected the income from his "patrimony." It was also usual for a chief to impose dues upon commercial transactions between his own people and others.[1] On the whole, taxation was irregular and determined by the ruler's wants, not by the capacity of the people to pay.[2] Thus, the Bantu were acquainted with the principles of both patrimonial and levied revenue, and were to some extent prepared for the introduction of the European fiscal system.

The Republic of Natalia

The first historical records on public finance in Natal come from the Boer Republic of Natalia.[3] The Voortrekkers, owing to internal jealousies, split into two groups. One of them, under Potgieter and Uys, settled west of the Drakensberg, in the present territory of the Orange Free State and the Transvaal. The other, headed by Piet Retief and Maritz, trekked to Natal. In 1838 possession was taken of Port Natal and a constitution was drawn up; in 1839 Pietermaritzburg was founded as the capital of the Republic.

The finances of the Voortrekker community of Natal reflected

1. G. McCall Theal, *History and Ethnography of Africa South of the Zambezi* (London: Swan, Sonnenschein & Co., 1910), pp. 82-83.
2. E. J. Krige, *The Social System of the Zulus* (Pietermaritzburg: Shuter and Shooter, 1950), p. 221.
3. The existence of the Republic of Natalia *de jure* may be questioned, but not its *de facto* existence. The minutes of the meetings of the Raad are the source of information on the finances of the Republic.

the primitive character of its agricultural and pastoral economy. Originally fines and court fees were a source of irregular revenue. Gradually these were supplemented by a large variety of fees.[4] In addition there was an erf tax[5] and a farm tax. Proceeds from the sale of land and income derived from trading licenses as well as liquor and timber licenses were important sources of revenue. Increasing imports yielded customs duties and harbor dues. Share of booty taken from Natives and voluntary contributions in money and services were somewhat unusual sources of revenue.

The expenditure of the Republic consisted mainly of salaries paid to some of the officials. The members of the Raad were also entitled to allowances during sessions. Other items included expenditure on public works, war material, and public buildings.

The administration of finance was the least of the Voortrekkers' preoccupations. Finance was a matter of expediency rather than of any systematic budgeting. Estimates of revenue and expenditure were hardly ever drawn up. There was no uniformity in the monetary unit: some taxes, fines, and fees were assessed in rixdollars,[6] others in the British currency. Exemptions from taxation were often granted, and permission to postpone payment for long periods of time was freely given. Considerable arrears in salaries were not infrequent, and debts to the government suppliers were a rule. In theory, surplus money in the possession of the landdrosts and the Port Administration should have been at the disposal of the central exchequer in Pietermaritzburg. In practice, however, deficits were more frequent than surpluses and consequently the Raad was often in debt to the local administration.[7]

In 1843 the short-lived Republic of Natalia came to an end when Natal was annexed by the British. Approximately two-thirds of the six thousand Voortrekkers left Natal.[8]

4. They included fees for inspection of farms, fees for title deeds, fees for bonds on immovable property, transfer fees, and auction fees.

5. Tax on land in an urban area.

6. Rixdollars were introduced by the Dutch East India Company and circulated at the Cape. They were used by the Voortrekkers as actual currency and as a unit of account along with the sterling. In 1867 the latter was declared legal tender in Natal.

7. J. J. Breanach, "The Development of the Public Finances of the South African Republic to 1877, and of the Antecedent Voortrekker Communities of Natal, Potchefstroom and Ohrigstad" (Master's thesis, University of South Africa, 1929).

8. R. J. Mann, *The Colony of Natal* (London: Jarrold & Son, 1860), p. 173.

The British Rule

In 1846 the first public accounts of the new British dependency appeared. They disclosed a revenue of £3,073, and an expenditure of £6,905. Such were the modest beginnings of public finance in a territory inhabited by a few thousand Europeans living among one hundred thousand tribal Africans. As shown in the previous chapter Natal progressed rapidly after 1870; this is reflected in the expanding public finance of the Colony.

Table 1.2. Ordinary Government Revenue and Expenditure of Natal, 1850-1889

Period	Annual average revenue (£000)	Annual average expenditure (£000)
1850-54	27.8	25.7
1855-59	38.3	35.5
1860-64	107.0	88.0
1865-69	101.6	127.4
1870-74	178.0	161.1
1875-79	328.2	346.1
1880-84	582.3	587.2
1885-89	907.5	821.7

Source: Natal, *Blue Books.*

Between 1855 and 1889 the total population increased fivefold and the European population sixfold; government expenditure increased fortyfold.[9] This is the measure of the Colony's progress. During the same period the per capita expenditure increased from £5s.2d. to £2.3.3 for the total population and from £4.5.6 to £30.13.0 for the European population.

Prior to the early 1880's taxation contributed more than one-half of the Colony's revenue. The earliest taxes imposed were similar to those found in the Cape Colony: in 1843, the customs tariff in force in the Cape was extended to Natal.[10] The revenue from this tax was largely contributed by the relatively small European popu-

9. Since population figures for 1850 are not available, the year 1855 was chosen for comparison.
10. Proclamation of September 28, 1843.

lation. Because Natal duties applied also to goods in transit, duties levied on such goods amounted to indirect taxation of foreigners. As early as 1855 it was estimated that about 25 per cent of the customs revenue was derived from re-exports. Between 1871 and 1880 one-third to one-half of the total revenue was derived from customs duties, and nearly half of these duties were obtained from goods in transit to the neighboring states.[11]

The dependence of the public revenue of the colony on the state of prosperity of the inland territories was intensified with the opening up of the Witwatersrand goldfields. Furthermore, the growth of competition for the inland trade between Natal and other coastal colonies added to the precariousness of the position of the former. Thus in 1886 low transit duties on certain leading re-exports replaced the customs duties.

The imposition of the customs tariff was followed in 1846 by several other taxes, which included a duty on the transfer of landed property,[12] licenses and stamp duties, and auction duties.[13] The latter tax, which was applicable to immovable property, was abolished in 1874.[14]

In 1849 a tax on Native huts, amounting to 7s. per annum on each hut, was the earliest form of direct taxation in Natal. The necessity for a direct tax was dictated by the fact that the Africans were not as yet consumers of imported goods and hence their contribution to the revenue from customs duties was negligible. A hut tax was preferred to a poll tax, the advantages of the former being the difficulty of evasion and the discouragement of polygyny: according to Native custom each wife had to have her own hut. In addition this tax was intended to familiarize the Africans with the advantages of using money. On European farms and in towns those huts inhabited by Africans in the actual receipt of monthly wages were exempted.[15] Originally this tax was expected to yield about £10,000. As the total quantity of currency in circulation in the colony was only slightly in excess of that amount, Africans were

11. C. E. Axelson, "The History of Taxation in Natal Prior to Union" (thesis submitted for the degree of Master of Commerce, University of South Africa, 1936), p. 23.
12. Cape Colony Ordinance No. 3, 1846.
13. *Ibid.*, No. 18, 1846.
14. Law No. 32 of 1874.
15. Proclamation of July 12, 1849.

permitted to make payments in kind.[16] In 1875, after an unsuccessful attempt to introduce a fee for the compulsory registration of
Native marriages,[17] the hut tax was increased to 14s. per hut per
annum.[18] The rate of this tax remained unchanged until the creation of the Union of South Africa. In 1856 an excise duty was added
to the already existing taxes. However, it remained a minor source
of revenue. Such was the basic structure of Natal's taxation until
the first years of the twentieth century.

The budget surpluses or deficits which appeared during the third
quarter of the nineteenth century were mainly due to business
fluctuations. These fluctuations had a strong influence upon the
imports of the Colony,[19] and in turn affected customs receipts.
Stamp duties, land sales, and transfer duties were also sensitive to
changes in the state of business. Transfer duties fluctuated directly
with the volume of transactions in fixed property. The yield of the
Native hut tax, on the other hand, depended on the size of the
African population.

The principle of "cutting one's coat according to one's cloth"
could not entirely be disregarded; yet, because of unforeseen
changes, balancing the budget was not always possible. Surpluses or
deficits were also partly due to the system of colonial bookkeeping.
The committee of inquiry into the working of the various public departments of the Colony reported in 1875 that "the Treasurer is
not at present in a position to take his proper high place as the
financial adviser to the Government."[20] The method of accounting

16. It is difficult to ascertain how much income in kind contributed to the hut
tax. In 1856 the secretary for Native affairs suggested that the hut tax should be paid
in cotton and taxes paid in money be raised to 10s. This proposal was never put
into effect. A year later the magistrates were instructed to accept payments in sesame
seed (Axelson, *op. cit.*, p. 59). In spite of this early policy of encouraging the cultivation of exportable crops by the Natives, payments in kind never became important.
The extensive use of money for tax payments is indicated by the fact that during
the period of three months preceding the payment of hut tax (the time of payment
took place between April and May), coins of smaller denominations used to disappear
from circulation (*Blue Book*, 1855, p. 245).

17. In 1869, in order to increase the Africans' contribution to revenue, the colonial
authorities imposed a marriage fee of £5. Since it was a very unsatisfactory form
of taxation and had a side effect of discouraging marriages, it was abolished in 1875.

18. Law No. 13 of 1875.

19. See Chapter 1, pp. 16-19.

20. *Report of the Committee appointed to enquire into the working of the various
public Departments of the Colony, with the view to placing them upon the most
efficient footing, and simplifying the Conduct of business*, 1875, p. 11.

prevented him from actually ascertaining at any moment how the amount voted had been expended, or what revenues had been received. Consequently, he could not prevent expenditures exceeding fiscal estimates, or submit reliable estimates based on past receipts. He had to rely on the auditor for up-to-date financial data, but as the report pointed out, "The Treasurer, not the Auditor, should be the financial adviser of Government, the Auditor being the authority on matters of book-keeping, not on matters of finance."[21] At a time when the Colony was under the watchful eye of the Mother Country, the principles of Gladstonian finance could not be ignored. Whenever it was necessary to balance the budget, retrenchment was invoked.[22] In the last quarter of the century public finance became more complicated with the inclusion of railway finances.

Originally, the main source of revenue was taxes, which consisted primarily of customs and excise duties as well as the Native hut tax. In 1880 these provided two-thirds of the Colony's revenue (Table 2.2). Until 1855 customs duties and Native taxation were equally important. Afterwards, because of the rapid expansion of imports, customs duties assumed major significance. Table 2.2 shows that from 1880 taxes and public services[23] contributed most of the revenue. Railway receipts increased rapidly from £74,000 in 1880 to £687,000 in 1890/1. In that year they contributed more than 50 per cent of the Colony's total revenue.

There was no uniformity in allocating railway expenditure to the current account or to the capital account. In 1886 the Natal railways for the first time showed an excess of receipts over ex-

21. *Ibid.*

22. The guiding principle of the financial relationship between the home and colonial governments was formulated as early as 1846 by Earl Grey, who wrote: "It is mainly for the benefit of the native inhabitants of Africa that this Colony is to be maintained, and, therefore, it is only just to require that no part of the cost of supporting it for which they can be made to provide, should be thrown upon this country. Nor do I think it impossible that the Colony of Natal may be so managed as to prevent it from bringing any considerable or permanent charge upon the British revenue." Sir John Robinson commented on this quotation: "That was the keynote of Imperial policy then and ever afterwards, and though it is true that Natal never has imposed any such charge upon the home taxpayer—apart from military expenditure—the result was at the time the failure of every effort to govern the natives on the lines of a large progressive policy" (Robinson, *op. cit.*, p. 294).

23. Public services in Table 2.2 include railway and postal receipts as well as receipts from the sale of arms and ammunition.

Table 2.2. Natal's Revenue, Excluding Loans, 1850-1890/1

	Year	Total revenue	Taxes	Public services	Fines & fees	Land sales	Other revenue
£000	1850	39.7	25.1	0.6	0.9	11.8	1.3
	1855	28.7	23.3	1.3	2.0	0.2	1.9
	1860	77.5	57.6	3.5	2.8	0.6	13.0
	1865	105.7	77.1	6.5	6.2	2.7	13.2
	1870	126.3	89.0	13.6	9.9	0.3	13.5
	1875	260.3	165.1	25.0	22.1	19.2	28.9
	1880	582.7	388.2	113.8	16.7	4.8	59.2
	1885	662.9	319.8	225.7	16.5	23.8	77.1
	1890/1	1,318.8	449.5	744.5	27.3	44.2	53.3
Percentages	1850	100.0	63.2	1.5	2.3	29.7	3.3
	1855	100.0	81.2	4.5	7.0	0.7	6.6
	1860	100.0	74.3	4.5	3.6	0.8	16.8
	1865	100.0	72.9	6.1	5.9	2.6	12.5
	1870	100.0	70.5	10.8	7.8	0.2	10.7
	1875	100.0	63.4	9.6	8.5	7.4	11.1
	1880	100.0	66.6	19.5	2.9	0.8	10.2
	1885	100.0	48.3	34.0	2.5	3.6	11.6
	1890/1	100.0	34.1	56.5	2.1	3.3	4.0

Note: Prior to 1890 the budget year coincided with the calendar year. Thereafter the budget year ran from July 1 to June 30.
Source: Natal, *Blue Books.*

penses. Railway surpluses were frequently used to pay the ordinary expenses of the government. On the other hand, surpluses from ordinary revenue were occasionally used for railway construction.

In the formative years expenditure by the Colony reflected the liberal ideas of the nineteenth century. Colonial authorities limited expenditure to the provision of defense against aggression, the maintenance of justice and internal order, the financing of public works, and the provision of services which were not undertaken by private enterprise.

In 1850 the expenditure on those four basic functions of government amounted to two-thirds of the budget. Twenty-five years later it fell to a little over one-half, although from the early sixties Natal had to contribute to the military expenditure which previously had been borne entirely by the Imperial Government. By 1890/1, this proportion fell to one-fifth. This was largely due to the growing expenditure on the railways, as well as to the substantial rise in the amount of interest on public debt. *Inter alia* expenditure on public health, education, and immigration (included under "other expenditure") was also increasing (see Table 3.2).

The public debt of Natal was created in 1860 when a loan of £50,000 was raised for improving the Durban harbor. During subsequent years additional sums were borrowed to finance further harbor works and the immigration of Indian laborers. After 1875 the public debt grew at a rapid pace because of loans for railway construction. The colonial debt rose to £268,000 in 1870, and ten years later it reached £1,632,000. By the end of 1892 the funded debt of Natal amounted to £7,170,000 and the sinking fund to £210,000.[24] The per capita debt for the total population was £12.18.0 and £167.13.8 for the European group. Since the public debt was largely reproductive, it cannot be regarded as excessive for the growing economy of the Colony. In 1892/3, £5,820,000 from loan account was invested in railroads. This amounted to well over four-fifths of the public debt. The balance of the public debt included expenditure on harbor improvements and other public works of a reproductive nature. Expenditure on the Zulu War amounted to £250,-000.[25]

Owing to the shortage of funds in the Colony and high local rates of interest, Natal had to raise her funds overseas in the London capital market. Originally rates of interest ranged from 4.5 to 6 per cent, but as the credit of the Colony improved and loanable funds became more abundant, the rates fell as low as 3.5 per cent. The average rate of interest on public loans was about 4 per cent in 1892. From 1866 a distinction was made between expenditure on loan account and ordinary expenditure. During the preceding five years the accounts of expenditure on public works had been in a confused state. It was also customary to borrow from the loan funds to supplement ordinary revenue.

In summary, the growth of the public sector of the economy prior to 1893 depended on the same vital factors as the growth of the private sector. Growth was determined by increase in popula-

24. *Blue Books.*
25. *Sessional Papers* of the Legislative Assembly, 1893, p. 34. Cost of the Zulu War incurred by 1880.

Table 3.2. Natal's Ordinary Expenditure, 1850-1890/1

		1850	1855	1860	1865	1870	1875	1880	1885	1890/1
£000	Civil establishments	5.7	7.4	12.4	15.3	17.2	30.3	37.7	32.6	45.6
	Justice, police, and jails	6.0	8.3	12.8	24.6	22.1	30.7	47.9	54.1	63.7
	Colonial defense	—	—	—	1.2	5.9	17.8	73.4	62.0	60.6
	Interest and sinking fund	—	—	—	—	22.9	25.2	—	190.1	225.1
	Public works	2.6	3.9	8.0	37.5	9.3	85.1	59.7	86.7	120.5
	Railways	—	—	—	—	—	—	89.3	229.0	607.5
	Other expenditure	7.5	8.7	23.7	64.2	39.6	117.9	169.1	119.7	270.9
	Total ordinary expenditure	21.8	28.3	56.9	142.8	117.0	307.0	477.1	774.2	1,393.9
Percentages	Civil establishments	26.2	26.0	21.8	10.7	14.7	9.9	7.9	4.2	3.3
	Justice, police, and jails	27.5	29.4	22.5	17.2	18.9	10.0	10.0	6.9	4.6
	Colonial defense	—	—	—	.8	5.0	5.8	15.4	8.0	4.3
	Interest and sinking fund	—	—	—	—	19.6	8.2	—	24.4	16.1
	Public works	11.9	13.8	14.1	26.3	7.9	27.7	12.5	11.6	8.6
	Railways	—	—	—	—	—	—	18.7	29.5	43.7
	Other expenditure	34.4	30.8	41.6	45.0	33.9	38.4	35.5	15.4	19.4
		100.0	100.0	100.0	100.0	100.0	100.0	100.0	100.0	100.0

Source: Natal, Blue Books.

tion, expansion of internal trade, and the impact of the mining dis-coveries of the seventies and eighties on the foreign trade of the Colony. The rapid development of the markets in the Orange Free State and the South African Republic acted as a powerful stimulus in expanding the Colony's trade. Overshadowing all expansion was the development of railways.

Finally, the influence on the private sector of the business fluctu-ations in South Africa and overseas was naturally transmitted to the public sector, thereby affecting the revenue and the borrowing powers of the government. The tariff and railway policies of the inland republics and coastal colonies of the Cape and Natal were strongly influenced by political considerations. The Colony also had to bear a portion of the expenditure on the military establishments as well as a share of the expenses of the Zulu War of 1879.

An important feature was the large measure of fiscal control by a small European minority because of the political power of this group and the inability of the Native population to participate in the affairs of the Colony. Although taxed by the Europeans, the Natives had no say in the public services provided for them.

Chapter 3. The Legislative Framework

From 1843 to 1845 Natal was an integral part of the Cape Colony. In the latter year it became a district with its own administration headed by a lieutenant-governor. In 1856 Natal was raised to the status of a colony, with representative government. Thus were realized the aspirations of the settlers, who strongly desired to have a share in the control over the territory they inhabited.

The Charter[1] enlarged the existing Legislative Council by including a number of elective members in addition to those nominated by the Crown.[2] The nominees constituted the Executive Council,[3] which was responsible to the Ministers of the Crown in Great Britain. The electorate consisted of all men above the age of twenty-one years possessing immovable property to the value of £50 or paying a yearly rental of £10 for hired property within any electoral district. Aliens were excluded.[4] The Indians enjoyed voting rights on the same basis as Europeans, after their period of indenture had expired.

In theory the electoral law did not discriminate between the races, but in practice the property qualification deprived the African population of the right to vote. Because it was contemplated granting Natives documentary titles to certain lands, additional restrictions on Natives were introduced in 1865 in order to prevent them from exercising the electoral franchise based on property qualification. In particular, only those could vote who had resided for twelve years in the Colony and had been exempted from the operation of Native law for a period of seven years.[5]

In 1883 an alternative to the property qualification was introduced.[6] The new legislation stipulated that every male inhabitant who was a British subject or a naturalized alien of three years' resi-

1. Letters Patent dated July 15, 1856.
2. According to the 1856 Charter, the Legislative Council consisted of 12 members elected for a period of four years and of 4 nominated members. Law No. 1 of 1873 increased the total number to 20 members, of whom 15 were elective. Law No. 3 of 1875 increased the number of the nominated members from 5 to 13. This measure applied for five years. Finally, Law No. 1 of 1883 increased the total number of the members to 30, of whom 23 were elective.
3. G. W. Eybers, *Select Constitutional Documents Illustrating South African History, 1795 to 1910* (London: George Routledge and Sons, Ltd., 1918), p. li.
4. Charter of Natal, 1856, Sec. 11.
5. Law No. 11 of 1865.
6. Franchise Amendment Law No. 2 of 1883.

dence in the Colony and whose income was £96 per annum could be enrolled on the voters' list. In the case of Africans the exemption from the operation of Native law was still required.

The provisions of the Charter dealing with financial powers stated that (a) any bill appropriating any part of the public revenue for any purpose had to be recommended to the Council by the governor of the Colony during the session in which it was proposed, before it was passed by the Legislative Council and assented to by the governor; (b) no part of the public revenue was to be issued except in pursuance of a warrant from the governor directed to the public treasurer of the Colony; (c) the treasurer was to account for all revenues to the Lords Commissioners of the Treasury of the United Kingdom. That part of the revenue used to cover the expenditure of the civil list was an exception. The salaries stipulated in the civil list were under the direct control of the Crown. The Charter set aside an amount of five thousand pounds from the consolidated revenue fund for Native purposes.

The governor was empowered to return bills passed by the Legislative Council for reconsideration and to make amendments as he saw fit. All bills had to have the governor's assent to become law, and all the laws thus assented to by him could be disallowed by the Crown within two years.[7] The introduction and passing of taxation bills followed the same procedure. In 1875 an amendment was introduced[8] whereby all laws which taxed Europeans required a majority of not less than two-thirds of the members present.

Such was the broad legal framework within which the public finance of Natal developed during the period of representative government, which lasted till 1893. The franchise laws deprived almost all Africans of their voting rights. Not more than five were ever on the common voters' roll.[9]

During the early nineties Indian participation in the government of the Colony was limited to three or four hundred persons who were enrolled as voters.[10] The Europeans considered even this

7. Charter of Natal, 1856.
8. Constitution Amendment Law No. 3 of 1875.
9. E. H. Brookes and J. B. Macaulay, Civil Liberty in South Africa (Cape Town, London, and New York: Oxford University Press, 1958), pp. 140-141.
10. Governor of Natal to the secretary of state, letter dated July 16, 1894. Sessional Papers of the Legislative Assembly, No. 6, p. 45.

small number a threat to their political power in view of the potential growth of Indian voters. This danger was voiced by the governor of Natal:

It is a question whether he [the Indian] should be allowed to exercise a voice, which will surely become a controlling voice, in the Government of the Colony of Natal, which, it must be recollected, contains in addition to its 40,000 European inhabitants, 450,000 natives, who are debarred, of necessity from the exercise of the Franchise.[11]

The Franchise Amendment Act of 1896, which disenfranchised the Indians, was an epilogue to the three-cornered struggle between the Natal legislature, the Indian community led by M. K. Gandhi, and the Colonial Office, whose disapproval of the original bill was met by an insignificant change in its wording.[12]

In short, only the Europeans could, on the basis of existing legislation, influence politically the budget and taxation. There was no mechanism whereby the non-Europeans could exercise any influence on fiscal policy. The European colonists conducted the fiscal system of Natal without regard to the other races and according to their own value judgments. Their guiding principle could perhaps be best illustrated by Sir John Robinson speaking in the Legislative Assembly in 1896: ". . . we believe . . . that the interests of the Colony demand that the control of its destinies should continue in the hands of men of European descent and race . . . ."[13]

The year 1893 brought a vital change in the constitutional framework of the Colony. Natal was granted responsible government. From now on, the Executive Council, on whose advice the governor was supposed to act, became responsible to the legislature. The elected members of the legislature were, in their turn, responsible to their electors in the matters of broad policy. The main problem was to what extent the governor would follow the advice of his minister: he could dissent from the opinions of the Council whenever sufficient reasons were present. This happened when there was conflict between Imperial and local interests, when the British had to fulfil international obligations, or when the Colony had to exercise its authority over the Imperial forces stationed

11. *Ibid.*
12. M. Palmer, *The History of the Indians in Natal (Natal Regional Survey)* (Cape Town, London, and New York: Oxford University Press, 1957), chap. iv.
13. *Legislative Assembly Debates,* 1896, p. 166.

there. Another source of conflict in Natal was the presence of an overwhelming number of non-Europeans who were practically debarred from exercising any influence upon the government.[14]

The new Constitution[15] replaced the former Legislative Council with a Legislative Assembly consisting of thirty elected members. Elections were to take place every four years, or earlier, if the Assembly happened to be dissolved by the governor. In addition to the Assembly there was a Legislative Council consisting of eleven members nominated for a period of ten years by the governor-in-council.[16]

The Executive Council was composed of six ministers appointed by the governor in the name of the Crown. All questions were to be decided by a majority of votes,[17] but the Crown had the power to disallow, within two years, any law passed by the legislature. These provisions were similar to those of the Charter of 1856.

The most important rules relating to public finance stipulated that all the revenues arising within the Colony, over which the legislature had power of appropriation, were to form one consolidated revenue fund. The fund was to be charged with all the costs, charges, and expenses incidental to its collection and management. Such costs, charges, and expenses were to be reviewed and audited in the manner prescribed by the legislature.

All bills for appropriating any part of the consolidated revenue fund or for imposing, altering, or repealing any tax or duty, etc., were to originate in the Legislative Assembly. The governor had to recommend them to the Assembly during the session in which they were to be discussed. The Legislative Council had the power of either accepting or rejecting any money bills passed by the Legislative Assembly, but could not alter them.

The Constitution Act of 1893 provided that an annual payment of £21,000 be made from the consolidated revenue fund for defray-

14. Eybers, op. cit., pp. lix-lx.

15. Law No. 14 of 1893, later referred to as "Constitution Act of 1893."

16. I.e., the governor acting on the advice of the Executive Council. On the annexation of Zululand, two members were added to the Legislative Assembly, and one to the Legislative Council. On the incorporation of the districts of Utrecht and Vryheid in 1902, three members were added to the Legislative Assembly, and two to the Legislative Council.

17. The quorum of the Legislative Assembly was twelve members, and that of the Legislative Council five members.

ing of the salaries of the governor, the ministers, and other high-ranking officials. The above sum also included £10,000 for the promotion of the welfare and education of the Natives.

The granting of responsible government to Natal was the result of persistent endeavors by certain sections of the colonists. Economic considerations were of prime importance. Ever since the first election for the Legislative Council in 1857 there had been a protracted struggle for increased self-government. The home government made concessions by increasing the number of the elected members of the Legislative Council. But the movement for responsible government was hardly appeased by these measures. The constitutional development of the Colony received a severe setback when the Imperial Government disapproved of the handling by Sir Benjamin Pine, the lieutenant governor, of the Hlubi rebellion led by Langalibalele. Sir Benjamin was recalled and the number of the nominated members of the Legislative Council was raised from five to thirteen, thus considerably strengthening, at least in theory, the power of the new governor. When, in 1880, the Legislative Council petitioned for responsible government, all it secured was the reversal to its former number of the nominated members. Natal was also given to understand that responsible government would be granted only if the Colony were prepared to provide for its own defense. This, of course, raised the question of heavy military expenditure, and the colonists decided against responsible government.[18] Apart from doubting whether the Colony could provide adequate financial resources, the government in London feared that under responsible government the white population would disregard the rights of Africans and Indians. Hence constitutional safeguards were necessary to protect the non-Europeans. The governor as supreme chief was invested with certain powers under the Code of Native Law, and hence it was not necessary for him to consult his Council. Under responsible government it would have been essential for him to retain these powers.[19]

The struggle for self-government gained new impetus when a large part of Northern Zululand was ceded in 1886 to the South

18. *The Cambridge History of the British Empire* (2nd ed., Cambridge: Cambridge University Press, 1963), VIII, 499.
19. Eybers, *op. cit.*, pp. liii-lix.

African Republic, an act which aroused dissatisfaction among the Natal colonists. A further issue arose when Natal desired to raise a new loan for the extension of railways and other public works. The secretary of state pointed out that this could be done only when Natal achieved responsibilities of self-government. Thus controversy continued. But it was not limited to the Colonial Office in London and the colonists as a whole; the latter were far from being united.[20] Responsible government had its supporters and opponents. The "Forwards," the party in favor of responsible government, emanated from the commercial section associated with the coastal districts. They were led in their fight for responsible government by the well-known Natal politician John Robinson. The "Country" party, the opponents, consisted mainly of farmers and planters; by nature more conservative, they were unwilling to take on the new responsibilities. They claimed that Natal would be unable to defend herself unless supported by the Imperial troops. They also maintained that the granting of self-government would adversely affect the credit of the Colony and would thereby hinder it from raising loans for public works.

The need for responsible government became more acute with the decline in Natal's lucrative overberg trade when the Cape railway was extended to Johannesburg in 1892. By means of diplomacy Natal attempted to gain a victory over the Cape by requesting permission from Pretoria to extend her railway line beyond the Transvaal border. President Kruger and the commercial interests on the Witwatersrand did not regard Natal claims with an unkindly eye. One more line would strengthen their bargaining power with the Cape. To the republican politicians, the stumbling block appeared to be the fact that Natal was still under direct Crown rule. They shrank from allying themselves with a community whose administrators were appointed by Britain.

Because the existing form of government proved an obstruction to railway extension, the influence of the "Forwards" was strengthened to such an extent that they gained a majority in the Legislative Council, thereby making the acceptance of responsible government an accomplished fact in 1893.[21] One of the first acts of the

20. Robinson, *op. cit.*, pp. 165-166.
21. *Ibid.*, pp. 249-250.

new government, headed by John Robinson, was to sign a convention with the Transvaal early in 1894, which allowed Natal to extend her railroad to the Witwatersrand.[22]

The constitutional reform of 1893 marked a new era in the history of the Colony. Prior to that the life of the community was shaped by an executive responsible to the Home Government. The administration had not always been in touch with the people, particularly in matters dealing with taxation, expenditure, and borrowing powers. The new constitution by improving the competitive position of Natal vis-à-vis the Cape enhanced the economy of the Colony. As later events proved, however, the attainment of self-government by the European element proved to be disadvantageous to the people of Zululand and the Indian and African population of Natal proper.

22. *The Cambridge History of the British Empire*, VIII, 542.

Part II

Part II

Chapter 4. Variations in Government Revenue and Expenditure

Receipts and Expenditures, 1892/3 to 1909/10

In economically advanced countries tax policy tends to accept the level of expenditure as its revenue goal.[1] Thus the sequence of decision runs from expenditure to taxes. In underdeveloped countries, on the other hand, the level of expenditure is largely determined by the ability of the tax system to place the required revenues at the disposal of the government.[2] It is for this reason that in the ensuing analysis precedence is given to the revenue side of the public accounts.[3] Total government revenue and expenditure during the period under review are shown in Table 1.4.

In this and the following two chapters the volume and composition of only the current government revenue and expenditure will be analyzed. The receipts originating from long-term borrowing and expenditure on capital account out of loan funds will be treated in Chapter 7.[4]

Receipts and expenditure of the colonial government, excluding loan funds, are shown in Table 2.4. Major expansion of government activities is reflected in the fiscal data of the table. During the war years 1899-1902 the increase in expenditure was partly due to inflation, which played no role between 1892 and 1899 or in the postwar years. Between 1892/3 and 1909/10 revenue and expenditure showed more than a threefold increase. During the same period the population of the Colony doubled; the recorded exports (including re-exports) rose eightfold, and imports nearly fourfold.

These developments form the broad background of the changes in public revenue and expenditure.

The Relationship between Revenue and Expenditure

Table 2.4 shows the actual surpluses and deficits. The last col-

1. It is assumed that considerations relating to the level of employment, prices, and economic activity are allowed for.
2. *Taxes and Fiscal Policy in Underdeveloped Countries* (New York: United Nations, 1954), p. 6.
3. Complete accounts of the public sector would also include the revenue and expenditure of the municipalities. See Appendix D.
4. See especially pp. 102-108.

umn of that table also shows expenditure expressed as a percentage of current revenue.

Our period begins with a series of budgetary deficits. The year 1891/2,[5] not included in the table, was the first in the series of three years showing an excess of expenditure over revenue. In 1894/5 this trend is reversed, and for five years surpluses were realized. Then there was a reversal, with a moderate deficit in 1899/1900, followed by two years of surpluses. During 1904/5 to 1907/8 we again have a series of deficits. We now proceed to examine the causes of these surpluses and deficits.

The Period of Falling Revenue

The year 1892/3 marks a revival after the depression which set

5. In 1891/2 the deficit amounted to £111,490.

Table 1.4. Total Government Revenue and Expenditure, 1892/3-1909/10 (£000)

Year	Current revenue	Loan receipts	Total revenue	Current expenditure	Loan expenditure	Total expenditure
1892/3	1,069.7	560.4	1,630.1	1,099.9	615.3	1,715.2
1893/4	1,011.0	856.6	1,867.6	1,082.4	620.7	1,703.1
1894/5	1,169.8	17.7	1,187.5	1,148.1	147.5	1,295.6
1895/6	1,457.3	125.0	1,582.3	1,282.5	232.7	1,515.2
1896/7	2,213.1	770.4	2,983.5	1,625.0	772.4	2,397.4
1897/8	1,964.3	1,366.7	3,331.0	1,812.3	1,369.8	3,182.1
1898/9	2,081.4	941.5	3,022.9	1,908.3	381.0	2,289.3
1899/0	1,886.7	10.7	1,897.4	1,955.1	816.2	2,771.3
1900/1	2,970.7	1,038.2	4,008.9	2,499.6	741.8	3,241.4
1901/2	3,439.8	2,122.4	5,562.2	3,052.6	1,240.7	4,293.3
1902/3	4,334.2	1,374.7	5,708.9	5,102.0	1,683.2	6,785.2
1903/4	4,160.1	1,491.0	5,651.1	4,071.4	1,292.4	5,363.8
1904/5	3,384.8	2,210.4	5,595.2	4,029.6	2,185.3	6,214.9
1905/6	3,666.0	1,415.2	5,081.2	3,670.6	2,004.9	5,675.5
1906/7	3,483.6	2,281.9	5,765.5	3,681.9	2,372.6	6,054.5
1907/8	3,510.4	1,871.8	5,382.2	3,689.8	1,814.1	5,503.9
1908/9	3,569.3	879.2	4,448.5	3,530.6	579.8	4,110.4
1909/10	4,293.7	792.0*	5,085.7*	3,530.3	1,250.5*	4,780.8*

*Estimate.
Source: Natal, Auditor-General's *Reports.*

in with the speculative "gold crisis" of 1899.[6] The growth of the gold mining industry in the Transvaal[7] was accompanied by an increasing demand for imports. It was expected in Natal that the growing prosperity of the goldfields would give rise to increased trade, part of which would come to the Colony.[8] Natal did not, however, share in the prosperity because of the loss of a substantial part of her rail traffic to the Cape (see Chapter 1).

The realized government revenue in 1892/3 was £30,000 short of expenditure. This difference was mainly due to a sharp fall in customs and railway receipts consequent upon declining imports. This deficit would have been larger if expenditure had not been curtailed. But this was only a half-measure, because the remedy lay in the extension of the Colony's railroad to the Witwatersrand. The year 1893/4 was also disappointing; the realized deficit rose to over £71,000. The deficits of 1892/3 and 1893/4 were made good from balances accumulated in the consolidated revenue fund during the previous years.

The financial position of the Colony was not alarming, but the loss of the Transvaal trade meant that the railway line, built in order to retain that trade, would not be able to pay for itself. There was a threat of higher taxation. The colonial authorities were, however, determined to bring back the diverted traffic and to increase revenue. It was in this spirit that the colonial treasurer concluded his 1893 budget speech with this hopeful remark: "The financial history of the Colony shows that it has in the past emerged from times of depression to times of advanced prosperity, and I have no doubt that history will again repeat itself in this respect."[9]

Prosperity and Depression, 1894/5 to 1898/9

The financial position in 1894/5 disclosed a modest surplus of nearly £22,000. Although there were no signs of a revival in the

6. The pattern of business fluctuations in South Africa, during the period under consideration, is taken from C. G. W. Schumann's *Structural Changes and Business Cycles in South Africa 1806-1936* (London: P. S. King & Son, Ltd., 1938).

7. Exports of gold increased from £67,500 in 1885 to £1,496,700 in 1889, and on February 15 of that year the market valuation of "thirty best known shares" amounted to £24,813,200 (*ibid.*, p. 28).

8. *Legislative Council Debates*, 1892, p. 28.

9. *Ibid.*, 1893, p. 24.

Colony, the budgetary deficit was eliminated. The tide turned in 1895/6 with the commencement of railway services between Durban and Johannesburg in January, 1896. In the financial year 1895/6 revenue reached £1,457,300, exceeding the previous year's figure by £287,500. The realized surplus of revenue over expenditure amounted to £174,800. The increases in receipts were shown mainly under the headings related to trade. In 1896/7 there was a further marked improvement in the financial position of Natal when revenue attained £2,213,100. Expenditure was £1,625,000 and

Table 2.4. Current Government Revenue and Expenditure, 1892/3-1909/10(£*000*)

Year	Revenue	Expenditure	Surplus	Deficit	Expenditure as percentage of revenue
1892/3	1,069.7	1,099.9	—	30.2	102.8
1893/4	1,011.0	1,082.4	—	71.4	107.1
1894/5	1,169.8	1,148.1	21.7	—	98.1
1895/6	1,457.3	1,282.5	174.8	—	88.0
1896/7	2,213.1	1,625.0	588.1	—	73.4
1897/8	1,964.3	1,812.3	152.0	—	92.3
1898/9	2,081.4	1,908.3	173.1	—	91.7
1899/0	1,886.7	1,955.1	—	68.4	103.6
1900/1	2,970.7	2,499.6	471.1	—	84.1
1901/2	3,439.8	3,052.6	387.2	—	88.7
1902/3	4,334.2	5,102.0*	—	767.8	117.7
1903/4	4,160.1	4,071.4	88.7	—	97.9
1904/5	3,384.8	3,829.6 200.0†	—	644.8	119.0
1905/6	3,666.0	3,670.6	—	4.6	100.1
1906/7	3,471.9 11.7‡	3,681.9	—	198.3	105.7
1907/8	3,510.4	3,689.8	—	179.4	105.1
1908/9	3,569.3	3,530.6	38.7	—	98.9
1909/10§	4,293.7	3,530.3	763.4	—	82.2

*Includes war expenditure of £1,139,793.
†Amount set aside as contingencies fund under Act No. 21 of 1904.
‡Cash surrenders treated in previous years as expenditure, and brought into revenue in 1906/7.
§Eleven months only.
Source: Natal, Auditor-General's *Reports;* Union of South Africa, *Finance Accounts, Appropriation Accounts, Loan Funds, and Miscellaneous Funds,* with the *Report* of the Controller and Auditor General of the Union (Natal), 1911.

the realized surplus rose to the remarkable figure of £588,100. Apparently the collapse of the stock market in September, 1895, which brought to a sudden end an intensive speculative boom in Kaffirs that was listed on the London stock exchange, had little influence on the general state of trade. Similarly, the famous "Jameson Raid" of December, 1895, left no lasting effect on the market.[10]

It was only in 1897 that the years of prosperity came to an end and a recession set in. The period of slack trade lasted until 1899, and in Natal it was aggravated by losses sustained through locusts, rinderpest, and drought.[11] The revenue fell by nearly a quarter of a million, as compared with the preceding year, and this was largely due to reduced railway receipts. Expenditure, on the other hand, showed an increase of £187,400; but there was still a surplus amounting to £152,000. In spite of the depression, both revenue and expenditure showed a marked rise in 1898; with revenue rising faster than expenditure, a surplus of £173,100 was realized.

Thus for five successive years Natal's revenue exceeded expenditure. The surpluses, which totaled over one million pounds, were advanced to the loan fund to finance current public works. The consolidated revenue fund had a credit of £639,800 in 1895, which increased to £1,554,800 in 1898. Because of the advances to the loan fund the credit balance fell to £180,800 in 1899 (see Appendix B). Subsequent events proved that this balance was wholly inadequate.

Revival and Prosperity of the War and Postwar Period, 1899/1900 to 1902/3

Trade began to improve slowly in 1899. Moreover, the customs receipts were expected to increase under the new customs convention. Thus, in spite of the political uncertainty on the eve of the war, the colonial treasurer was inclined to frame his estimates for the coming year "in a spirit of cautious hopefulness, begotten of the experience of recent years."[12]

10. There is a strong suspicion that the sales of shares were started by those who had the "inside information" on the approaching political action undertaken by Dr. Jameson. (See P. H. Emden, *Randlords*, London: Hodder & Stoughton, 1935, p. 199.)

11. *Legislative Assembly Debates*, 1899, p. 58.

12. *Ibid.*, p. 70.

The Anglo-Boer War broke out in October, 1899. Its effects on the two republics and the colonies of the Cape and Natal were markedly different. On the one hand, we find wartime destruction in the Transvaal and the Orange Free State, which affected especially the farming community. There was also an almost complete cessation in the production of gold.[13] On the other hand, the Cape Colony and Natal enjoyed prosperity. The internal purchasing power of these territories was increased tremendously by the upkeep of an army of 250,000, which represented nearly one-quarter of the white population of South Africa.[14] The full measure of wartime prosperity reached Natal only after 1900. The financial estimates for the budget year 1899/1900 were upset by the disorganization of the overland trade and the invasion of the northern districts of the Colony by enemy forces. Revenue fell to £1,886,700, but expenditure continued to increase, resulting in a deficit of £68,400.

Heavy extraordinary expenditure caused by the war was separately accounted for under the heading of "Advances made in connection with the South African Crisis."[15] The proportion of these advances to be borne by Natal was to be decided upon at a future date.[16] A loan was granted by the Bank of England to cover the deficiency.[17] The extraordinary expenditure was met out of advances, as the Constitution prohibited the appropriation of any part of the consolidated revenue fund, except by an act of Parliament.

In 1900/1 the revenue rose to £2,970,700, or 57 per cent above the previous year's level. Such an amount had never before been collected in the Colony. This unexpected rise was largely the result of an increase in railway earnings caused by the military traffic. But in order to increase revenue new expenditure had to be in-

13. Gold output fell from £15,452,000 in 1899 to £1,481,000 in 1900 and to £1,097,000 in 1901; it increased to £7,297,000 in 1902 and £12,622,000 in 1903 (Schumann, *op. cit.*, p. 92).

14. *Ibid.*

15. On June 30, 1900, it reached £449,100.

16. *Legislative Assembly Debates*, 1901, pp. 41-42.

17. After the commencement of hostilities, treasury balances decreased rapidly and it was necessary to seek assistance from the Bank of England. Credit was arranged up to one million pounds and was utilized for the extraordinary expenditure incurred by the war, and to carry on works chargeable to loan funds. It was impossible to raise loans elsewhere at an acceptable rate of interest (*ibid.*, pp. 45-46).

curred. Hence the increased railway disbursements were mainly responsible for the rise of the total expenditure to £2,499,600. Despite this, a substantial surplus of £471,100 was realized.

In 1901 the extraordinary expenditure caused by the war reached £900,000, and this was still accounted for under "Advances." In 1901/2 the favorable trend continued and the budgetary surplus reached £387,200.

The close of hostilities evoked a general feeling of optimism both in South Africa and in England. There was an inflow of capital and immigrants; stocks of imported goods were built up by the traders in anticipation of increased demand. There were also increased dealings in fixed property.[18] A typical postwar boom developed, accompanied by some inflation. The retail price index rose from 116.5 in 1900 to 131.4 in 1901; thereafter it fell to 127.5 in 1902 and to 118.8 in 1903.[19]

Government revenue for 1902/3 attained a figure of £4,334,200 while current expenditure amounted to £3,962,200. A surplus of £372,000 could have been realized, had it not been for the fact that Natal had agreed to pay some of the war expenses, which had reached £1,139,800. Consequently total current expenditure rose to £5,102,000, resulting in a deficit of £767,800. This was met from the accumulated balance of the consolidated revenue fund. Thus by the end of the budget year 1902/3 Natal succeeded in wiping out all the expenditure described as "Expenditure connected with the South African Crisis."

The Depression of 1903-9 and the Revival of 1909/10

In 1903 the first signs of a recession had already appeared. The recession was partly due to the falling off of war expenditure, which had engendered large profits and other income in the Colony, and the cessation of large sums devoted to the repatriation and resettlement of refugees. In 1903/4 the finances of the Colony were, however, not wholly unsatisfactory although there were six months of depression: the revenue of £4,160,100 still exceeded expenditure

18. Schumann, op. cit., p. 93.
19. Index of Retail Prices, *Official Year Book of the Union of South Africa*, No. 6, 1923, p. 344 (see Appendix F).

by £88,700. This favorable outcome was due to the buoyancy of railway receipts in the first half of the year.

In 1904/5 no retrenchment was contemplated by the colonial treasurer, who budgeted for a modest deficit of £56,000. However, the actual excess of expenditure over revenue reached £444,-800, but a transfer of £200,000 to the newly created contingencies fund increased the deficit.[20] The credit balance in the consolidated revenue fund amounted to only £293,000. Thus, as a result of the deficit at the end of the budget year there appeared a debit balance of £351,800 (see Appendix B). Thereafter shortfalls in the revenue fund became a marked feature until 1909. In 1905/6 revenue showed an increase of some £281,000 and expenditure was drastically curtailed. There was an insignificant deficit of £4,600, and the budget was nearly balanced.

The financial year 1906/7 began with an outlook which was by no means encouraging. The Native rebellion[21] and the ravages of East Coast Cattle Fever, together with the generally depressed conditions of trade, combined to reduce revenue and increase the expenses of administration.[22] The budgetary deficit for that year reached £198,300, which increased the debit balance on the consolidated revenue fund to £554,700 (see Appendix B).

During 1906/7 a tendency toward improvement of business conditions in South Africa was reversed under the impact of the world crisis which broke out in 1907. In the course of the following year the depression deepened.[23] The attempts of the Natal government to increase revenue by new taxation were of little avail. The desired reduction of expenditure was prevented by the costs incurred in connection with the continuing epidemics of the East Coast Fever.[24] With a deficit of £179,400 in 1908/9 the financial position of the colonial government deteriorated and was reflected in a further increase of the debit balance on the consolidated revenue fund to £734,100.

20. The contingencies fund was created by Act No. 21 of 1904. Its purpose was to enable the executive to incur expenditure on such unforeseen services as could not be postponed without serious injury to public interest. Temporary advances to meet such expenditure could be charged to this fund.

21. Known as Bambata Rebellion of 1906.

22. *Legislative Assembly Debates*, 1907, p. 291.

23. Schumann, *op. cit.*, p. 96.

24. *Legislative Assembly Debates*, 1908, p. 510.

Thus the government's attempts to balance the budget proved a failure. The colonial treasurer in his budget speech of 1908/9 stressed the fact that the Colony's income from the main source of taxation (customs duties) had decreased during the last years by reason of the growth of local industry, and it had become necessary to replace the revenue thus lost from some other sources.[25] What he had in mind was obviously new taxation.[26] The year 1907/8 was, however, the last of a series of the four years of depression with a budgetary deficit. The financial results which for the year 1908/9 disclosed a revenue of £3,569,300 and an expenditure of £3,530,600, showed a realized surplus of £38,700 instead of the expected deficit of £167,600. Compared with the previous year's results, revenue improved to the extent of nearly £60,000, whereas expenditure fell by £159,200.

During 1909 South Africa followed England on her way to recovery.[27] In his last budget speech, on the eve of the union of the South African colonies, the treasurer of Natal was able to present what he called "a satisfactory statement of the Colony's position."[28] In his opinion, "by severe retrenchment and economies in the management of the Government and of private business concerns, and by some fresh taxation of the people, the Colony has successfully pulled through a most difficult time."[29] He also suggested that with the returning prosperity the removal of some of the recently imposed taxes should receive careful consideration.[30] Such were the views of a statesman who shaped the financial destinies of Natal according to the then widely recognized principles of "sound finance."

The accounts for 1909/10 referred to the period ending on May 31, 1910. The revenue realized for the eleven months was £4,293,700 and the actual expenditure £3,530,000, with a resulting surplus of £763,400. This made it possible to wipe out the debit balance of £695,400 on the consolidated revenue fund, which at the date of the closing of the fund was converted into a credit balance of £67,900. On June 1, 1910, the colonial accounts were taken over

25. *Ibid.*, p. 517.
26. See Chapter 5, pp. 80-82.
27. Schumann, *op. cit.*, p. 96.
28. *Legislative Assembly Debates*, 1909, p. 291.
29. *Ibid.*
30. *Ibid.*, p. 292.

by the Ministry of Finance of the newly formed Union of South Africa.

During the eighteen years under review, the revenue and expenditure of Natal were strongly influenced by business fluctuations. But superimposed upon these fluctuations were other factors which were at times powerful enough to interfere seriously with the cyclical pattern. The first of these was the diversion of trade to the Cape route in 1892; the second was the Anglo-Boer War. The impact of the latter on the South African economy extended over nearly five years and overshadowed all other influences.

Out of the ten years in which budgetary surpluses were present, five fell during the nineties, while an equal number of deficit years occurred after the turn of the century. With the exception of the war period, year-to-year fluctuations in revenue were much more marked than those in expenditure. Thus in the short run, expenditure was less sensitive to changes in income, a phenomenon which can be explained by a certain fixity of government spending, as determined by the institutional set-up. Revenue, on the other hand, depended on the state of trade, a highly changeable factor in the colonial economy.

In order to obtain an insight into the phenomena described in this chapter, we shall pass to a more detailed analysis of the fluctuations and the structure of revenue and expenditure.

Chapter 5. The Revenue

Introduction

The sources of the data of government income are the annual statements of actual receipts published by the colonial treasurer. The sources of revenue are analyzed in broad groups in Table 1.5. Unlike the preceding period, when taxes were the principal source of government receipts (compare Table 2.2, Chapter 2), public services came to the fore during the years 1892/3 to 1909/10. Moreover, during this period the revenue derived from public services increased more than fourfold, while the revenue from taxes was slightly more than half of the latter. In 1892/3 public services accounted for one-half of the total revenue; by 1910 they rose to nearly two-thirds. The growth of public services was primarily due to the extension of the railway system, though postal and telegraphic services did not lag far behind. Other receipts were largely provided by taxes and only to a small extent by other sources, of which the sale of Crown lands was the most important single source.

Variations in total tax receipts fall into two distinct periods. The first, between 1893/4 and 1902/3, discloses a steady increase in the sums collected. Tax receipts were subject to rather wide fluctuations during the following period, 1903/4-1909/10. To explain these movements it is necessary to analyze the structural changes in the tax system, and the changes in the yields from particular taxes. In 1892/3, Natal's tax system included the following taxes:[1]

Import duties. Customs tariffs included three categories of goods: dutiable goods, goods free of duty, and goods subject to transit dues.[2] Dutiable goods included a wide range of merchandise subject to either specific or ad valorem duties. Goods not enumerated, and not exempted from duty, were charged a flat ad valorem rate of 5 per cent. The "free" list enumerated about forty items consisting largely of raw materials, machinery and spare parts, and also coin and bullion. These were exempt from duty but were subject to registration charges which, if not otherwise specified, amounted to 2s. per ton, or 6d. per package. Finally, goods enumerated as removable from any bonded warehouse for conveyance beyond

1. This description is based on the information given in the *Blue Book* for 1892/3.
2. Law No. 4 of 1886, as amended.

Table 1.5. Government Revenue, Excluding Loans, by Sources, 1892/3-1909/10

Fiscal year	Total £000	Taxes £000	Taxes Per cent of total	Public services £000	Public services Per cent of total	Fines and fees £000	Fines and fees Per cent of total	Other revenue £000	Other revenue Per cent of total
1892/3	1,069.7	366.1	34.2	583.9	54.6	27.3	2.6	92.4	8.6
1893/4	1,011.0	342.9	33.9	550.1	54.4	25.5	2.5	92.5	9.2
1894/5	1,169.8	347.5	29.7	656.0	56.1	27.2	2.3	139.1	11.9
1895/6	1,457.3	425.6	29.2	883.0	60.7	32.4	2.2	116.3	7.9
1896/7	2,213.1	601.9	27.2	1,460.6	66.0	36.2	1.6	114.4	5.2
1897/8	1,964.3	611.9	31.2	1,169.2	59.4	44.8	2.3	138.4	7.1
1898/9	2,081.3	678.0	32.6	1,221.2	58.6	34.9	1.7	147.2	7.1
1899/0	1,886.7	711.5	37.7	997.0	52.8	29.3	1.6	148.9	7.9
1900/1	2,970.7	951.7	32.0	1,823.2	61.5	60.7	2.0	135.1	4.5
1901/2	3,439.8	1,187.2	34.5	2,022.5	58.8	58.9	1.7	171.2	5.0
1902/3	4,334.2	1,379.1	31.8	2,654.0	61.3	67.1	1.5	234.0	5.4
1903/4	4,160.1	1,114.8	26.8	2,817.2	67.7	57.6	1.4	170.5	4.1
1904/5	3,384.8	935.7	27.6	2,206.3	65.3	66.9	2.0	175.9	5.1
1905/6	3,666.0	1,016.8	27.7	2,404.7	65.6	68.6	1.9	175.9	4.8
1906/7	3,471.9	1,015.3	29.2	2,192.0	63.2	95.7	2.8	168.9	4.8
1907/8	3,510.4	929.5	26.5	2,357.4	67.2	54.0	1.5	169.5	4.8
1908/9	3,569.3	1,018.2	28.5	2,346.8	65.8	49.9	1.4	154.4	4.3
1909/10*	4,293.7	935.3	21.8	2,819.6	65.7	52.2	1.2	486.6	11.3

*Eleven months only.
Source: Natal, Colonial Treasurer's Accounts and Auditor-General's Reports.

the borders of Natal were charged transit dues. These were considerably lower than customs duties on goods destined for home consumption. For example, whereas the duty on blankets, sheets, shawls, etc., was 5 per cent ad valorem, and 4s. per gallon of wine, transit dues on these commodities were 3 per cent and 6d. respectively. The object was, of course, to foster the Colony's transit trade.

Consumption taxes. The only consumption tax in existence was the excise duty levied on rum and other spirits distilled in the Colony.[3] On spirits destined for local consumption, it was assessed at a rate of 4s.6d. per proof gallon, but on spirits produced for export the charge was only 6d. per liquid gallon. In the latter case the charge was rather in the nature of an export tax, but since the statistics data do not show separate amounts collected on the basis of these two rates, this tax is included under the heading of "consumption taxes."

Direct taxes. In 1892/3, the only direct tax was the Native hut tax assessed on all Native huts in the Colony at a rate of 14s. per hut.[4] Other taxes classified by the colonial authorities as direct taxes cannot be treated as such. An example is supplied by the dog tax, which was of the nature of a license.

License and other business taxes. The main taxes included under this heading were licenses, stamp duties, and transfer dues. License taxes included the dog tax, which amounted to 5s. per dog. It was not a revenue measure but was intended to keep a check on the number of dogs, which constituted a danger to sheep.[5]

Stamp duties were charged for carrying on certain specified trades and professions in the Colony. Stamp duties applied also to transfers passed by the register of deeds, and to various other documents. Transfer dues were chargeable at a rate of 2 per cent on any sale or exchange of landed property and at a rate of 4 per cent also on the purchase price of a lease. In addition a charge amounting to 2 per cent was payable on one-third of the rent of landed property. The composition of government tax receipts in the period under consideration is shown in Table 2.5.

3. Law No. 16 of 1884.
4. This tax is considered as a direct tax, since taxes on dwellings, like those on land or wages, are levied on a given part of the taxpayer's general income.
5. Government House Minute Book, No. 12, 1875. Government House Records.

Table 2.5. Composition of Government Tax Receipts, 1892/3-1909/10

Fiscal Year	Total £000	Direct taxes		Import duties		Consumption taxes		Licenses & other business taxes	
		£000	Per cent of total	£000	Per cent of total	£000	Per cent of total	£000	Per cent of total
1892/3	366.1	79.5	21.7	219.7	60.0	20.9	5.7	46.0	12.6
1893/4	342.9	82.4	24.0	194.1	56.6	20.2	5.9	46.2	13.5
1894/5	347.5	84.9	24.4	192.8	55.5	20.4	5.9	49.4	14.2
1895/6	425.6	76.8	18.0	269.5	63.3	19.6	4.6	59.7	14.1
1896/7	601.9	94.0	15.6	418.9	69.6	20.2	3.4	68.8	11.4
1897/8	611.9	129.6	21.2	389.0	63.6	21.9	3.6	71.4	11.6
1898/9	678.0	135.4	20.0	440.7	65.0	28.3	4.2	73.6	10.8
1899/0	711.5	102.0*	14.3	527.8	74.2	28.9	4.1	52.8	7.4
1900/1	951.7	168.1	17.7	659.4	69.3	41.9	4.4	82.3	8.6
1901/2	1,187.2	142.2*	12.0	851.0	71.7	50.4	4.2	143.6	12.1
1902/3	1,379.1	149.3	10.9	1,023.6	74.2	54.4	3.9	151.8	11.0
1903/4	1,114.8	156.2	14.0	760.9	68.3	69.1	6.2	128.6	11.5
1904/5	935.7	173.5	18.5	569.5	60.9	69.2	7.4	123.5	13.2
1905/6	1,016.8	269.2	26.5	569.6	56.0	65.7	6.5	112.3	11.0
1906/7	1,015.3	298.4	29.4	539.9	53.1	60.5	6.0	116.5	11.5
1907/8	929.5	281.6	30.3	482.1	51.9	51.3	5.5	114.5	12.3
1908/9	1,018.2	367.4	36.1	477.2	46.8	46.5	4.6	127.1	12.5
1909/10†	935.3	305.2	32.6	459.3	49.1	45.6	4.9	125.2	13.4

*The actual accounts did not provide figures for the hut tax. Data were obtained from the magisterial reports and the budget speech of 1900 and adjusted to correspond to the budget year. They can, therefore, be considered as close estimates.
†Eleven months only.
Source: Natal, Colonial Treasurer's Accounts and Auditor-General's Reports.

Generally, it may be noted that import duties and direct taxes formed a vital source of Natal's tax revenue. The former contributed between one-half and three-quarters, and the latter between one-tenth and one-third of the tax receipts. The remaining taxes, which included consumption taxes and licenses and other business taxes, were relatively less important.

During the nineties receipts from direct taxes were erratic, but after the Anglo-Boer War they contributed an increasing proportion of the total tax revenue. On the other hand, revenue from import duties, which prior to the war showed irregular increase, dropped considerably between 1902/3 and 1908/9. A similar trend was discernible in consumption taxes.

Receipts from government services are analyzed in Table 3.5. During the period under review railway receipts furnished between 82 and 90 per cent of the revenue from government services. Next in importance were postal and telegraph services, followed by port and harbor services, and other services.

The Relationship between Revenue and Imports

Very helpful in tracing the main causes of fluctuations in the total revenue of the Colony are changes in the revenue from customs, railways, and port and harbor services as compared with imports. Table 4.5 reveals that the receipts from customs, railways, and port and harbor services ranged between 66.2 and 81.2 per cent of the total revenue. Hence they were of crucial importance in determining the level of the Colony's total revenue. Column 5 of Table 4.5 shows the revenue from these three sources as percentages of imports. With the exception of four years, receipts from the above sources ranged between 25.7 and 32.7 per cent of imports, despite considerable fluctuations in the total revenue and imports. It follows, therefore, that the bulk of the Colony's revenue, being closely related to trade in general and imports in particular, was highly sensitive to the state of business conditions in Natal and in the adjoining territories whose imports passed through Durban.

The purpose of the ensuing analysis is to trace the causes of the fluctuations in the various sources of revenue.

Table 3.5. Composition of Revenue from Government Services, 1892/3-1909/10

Fiscal Year	Total £000	Railways		Port & harbor		Posts & telegraphs		Other	
		£000	Per cent of total	£000	Per cent of total	£000	Per cent of total	£000	Per cent of total
1892/3	583.9	479.4	82.1	45.3	7.8	53.0	9.1	6.2	1.0
1893/4	550.1	447.0	81.3	47.0	8.5	50.4	9.2	5.7	1.0
1894/5	656.0	536.4	81.8	45.5	6.9	70.5	10.8	3.6	0.5
1895/6	883.0	745.7	84.5	65.4	7.4	68.0	7.7	3.9	0.4
1896/7	1,460.6	1,285.2	88.0	89.3	6.1	79.7	5.5	6.4	0.4
1897/8	1,169.2	1,000.3	85.6	78.4	6.7	84.5	7.2	6.0	0.5
1898/9	1,221.2	1,053.4	86.3	74.6	6.1	86.0	7.0	7.2	0.6
1899/0	997.0	792.4	79.5	84.7	8.5	112.9	11.3	7.0	0.7
1900/1	1,823.2	1,579.9	86.7	99.1	5.4	137.2	7.5	7.0	0.4
1901/2	2,022.5	1,726.5	85.4	107.0	5.3	182.0	9.0	7.0	0.3
1902/3	2,654.0	2,287.0	86.2	122.9	4.6	237.1	8.9	7.0	0.3
1903/4	2,817.2	2,499.3	88.7	115.9	4.1	194.8	6.9	7.2	0.3
1904/5	2,206.3	1,884.4	85.5	110.7	5.0	206.1	9.3	5.1	0.2
1905/6	2,404.7	2,086.0	86.8	114.6	4.8	195.8	8.1	8.3	0.3
1906/7	2,192.0	1,881.6	85.8	108.6	5.0	173.9	7.9	27.9	1.3
1907/8	2,357.4	2,019.5	85.7	120.9	5.1	175.6	7.4	41.4	1.8
1908/9	2,346.8	1,989.2	84.8	157.9	6.7	157.8	6.7	41.9	1.8
1909/10*	2,819.6	2,409.3	85.4	204.6	7.3	151.9	5.4	53.8	1.9

*Eleven months only.
Source: Natal, Colonial Treasurer's Accounts and Auditor-General's Reports.

Table 4.5. Revenue from Customs, Railways, and Port and Harbor Services, 1892/3-1908/9 *(as percentages of total revenue and imports)*

| Year | Imports (1) £000 | Revenue | | (3) as % of (2) (4) | (3) as % of (1) (5) |
		Total (2) £000	Customs, railways, port & harbor (3) £000		
1892/3	2,456.6	1,069.7	744.4	69.6	30.3
1893/4	2,171.3	1,011.0	688.1	68.1	31.7
1894/5	2,370.0	1,169.8	774.7	66.2	32.7
1895/6	3,904.0	1,457.3	1,080.6	74.2	27.7
1896/7	5,710.8	2,213.1	1,793.4	81.0	31.4
1897/8	5,654.4	1,964.3	1,467.7	74.7	26.0
1898/9	5,341.3	2,081.4	1,568.7	75.4	29.4
1899/0	5,687.7	1,886.7	1,404.9	74.5	24.7
1900/1	7,869.5	2,970.7	2,338.4	78.7	29.7
1901/2	11,626.2	3,439.8	2,684.5	78.0	23.1
1902/3	14,401.8	4,334.2	3,433.5	79.2	23.8
1903/4	13,132.8	4,160.1	3,376.1	81.2	25.7
1904/5	10,980.0	3,384.8	2,564.6	75.8	23.4
1905/6	10,337.0	3,666.0	2,770.2	75.6	26.8
1906/7	9,204.8	3,471.9	2,530.1	72.9	27.5
1907/8	8,303.8	3,510.4	2,622.5	74.7	31.6
1908/9	8,577.5	3,569.3	2,624.3	73.5	30.6

Source: Natal, Colonial Treasurer's *Accounts* and Auditor-General's *Reports.*

The Period of Railway Rivalry and Growing Revenue, 1892/3 to 1898/9

The fall of the Colony's revenue between 1892/3 and 1893/4[6] can be traced to external causes. Receipts from internal sources remained practically unchanged. The decline in Natal's imports (including transit trade) from £3.7 millions in 1891/2 and £2.2 millions in 1893/4[7] reduced tax receipts because of the loss of customs and transit dues, which fell from £301,000 to £191,000. Moreover, in the period under review reduced imports led to a decline of railway receipts from £665,300 to £447,000. There was also a

6. See Table 1.5, p. 60.
7. See Table 8.1, p. 17.

reduction in post office revenue due largely to Natal's entry into the Universal Postal Union in 1892. The Colony adopted the Union's postal rates and a new system of international settlements.

To deal with the problem of dwindling revenues two measures were applied. First, reductions in railway rates ranging from 15 to 56 per cent were introduced by Natal.[8] Second, certain goods were included in the transit list and subjected to an ad valorem duty of 5 per cent.[9] The colonial treasurer, in his 1895 budget speech,[10] stated that this caused a loss of nearly £20,000 in customs receipts, but prevented a large loss of trade to the Colony and to the railways.

These were, however, temporary measures. A promise of a more lasting solution of the financial difficulties of the Colony's Treasury was found in the railway convention concluded with the Transvaal in 1894. It was agreed to establish direct connection between Durban and Johannesburg by line constructed by Natal from the Charlestown end, and from the Elsburg end by the Netherlands Company. It was furthermore agreed that

1. the railway rates should be adjusted so as to insure a proper proportion of the Transvaal traffic to the Natal and the Delagoa Bay lines. The "proper proportion" of the traffic for either line was defined as not more than half and less than one-third of the gross goods traffic to the Transvaal;

2. Natal would not impose duties upon goods destined for the Transvaal higher than the transit dues then in force, nor lower than the transit dues payable at Delagoa Bay. The Transvaal in return would give Natal most-favored-nation treatment at her borders.[11]

The railway convention of 1894 saved Natal from a major financial crisis. It also strengthened the position of the South African Republic vis-à-vis the Cape Colony and Mozambique by introducing a third competitor. But it must be remembered that the ultimate

8. *Legislative Council Debates*, 1893, pp. 20-21; *Legislative Assembly Debates*, 1895, p. 131.
9. Law No. 23 of 1894.
10. *Legislative Assembly Debates*, 1895, p. 132.
11. Van der Poel, *op. cit.*, pp. 76-77.

control over the proportion of traffic carried by each line rested with the Netherlands Company, which ran the terminal sections where it could impose its own rates.[12] Natal had to wait for two years before the agreement of 1894 began to bear fruit.

In 1894/5 there was only a small improvement in the value of imports, which reached a total of £2.4 millions. Railway revenue increased by nearly £90,000 over 1893/4. This was mainly due to the transport of construction material for the Charlestown-Johannesburg railway. On the other hand, there was little change in customs receipts. The over-all revenue for the year increased by £159,000 to reach £1.2 millions.

A marked rise in imports, which in 1895/6 attained a figure of £3.6 millions, was reflected in a further increase of Natal's revenue to £1.5 millions. The principal increases in revenue had their sources in trade. Railway receipts were responsible for the largest increase, which amounted to £209,000. The advance of customs receipts from £190,000 in 1894/5 to £265,000 in 1895/6 was accompanied by marked increases in port and harbor dues. Higher receipts from transfer and stamp duties originated from a general improvement in the Colony's trade. These were considered as reliable indices of the economy's well-being.[13] This marked improvement in revenue occurred in the second half of the financial year, when the railway connection with Johannesburg was established. For Natal the difficult period was over, and the revenue was rising without additional taxes being imposed. In contrast, reductions in the rates of indirect taxes enabled the Colony to weather the worst years.

Paradoxically, the high degree of dependence of the Colony's revenue on the trade with the Transvaal must be regarded as a source of both weakness and strength. The weakness lay in the wide annual fluctuations in government receipts, which depended on fluctuating revenues from railways and customs duties. Natal's source of strength lay in the long-run economic development of the Witwatersrand. Natal possessed wealth sufficient to raise her economy to that level which she eventually attained.

Having secured outlets for her traffic, and with the return of

12. *Ibid.*, p. 79.
13. Auditor-General's *Report*, 1896, p. iii.

economic prosperity, Natal showed renewed interest in regaining and developing her trade with the Orange Free State, Basutoland, East Griqualand, and Pondoland, from whose trade she had been largely cut off by remaining outside the Customs Union of 1889.[14]

In September, 1896, Natal attended a customs conference at Bloemfontein, where the Orange Free State proposed a uniform tariff with free trade in South African products. Natal, anxious to preserve control over her tariffs in order to continue her policy of low duties, withdrew from the conference.[15]

Times were changing, however, and the events of the next two years made plausible the idea of a wider customs union for the South African territories. Toward the close of 1896, the deep levels "boom" in Witwatersrand, which had kept the railway lines working at full capacity, came to an end. The Cape, handicapped by a longer route and prohibitive charges over the terminal section, was losing her traffic.[16] The changing position of the Cape ports as compared with Durban and Delagoa Bay is illustrated by the figures in Table 5.5.

Table 5.5. **Tonnage of Traffic from the Coast Ports to the Transvaal, 1895-1898** (*percentages of total*)

Year	Cape ports	Durban	Delagoa Bay
1895	75	2	23
1896	44	32	24
1897	38	32	30
1898	33	33	34

Source: C. Verburgh, "The Competition of South African Harbours and Lourenço Marques for the Ocean-borne Imports of the Transvaal: 'Competitive Areas'," *South African Journal of Economics,* XXV (Dec., 1957), 264-274.

In contrast to the Cape, Natal showed a dramatic improvement. Imports rose from £2.4 millions in 1895 to £6.0 millions in 1897. The Colony's revenue moved in the same direction as her trade. In 1896/7 government receipts reached £2,213,000, thus exceeding the previous year's figure by £756,000.

14. Van der Poel, *op. cit.,* p. 94.
15. *Ibid.,* p. 95.
16. *Ibid.,* pp. 97-98.

The economic depression of 1898 had an adverse effect on the level of imports, which fell to £5.3 millions. The 1897/8 revenue was reduced to £1,964,000, railway revenue fell by £285,000, and customs duties by £29,000. On the other hand, there was an increase of £36,000 in hut tax receipts, a financial consequence of the annexation of Zululand in 1897. A small balance was also transferred from the Zululand government.

At that time the Colony's attitude toward the South African Customs Union began to change. This change did not stem from any immediate difficulties but rather from anticipation of future difficulties. In the face of an approaching political conflict in South Africa, Natal desired to make her peace with the Union. Her politicians were also influenced by the opinions of Cecil Rhodes, who had not abandoned his belief that a South African federation would soon become a reality. In these circumstances compromise was a keynote of the conference held in April, 1898, from which the Transvaal was significantly absent. The Cape and the Orange Free State reduced the general ad valorem rate to 7.5 per cent. It was still ½ per cent higher than that proposed by Natal, but by accepting the former rate, the Colony found herself able to enter the Union.[17]

On a large number of commodities the new tariff rates were above those previously in force in the Colony. In addition, Natal had to hand over to the territory where the importers resided 85 per cent of the duties collected on goods in transit.[18] Free trade in South African products was extended to Natal by the Customs Union. In order to protect the grain farmers of the Orange Free State, free trade in flour manufactured from South African wheat was prohibited. Since Natal did not grow wheat, she refused to burden her population with a duty of 4s.6d. per 100 lbs. imposed by the Convention. The Colony, however, agreed to pay a bounty equal to the above duty on her imports of flour made from wheat grown in South Africa.[19] This arrangement was in force until 1903,

17. *Ibid.*, pp. 99-101.
18. The Customs Convention of 1898 stipulated that 85 per cent of the customs duties collected by Natal on goods in transit to any other member of the Customs Union should be handed over to the importer's government. This, however, did not apply to the Transvaal, which remained outside the Union. Transit dues and 15 per cent of the duties collected by Natal were meant to cover the administrative costs of handling the goods by customs authorities (Act No. 50 of 1898).
19. Act No. 50 of 1898.

when the new South African Customs Union was concluded.[20] Spirits were also excluded from the Convention's free trade, in order to safeguard the interests of the Cape wine-growers. Natal by special arrangement was allowed to charge a duty on her imports of South African-produced spirits which was equal to the excess, if any, of the Colony's excise duty over and above the excise duty paid on such spirits at the place of distillation.[21] Thus the new legislation insured that all South African producers of spirits could compete on an equal footing.

In 1898/9 Natal's revenue of £2,081,000 showed an increase of £117,000 over the previous year. There was a modest improvement in customs duties of £53,000, and a similar increase in railway receipts. This was largely caused by imports into the Colony during the last quarter of 1898 of goods which were liable to the higher duties leviable under the Customs Convention.[22] On the other hand, customs receipts from the Transvaal trade were adversely affected by reducing transit dues to 3 per cent on goods destined for that territory.[23] This was done in order to meet the increasing competition of the Cape and Delagoa Bay.[24] However, trade did not respond to this measure.[25]

The period 1892 to 1899 was marked by Natal's intensive efforts to secure and maintain her share of the forwarding trade of the South African Republic and other inland territories. For this reason, customs and railway policies were of primary importance, and other fiscal problems received little attention. By joining the Customs Union, Natal solved her tariff problems with regard to her other partners. But for the time being, the competition for the traffic with the Transvaal remained a source of anxiety to the fiscal authorities of the Colony.

Revenue during the Anglo-Boer War, 1899/1900 to 1902/3

The changes in Natal's revenue during the period 1899/1900 to 1902/3 were largely due to the war and the impact of the Customs

20. Extended by Acts No. 11 of 1901 and No. 19 of 1902.
21. Act No. 50 of 1898.
22. *Legislative Assembly Debates*, 1899, p. 58.
23. Act No. 7 of 1898.
24. Van der Poel, *op. cit.*, p. 104.
25. *Sessional Papers* of the Legislative Assembly, No. 3, 1899.

Union upon her trade. The revenue fell from £2,081,000 in 1898/9 to £1,887,000 in 1899/1900. The largest reduction was in railway receipts, which declined by £261,000, accompanied by a serious decline in direct taxes, licenses, and other business taxes. Railway receipts fell sharply on account of the cessation of trade with the South African Republic following the outbreak of the war. Military traffic enabled the Railway Department to earn a large part of the revenue accruing to it. The disadvantage of this traffic was, however, that the bulk of it was transported inland from the coast, and few of the returning vehicles carried any payloads. The occupation of the northern districts of Natal by enemy forces deprived the Treasury of revenue consisting largely of the hut tax, licenses, stamp duties, fines and fees of office, transfer dues, and land revenue.

The increase in receipts from customs duties was due to the general improvement in trade in the Colony and in other parts of South Africa not directly affected by the war, as well as to the stimulating effects of the Customs Union. In addition, the presence of the Imperial troops and large numbers of refugees from the Transvaal increased the demand for imported goods, which rose from £5,359,000 in 1899 to £6,016,000 in 1900.

The rise in the cost of living caused by higher customs duties was largely offset by rising incomes and employment.[26] To reduce the burden of indirect taxes, duties on frozen meat were suspended. However, the upward trend of exports was temporarily arrested. Exports initially rose from £2,202,000 in 1898 to £3,185,000 in 1899, but fell to £1,343,000 in 1900, owing to the cessation of trade with the South African Republic.

In 1900/1 the revenue of the Colony rose by over a million pounds to £3.0 millions. This was owing to the fact that as the invaders retreated, more territory had been opened up for trade and railway traffic. Moreover, the economy of Natal recovered from the first impact of the war and began to share in the prosperity of those parts of South Africa where peace prevailed. Thus the portion of the Native hut tax and other dues, which could not have been collected because of the Boer invasion, was now paid. Conse-

26. It was estimated that the new tariff exceeded the pre-Convention rates on foodstuffs by less than 2 per cent (*Legislative Assembly Debates*, 1901, p. 44).

quently direct taxes, licenses, and other business taxes increased
to £123,000.

Imports were continuously rising and reached £9.7 millions in
1901, thereby increasing customs receipts to £681,000. The loss
of receipts from the transit dues on goods sent to the Transvaal
was compensated by increased local consumption of imports which
paid the full duties.[27] By far the largest increase was in railway
receipts, again a result of military traffic. The amount of £1,580,000
in 1900/1 exceeded the 1899/1900 level by £788,000.

The rapid growth of the private sector of Natal's economy and
the extraordinary requirements of the war placed a strain on the
public services. This was admitted in the treasurer's budget speech
for 1901, where he expressed the opinion that

in order to build up the Colony, it is, and will be for years to come, necessary that a large revenue be raised. Durban as a port, must be continuously improved . . . . the Railways must be extended and agriculture
must be encouraged. For these things people must pay.[28]

At the same time he explained that "taxation through the Customs
is far and away the most simple and most sure method."[29] Thus the
fiscal policy envisaged by the colonial treasurer was one of indirect
taxation based on the expectation of growing trade arising from
a South African Customs Union.[30] The obvious danger was the
embarrassing instability of the revenue derived from such a source
in view of the violent business fluctuation in South Africa. But this
was disregarded, at least for the time being.

In 1901/2 revenue continued to increase. The realized amount
of £3,440,000 was £469,000 higher than during the previous budget year. Increases occurred under nearly all the important heads
of revenue. In 1902 imports rose to £13,529,000. In addition to the
requirements of the Imperial troops and refugees in the Colony,
merchants began to accumulate imported goods for the anticipated
trade with the Transvaal. They considered it worthwhile to keep
them as open stocks and pay the full Natal duty, instead of storing
the goods in bonded warehouses, where they would have been sub-

27. *Ibid.*, pp. 41-42.
28. *Ibid.*, p. 43.
29. *Ibid.*
30. *Ibid.*

ject only to a transit duty of 3 per cent.[31] Customs receipts rose during the year by £180,000, and the revenue from public services by £202,000. Of the latter amount the railways were responsible for £147,000. These increases were caused by the military traffic, the needs of a larger population, and higher imports.[32]

The general trends of the previous years continued during 1902/3, when Natal's revenue increased by nearly one-third to £4,334,000. About one-half of this increase was due to the railways. A substantial rise in customs receipts was also maintained. The colonial treasurer, in his 1903 budget speech, described the financial position as "highly satisfactory, indicating . . . the growth and prosperity of the Colony."[33] In 1903 imports reached an unprecedented level of £15.3 millions as a result of the reconstruction requirements of the Transvaal. Natal merchants continued to accumulate stocks. This was partly the result of the anticipated higher duties under the new Customs Convention, and of the overly optimistic expectations of a rise in the volume of trade after the war. Railway receipts, which increased by £560,000 in 1901/2, were influenced by the heavy military requirements after the armistice, and by the larger proportion of commercial traffic at rates higher than those charged on the military traffic. A considerably larger contribution to the revenue was made by the post office because of the incorporation of the new territories and the general increase in business.[34]

In March, 1903, a conference assembled at Bloemfontein to deal with the problem of the revision of railway rates and customs tariffs. Conditions had changed and the participation of the Transvaal in the Customs Union had become a necessity.

The first problem settled by the conference was a *modus vivendi* with regard to railway rates. A through rate on imported produce from East London and Durban to Johannesburg was fixed at £3.10.0 per ton. In compensation for a larger maritime route the Portuguese were offered a preference of ten shillings per ton on

31. *Ibid.*, 1902, p. 62.
32. Auditor-General's *Report*, 1902, p. 23.
33. *Legislative Assembly Debates*, 1903, p. 315.
34. Auditor-General's *Report*, 1903, p. 21.

imported products carried from Delagoa Bay.[35] Secondly, the conference dealt with tariffs. It provided for

1. A rise in the general ad valorem rate from 7.5 to 10 per cent, and the protection of important industries by special rates on imported grain, flour, spirits, sugar, tea, and tobacco.
2. Free trade in South African products.
3. Preferential treatment of British goods to the extent of 25 per cent of the duty chargeable at the ad valorem rate, and free entry of machinery, railway, and telegraph material from Britain; similar goods from other countries paid 2.5 per cent ad valorem duty.
4. Preferential treatment of any British territory which would give the Union reciprocal advantages.
5. The imposition of an additional duty equivalent to the bounty granted on sugar imported from any country which was not a party to the Brussels Convention of 1902.[36]
6. The suspension of the duties on foreign flour and wheat upon payment by the government of the importer of a bounty on South African-produced flour and wheat equivalent to the suspended duty.
7. The suspension of the duties on fresh and frozen meat, and on animals for slaughter, until the majority of the parties to the Union should agree to the removal of the suspension.
8. The refund to the consuming country by the collecting member of 95 per cent of the Union duty.
9. The abolition of the existing transit dues.[37]

The tariff agreement was to run for two years, but the railway rates were fixed for only one year. Thus the prospects of further co-operation between the South African territories depended on the continuation of the existing arrangements. Nevertheless, the Customs Convention of 1903, which extended its membership to the Transvaal, was an important step toward the economic unity of British South Africa. A basis was created for a common policy. This

35. Van der Poel, *op. cit.*, p. 122.
36. Convention relating to the bounties on sugar signed in Brussels on May 5, 1902, between the United Kingdom and certain other countries.
37. Act No. 14 of 1903.

new policy found its expression in an increase in tariffs to provide for more revenue as well as the protection of local industries.

Compared with the last prewar budget year, 1898/9, the total revenue in 1902/3 had more than doubled. So had the income from public services and the receipts from taxes. All this was achieved without the introduction of new taxation or an increase in the rates of existing taxes, with the exception of customs duties. Future years were to create new economic problems. These, in turn, would lead to the implementation of new fiscal measures.

The Postwar Period of Falling Revenue, 1903/4 to 1909/10

During the first two postwar budget years government receipts fell from £4,334,000 in 1902/3 to £3,385,000 in 1904/5. In 1903/4 customs receipts declined by as much as one-third. The disappointed expectations of importers who had accumulated excessive stocks of foreign goods, together with the dumping on the market of a large surplus of military stores, had unfavorable influence on imports.[38] There was a loss of transit dues, which were discontinued under the new Convention; also a higher proportion of duties had to be refunded on imports by the inland territories.

In spite of the depression the railways and Excise Department showed increases. The revenue from the former rose by £212,000 as the result of the pressure of traffic in the early months of 1903, when war was concluded.[39] The increase in excise receipts was largely due to the imposition in 1903 of an excise duty on beer amounting to 4d. per gallon.[40] In the same year an excise duty on spirits was raised from 7s.6d. to 7s.10d. per gallon.[41]

In the budget year 1904/5 all the main heads of revenue showed a decrease. Railway receipts fell from £2,499,000 to £1,884,000, thus showing a reduction of £615,000. Customs revenue decreased by £196,000 owing to the deepening economic depression and the continuing diversion of through traffic to Delagoa Bay. The unfavor-

38. *Legislative Assembly Debates*, 1905, p. 247.
39. Auditor-General's *Report*, 1904.
40. Originally an excise duty of 2d. on beer was imposed by Act No. 37 of 1901, but it did not take effect until October 1, 1903. The duty was then raised to 4d. per gallon (Act No. 35 of 1903) and an equal amount of duty was imposed on beer imported from the other members of the Customs Union.
41. Act No. 34 of 1903.

able change in the distribution of traffic to the Transvaal is illustrated in Table 6.5. The only important increase was in direct taxes due mainly to the amounts of the Native hut tax collected from the newly annexed northern territories.

Table 6.5. Tonnage of Traffic from the Coast Ports to the Transvaal, 1903-1909 *(percentages of total)*

Year	Cape ports	Durban	Delagoa Bay
1903	26	44	30
1904	18	40	42
1905	13	36	51
1906	15	33	52
1907	14	30	56
1908	13	24	63
1909	12	22	66

Source: Verburgh, op. cit., p. 65, and D. M. Goodfellow, A Modern Economic History of South Africa (London, 1931), p. 190.

In view of the falling revenue and unduly high expenditure, the colonial treasurer in his budget speech of 1905 anticipated that the financial year 1905/6 would begin with a deficit of some £400,000[42] on the consolidated revenue fund. In order to wipe off this debit balance he proposed new taxes. He did not, however, expect to raise the whole amount needed for that purpose in a single year. The target for the coming budget year was £200,000.

The proposal included four new taxes:

1. A poll tax of £1 on all adult males, with the exception of indentured Indians and certain categories of Africans. This tax was expected to yield in 1905/6 £165,000.

2. A tax of 10s. per hut in private locations, payable by the landowner. Huts occupied by Natives employed by the owners of the land were exempted. The estimated yield of this tax was £25,000.

3. A tax of ½d. per acre of unoccupied rural lands. It was expected to yield £5,000.

42. One-half of this deficit was due to a transfer of £200,000 to a newly created contingencies fund. This amount, being unspent, was still available (see Chapter 4, p. 56).

4. A succession duty, which was expected to yield £5,000.[43]

The bill introducing the tax on unoccupied lands was passed by the Legislative Assembly, but was rejected by the Legislative Council. The hut tax of 10s. payable in private locations was also discarded. Only two out of the four taxes proposed in 1905 were enacted. One of them was the succession duty.[44]

The other tax enacted in 1905 was a poll tax[45] of £1 per annum on all males eighteen years of age or more. Natives liable for hut tax, and those employed in the Colony but domiciled elsewhere, did not pay the tax; exemptions were also granted to indentured Indians and to persons who could prove their inability to pay the tax due to poverty. Persons residing in the Colony for less than six months were excluded by the Act.[46]

The receipts from the poll tax, together with the increased railway revenue, helped to balance the 1905/6 budget.[47] The actual revenue of the Colony rose to £3,666,000, as compared with £3,385,000 during the previous financial year. Railways reported the largest increase, £202,000.

The increase in direct taxes resulted from poll tax receipts, which amounted to £125,000. The succession duty yielded only £3,000 instead of the estimated £5,000. There were, on the other hand, reductions in the receipts from other sources. A fall in imports from £10.9 millions in 1904/5 to £9.7 millions in 1905/6 was reflected in a reduction of customs receipts by £10,000. In 1905 Delagoa Bay definitely out-distanced Durban in the Transvaal trade (Table 6.5). The receipts from posts and telegraphs showed the same decline as the customs duty.

The poll tax, introduced in order to reduce the deficit in the Colony's revenue, became one of the important causes of the Bam-

43. *Legislative Assembly Debates*, 1905, p. 253. At that time the only death duty in Natal was a stamp duty of ¼ per cent on administration accounts. Such accounts were usually dispensed with, and the bulk of property passing at death was, therefore, exempt from taxation. The succession duty proposed in 1905 was based on the Cape Act of 1864.
44. Act No. 35 of 1905.
45. Act No. 38 of 1905.
46. *Ibid.*
47. The deficit reached an insignificant figure of £4,600. This could have been converted into a surplus had certain items of revenue received during 1905/6 been taken into account instead of having been either placed in a suspense account or held over till the year 1906/7.

bata uprising in Zululand. The cost of suppressing this rebellion aggravated the already difficult financial position of the government.

The deteriorating conditions of trade led to the appointment in 1906 of a commission whose task was to inquire into the problem of protecting the manufacturing industry of the Colony, and to revise the existing customs tariffs.[48] The report, being in favor of protection, strongly criticized the Customs Union tariff introduced in 1903 on the grounds that it was ill-designed to protect local industries.

In order to rearrange her tariffs Natal gave notice of withdrawal from the Customs Union, but was prevented from leaving the Union by a new tariff agreement concluded at a conference which was summoned to Pietermaritzburg in March, 1906.[49] There was an increase in the customs duties on a number of articles, and the general ad valorem rate on non-enumerated commodities was raised from 10 to 15 per cent. British goods were to receive a preferential treatment to the extent of 3 per cent in the case of the ad valorem rates. Individual reductions were stipulated in the case of specific rates. The increase in the customs tariff was also followed by an adjustment in the excise duty on spirits to 9s. per gallon.[50] In addition the conference attempted to settle the vexed problem of the railway rates. It was decided that any railway agreement was to be regarded as part of the general agreement embodied in the Customs Union, and no government was supposed to make any alterations in the rates without consulting its neighbors.[51] However, railway rates remained a bone of contention between the South African colonies until the final unification of the railways in 1910.

The financial position of the Colony deteriorated when revenue fell by £194,000. The receipts for the budget year 1906/7 amounted to only £3,472,000 and imports fell by a million to £8,704,000. There was a marked decrease in goods imported for consumption within the Colony and for transmission to the neighboring states. Goods produced locally displaced many imports. An addi-

48. *Report of Industries and Tariff Revision Commission,* 1906.
49. Van der Poel, *op. cit.,* p. 130.
50. Act No. 10 of 1906.
51. *Ibid.*

tional reason for the decrease in imports was the reduction of stocks held by merchants.[52] Thus the most affected sources of revenue were those influenced by the state of trade, namely customs and railway receipts. The former fell by £20,000 and the latter by £204,-000. The collection of the arrears in the poll tax and hut tax, which could not be gathered during the Bambata Rebellion, helped to increase the amount of the direct taxes.[53]

The fall in poll tax receipts to £104,000 in 1906/7 and the further decline in subsequent years can be explained by the increasing number of successful applications for exemption and the payment by Natives of the hut tax.[54] Evasions were also not uncommon.[55]

Attempts to increase the revenue by the introduction of new taxes or raising rates of existing taxes were unsuccessful, with the exception of the transfer duty, which increased from 2 to 3 per cent.[56] The proposals included an income tax (Bill No. 1, 1906), an unoccupied land tax (Bill No. 2, 1906), and a land tax (Bill No. 14, 1907). It was also proposed to consolidate the license and stamp laws (Bill No. 28, 1907), thereby raising the yield from these taxes by £35,000 per annum. The bills introducing the abovementioned taxes were not proceeded with.[57]

In 1907/8 the revenue was £3,510,000. It exceeded the previous year's figure by only £38,000. The gap of £179,000 between revenue and expenditure was present largely because most of the taxes proposed in the previous year were not introduced. The fall in tax receipts and fines and fees was offset by an increase in the revenue from public services, a result of steadily increasing railway traffic in coal and other colonial goods.[58] Customs, on the other hand, were largely responsible for the decline in tax receipts. Imports continued to fall, and in 1908 they dropped to £7,903,000. From 1903/4 revenue from customs duties declined continuously;

52. Legislative Assembly Debates, 1907, p. 291.
53. Auditor-General's Report, 1907.
54. J. Stuart, A History of the Zulu Rebellion, 1906, and of Dinizulu's Arrest, Trial, and Expatriation (London: Macmillan and Co., Ltd., 1913), p. 131.
55. Auditor-General's Report, 1907/8, p. XIII.
56. Act. No. 10 of 1906.
57. Auditor-General's Report, 1906/7, p. 6.
58. Legislative Assembly Debates, 1908, pp. 511-513.

the amount collected in 1907/8 was less than half of the amount obtained six years earlier.

The colonial treasurer in his 1908 budget speech insisted that "the loss to the Treasury of revenue derived from Customs duties must be made good from some other and new sources, if the administration of the Government is to be efficiently carried on . . . ."[59] He reasoned that, since the protection afforded in recent years by increased customs duties had given rise to the development of local industries and manufactures, it was not unfair to propose that the people who benefited thereby should pay taxes in lieu of customs duties. In support of this view he stated that imports were gradually replaced by locally produced commodities, and exports of colonial goods were increasing.[60] On the other hand, the taxable capacity of the population was being impaired by a severe economic depression and by the disastrous East Coast Fever.

While considering ways of increasing the revenue, the treasurer stressed the political factors which made any increase in railway rates extremely difficult; furthermore, the desirability of maintaining a customs union excluded the possibility of raising customs duties. The treasurer, therefore, stressed the revenue which could be derived from additional taxation. He admitted the need for a more equitable tax system and expressed the hope that the poll tax would be removed as soon as other more legitimate sources of taxation could be introduced.[61] The proposed legislation included an income tax (estimated to yield £50,000 per annum), a land tax chargeable on the unimproved value of land (estimated to yield £65,000 per annum), and an increase in wharf dues from 5s. per £100 to £1 per £100 on goods imported for home consumption (estimated to yield £21,000 per annum).

The personal income and company taxes together with the land tax were introduced in 1908.[62] Income taxes for the fiscal year 1909 were levied at the following rates:

59. *Ibid.*, p. 512.
60. *Ibid.*
61. *Ibid.*, pp. 514-515.

1. On private incomes:

   a. Married men:[63]

      Incomes not exceeding £240 per annum............nil.
      For every pound in excess of £240
      but below £750 per annum ....6*d.*
      For every pound in excess of £750
      but below £1,000 per annum ....9*d.*
      For every pound in excess of £1,000
      per annum ....1*s.*

   b. Unmarried men:

      Incomes not exceeding £150 per annum...........nil.
      For every pound in excess of £150
      but below £750 per annum ....6*d.*
      For every pound in excess of £750
      but below £1,000 per annum ....9*d.*
      For every pound in excess of £1,000
      per annum......................................1*s.*

2. On income of companies:

      For every pound of the taxable income.............1*s.*

Income was defined as any gains or profits excluding capital gains such as the natural increase of livestock, increase in the market value of securities, investments of other property. Permissible deductions were:

   a. Losses and outgoings incurred in the production of income;
   b. Repairs to premises and machinery;
   c. Depreciation to machinery, buildings, etc.;
   d. Life insurance premiums, not exceeding £50 per annum;
   e. Interest on bonds on immovable or movable property.

The income tax did not apply to income from land situated outside a municipality or township. If such land was "beneficially occupied"[64] by European tenants, it was subject to the land tax. There

62. Acts No. 33 and No. 34 of 1908.

63. Widowers with children dependent on them and other persons supporting a parent or other relative in Natal were treated as married men.

64. Beneficial occupation was defined by Act No. 33 of 1908 as "an active and reasonably sufficient utilization, according to civilized methods, for agricultural,

was, however, an exception to this rule: whenever the income tax assessed on the income derived from the land exceeded the land tax, the former and not the latter was applicable. The income tax was introduced in 1908 for one year only; it was discontinued in view of the improving financial position of the Colony.

The land tax introduced in 1908[65] varied according to whether the land was "beneficially" occupied or not. On beneficially occupied land the ordinary land tax was charged, while on other land an additional charge was made, in the form of the special land tax. The ordinary land tax amounted to ½d. for every pound sterling of assessed value. This tax was payable on the total unimproved value of all the land owned by the taxpayer. In order to arrive at the taxable value of lands beneficially occupied and used by the owner or a European tenant, a deduction of £2,000 from the total value, and an allowance for the value of land sufficient for a residence, was to be made. Mortgaged amounts were also deductible. In addition to the ordinary land tax, a special land tax was levied on land not beneficially occupied at a rate of 1½d. per pound sterling of value assessed, and 2d. in the case of absentee owners.[66] A Select Committee on the Income and Land Assessment Act reported that the act had worked smoothly, and that the Commissioner for Income and Land Tax had adopted a common-sense method of deciding whether land was beneficially occupied or not.[67] This method, although perhaps the only one practicable, can scarcely have made for exactness and impartiality in the assessment of taxes.

The financial results for 1908/9 disclosed a revenue of £3,569,-

pastoral or industrial purposes, or for any lawful purpose of utility or enjoyment." Land owned by a European was not considered to be beneficially occupied if it was occupied solely by Africans or Indians, unless such land was not suitable for European occupation.

65. The idea of a land tax was not new to the Colony. A number of proposals were put forward, the first of which went as far back as 1868. The subsequent proposals were made in the years 1880, 1885, and 1887. Afterwards the idea of a land tax was temporarily forgotten, but it was revived again in 1905, when the need for more revenue forced the colonial treasurer to investigate new sources of taxation. In that year two bills (No. 2 and No. 56) advocating taxation of unoccupied land were introduced. Another bill was introduced in 1907 (No. 14) proposing a land tax with an estimated yield of £100,000 per annum (Auditor-General's *Report*, 1906/7, p. 6). Neither of these bills was proceeded with.

66. An absentee landowner was defined by Act No. 33 of 1908 as an owner who had not been present in Natal for a least half the previous four years, unless he had beneficially occupied his land within twelve months of buying it.

67. *Sessional Papers* of the Legislative Assembly, No. 12, 1909/10.

000, which was £59,000 in excess of the last year's figure. This improvement was largely attributable to the new taxation. As compared with 1907/8 the revenue from direct taxes for 1908/9 increased by £85,000, of which the income tax yielded £69,000 and the land tax £11,000. However, there were considerable arrears of these taxes. The revenue from indirect taxes showed an insignificant decrease. In 1909 imports increased to £9,252,000. This helped to arrest a rather sharp rate of decline in customs revenue during the previous five years.

In spite of the improvement in the general conditions of trade in 1909, the receipts from government services decreased by some £10,000, railway revenue declined by £31,000, and post and telegraph receipts by £22,000. These reductions were partly offset by increased receipts from the Port and Harbor Department, following the imposition of higher wharf dues.

The prospects for the budget year 1909/10 were assessed by the colonial treasurer in the light of the expanding traffic in the Transvaal competitive area.[68] He also anticipated an improvement in the local trade. Nevertheless, government found it advisable to ask Parliament to re-impose the income and land taxes at reduced rates.[69] But no legislation to this effect was ever promulgated, and the revenue of some £26,000 from these taxes collected in 1909/10 represented the previous year's arrears.

The main feature of the revenue, representing eleven months of the last colonial budget year, was a marked increase of £420,000 in railway receipts. There was also a further improvement of some £47,000 in port and harbor revenue. Thus the treasurer's expectations were largely fulfilled.

The transfer of £300,000 from the consolidated loan fund to the consolidated revenue fund caused revenue for 1909/10 to rise to £4.3 millions. This transfer pertained to general stores accumulated from past revenue. Its object was to wipe out the deficiency of the consolidated revenue fund and, in the treasurer's words, "to enter Union with a clean sheet."[70]

To conclude, the heavy reliance on the receipts from the public

68. This was in spite of an increasing proportion accruing to Lourenço Marques (Delagoa Bay).

69. *Legislative Assembly Debates*, 1909, pp. 282-292.

70. *Ibid.*, p. 292.

services persisted in the postwar period. But this was not sufficient to offset the reduction in the proceeds from indirect taxation. Four years of consecutive deficits forced the legislature to approve the introduction of additional direct taxes in an attempt to maintain the revenue at the previous level. Nevertheless, the revival of 1909 lessened the importance of this new source of revenue.

The financial difficulties during the last years of colonial rule and the desire to find a permanent solution to the competitive customs and railway tariffs of the neighboring territories were among the important economic factors which influenced Natal's entry into the Union of South Africa.

Chapter 6. The Expenditure

Departmental Expenditure

The preceding chapter has presented a survey of the sources of government revenue in Natal. The present chapter examines the opposite side of the government accounts and presents a survey of current expenditure together with a brief discussion of its most significant features. As in the case of revenue, the analysis of expenditure which follows focuses attention on the change in its size and composition. Expenditure by the colonial government is shown in the accounts of the auditor-general. It consists of the amounts that were approved by the budget, and represents actual disbursements in each fiscal year. For the purpose of this study government expenditure has been grouped into six categories which reflect the principal functions of government. Items not accounted for under any of the following six categories are grouped under "Miscellaneous."

"General government and legislature" includes expenditure connected with the offices of the governor, the colonial secretary, the auditor, and the agent-general. Expenditure on the several departments of the Treasury, the Legislative Assembly, and Legislative Council are covered by this heading.

"Law and order" includes expenditure on the office of the attorney-general, various law courts, legal offices, and police and prisons. Expenditure on the offices of the magistrates is also accounted for under this heading. In addition to purely legal and administrative duties, these officials were responsible for collecting Native taxes and performing a variety of other functions in their respective districts.

"Colonial defense" refers to the expenditure on the maintenance of colonial troops and military establishments, as well as to the allowances paid by the colonial government to the Royal and Imperial troops stationed in the Colony.

"Public services" includes a fairly large number of items of which railways, post and telegraphs, port and harbor, education, agriculture, and mining are the most important.

"Public works" includes expenditure on buildings, roads and bridges, waterworks, and power stations. This expenditure comprised the cost of buildings and provision of new services, as well as the maintenance of existing ones. Expenditure on public works out of general revenue was separated from the expenditure on public works from loan funds. Only the former is included here.

"Public debt service" covers the payment of interest on the public debt, repayments of the principal, and contributions to the sinking fund.

A comprehensive picture of the expenditure of government funds is provided in Table 1.6. The most important fact revealed in the table is the growth of total government expenditure from roughly one million pounds in 1892/3 to over three and a half million pounds in 1908/9.

Between 1893/4 and 1902/3 there was a continuous rise of expenditure. The peak figure of £5,102,000, reached in the latter year, was the result of the combined impact of the large extraordinary expenditure caused by the Anglo-Boer War, the high level of economic activity, and an increase in prices. Thereafter, with the exception of 1906/7 and 1907/8, expenditure showed a downward trend. It fell to £3,530,600 in 1908/9.

It should be noted that during the postwar period expenditure never reverted to its prewar level. This was the result of the expansion of existing government activities and the establishment of new ones occasioned by population growth and the development of Natal's economy, as well as by economic progress in the neighboring territories.

Throughout the period under review expenditure presented a fairly stable pattern. Public services occupied the most prominent place. Their share in the total expenditure fluctuated between 40 and 55 per cent. Next was the public debt service, which ranged between 10 and 30 per cent. There is a close connection between the two items because the development of public services was largely financed from public loans.

The expenditure on "general government and legislature," "law and order," and "colonial defense" was of comparatively minor significance. These "traditional" functions of government never accounted for more than 20 per cent of total expenditure. On the other hand, expenditure on public works never fell below 6 per

Table 1.6. Government Expenditure, Excluding Loan Funds, by Purposes, 1892/3-1909/10 (£000)

Year	Total expenditure	Gen. govt. and legislature	Law and order	Colonial defense	Public services	Public works	Public debt service	Miscellaneous
1892/3	1,099.9	34.9	107.5	33.2	503.4	65.6	304.3	51.0
1893/4	1,082.4	38.2	103.0	32.1	457.4	63.4	324.9	63.4
1894/5	1,148.1	39.9	121.8	40.4	460.9	73.6	331.4	80.1
1895/6	1,282.5	43.0	130.6	45.6	563.4	77.0	329.4	93.5
1896/7	1,625.0	48.7	158.1	71.6	740.6	101.8	329.4	174.8
1897/8	1,812.3	51.1*	204.4*	51.8*	744.8*	94.4*	324.9*	340.9*
1898/9	1,908.3	59.5	236.1	58.8	905.5	217.2	340.9	90.3
1899/0	1,955.1	62.9	235.8	76.8	979.3	161.9	360.3	78.1
1900/1	2,499.6	72.9	269.6	78.7	1,384.5	220.7	390.8	82.4
1901/2	3,052.6	68.3	289.7	104.9	1,661.2	248.2	456.8	223.5
1902/3	5,102.0	94.5	469.0	94.5	2,088.5	350.4	522.1	1,483.0
1903/4	4,071.4	135.3	434.6	153.9	2,260.7	367.6	545.3	174.0
1904/5	3,814.6	108.5	450.7	203.8	1,912.3	333.2	651.3	154.8
1905/6	3,674.0	85.7	408.7	165.4	1,804.8	250.9	760.4	198.1
1906/7	3,681.9	81.8	427.2	126.1	1,878.2	231.2	805.4	132.0
1907/8	3,689.8	86.6	431.8	107.2	1,916.0	147.5	865.8	134.9
1908/9	3,530.6	89.4	424.5	86.6	1,783.2	115.9	898.7	132.3
1909/10†	3,530.3	101.9	395.6	102.5	1,897.3	154.3	725.8	152.9

*Estimate.
†Eleven months only.
Source: Natal, Auditor-General's Reports.

cent of the total. The residual group "miscellaneous" showed rather wide fluctuations.

Table 2.6. Government Expenditure, Excluding Loan Funds, by Purposes, 1892/3-1909/10 *(percentages of total expenditure)*

Year	Gen. govt. and legis- lature	Law and order	Colonial defense	Public services	Public works	Public debt service	Miscella- neous
1892/3	3.2	9.7	3.0	45.8	6.0	27.7	4.6
1893/4	3.5	6.4	6.1	42.3	5.8	30.0	5.9
1894/5	3.5	10.6	3.5	40.1	6.4	28.9	7.0
1895/6	3.4	10.2	3.6	43.9	6.0	25.7	7.2
1896/7	3.0	9.7	4.4	45.5	6.3	20.3	10.8
1897/8	2.8*	11.3*	2.9*	41.1*	5.2*	17.9*	18.8*
1898/9	3.1	12.4	3.1	47.4	11.4	17.9	4.7
1899/0	3.2	12.1	3.9	50.1	8.3	18.4	4.0
1900/1	2.9	10.8	3.1	55.5	8.8	15.6	3.3
1901/2	2.2	9.5	3.4	54.5	8.1	15.0	7.3
1902/3	1.9	9.2	1.9	40.9	6.9	10.2	29.0
1903/4	3.3	10.7	3.8	55.5	9.0	13.4	4.3
1904/5	2.8	11.8	5.3	50.2	8.7	17.1	4.1
1905/6	2.3	11.1	4.5	49.2	6.8	20.7	5.4
1906/7	2.2	11.6	3.4	51.0	6.3	21.9	3.6
1907/8	2.3	11.7	2.9	51.9	4.0	23.5	3.7
1908/9	2.5	12.0	2.5	50.5	3.3	25.5	3.7
1909/10†	2.9	11.2	2.9	53.7	4.4	20.6	4.3

*Estimate.
†Eleven months only.
Source: Natal, Auditor-General's *Reports.*

In view of their importance in relation to the other groups of expenditure, public services deserve particular attention. They are analyzed in Table 3.6.

Expenditure on railways was as important as the revenue obtained from their services. The railways were, as a rule, responsible for over two-thirds of the total expenditure on public services. There was a lack of uniformity in the allocation of railway expenditure to revenue and loan account. Certain works of a capital nature were, in some cases, included in the revenue account. Also, since the railway accounts were not separated from other government

Table 3.6. Expenditure on Public Services, 1892/3-1909/10

Year	Total public services £(000)	Railways £(000)	Railways % of total	Port and harbor £(000)	Port and harbor % of total	Posts and telegraph £(000)	Posts and telegraph % of total	Agriculture and mining £(000)	Agriculture and mining % of total	Education £(000)	Education % of total	Public health £(000)	Public health % of total	Other £(000)	Other % of total
1892/3	503.4	343.3	68.2	25.0	5.0	72.2	14.3	10.2	2.0	38.1	7.6	9.3	1.8	5.3	1.1
1893/4	457.4	294.7	64.4	26.0	5.7	74.0	16.2	9.8	2.1	38.3	8.4	9.2	2.0	5.4	1.2
1894/5	460.9	303.2	65.8	21.2	4.6	76.1	16.5	9.9	2.1	36.3	7.9	10.0	2.2	4.2	0.9
1895/6	563.4	391.1	69.5	24.4	4.3	81.1	14.4	10.5	1.9	41.4	7.3	10.4	1.8	4.5	0.8
1896/7	740.6	560.5	75.6	39.8	5.4	66.3	9.0	12.6	1.7	40.9	5.5	12.5	1.7	8.0	1.1
1897/8	744.8	538.3	72.3	41.6	5.6	74.6	10.0	18.6	2.5	47.9	6.4	14.6	2.0	9.2	1.2
1898/9	905.5	674.3	74.5	19.9	2.2	92.4	10.2	34.7	3.8	52.0	5.7	21.3	2.4	10.9	1.2
1899/0	979.3	756.0	77.2	22.8	2.3	88.9	9.1	29.4	3.0	54.0	5.5	19.6	2.0	8.6	0.9
1900/1	1,384.5	1,134.8	82.0	25.7	1.9	100.3	7.2	34.6	2.5	57.1	4.1	23.4	1.7	8.6	0.6
1901/2	1,661.2	1,317.4	79.4	32.1	1.9	128.1	7.7	80.3	4.8	70.2	4.2	26.2	1.6	6.9	0.4
1902/3	2,088.5	1,628.0	78.0	38.3	1.8	170.3	8.2	88.4	4.2	84.2	4.0	67.6	3.2	11.7	0.6
1903/4	2,260.7	1,753.8	77.6	37.0	1.6	170.8	7.6	125.1	5.5	101.0	4.5	62.9	2.8	10.1	0.4
1904/5	1,912.3	1,357.6	71.0	40.7	2.1	191.0	10.0	131.4	6.9	108.9	5.7	74.3	3.9	8.4	0.4
1905/6	1,804.8	1,337.7	74.0	37.9	2.1	178.5	9.9	100.3	5.6	100.3	5.6	41.5	2.3	8.6	0.5
1906/7	1,878.2	1,391.0	74.1	35.5	1.9	159.6	8.5	139.9	7.4	103.3	5.5	39.9	2.1	9.0	0.5
1907/8	1,916.0	1,395.8	72.8	61.4	3.2	165.7	8.6	145.1	7.6	106.6	5.6	36.0	1.9	5.4	0.3
1908/9	1,783.2	1,317.2	73.8	65.4	3.7	161.7	9.1	91.0	5.1	109.1	6.1	35.7	2.0	3.1	0.2
1909/10	1,897.3	1,380.0	72.7	75.6	4.0	161.7	8.5	125.6	6.6	113.7	6.0	37.0	2.0	3.7	0.2

Source: Natal, Auditor-General's Reports.

accounts, railway profits were often used to pay the ordinary expenses of other government departments.

Posts and telegraphs came next in importance, with expenditure ranging from 7 to over 16 per cent of total public services.

Expenditure on harbor works is consistently included under the heading of "public works," whereas the expenditure on the administration and working of the harbor services is included under "port and harbor." Port and Harbor Department expenses never exceeded 6 per cent of the total expenditure on public services.

Finally, in order of importance, expenditure on education was followed by agriculture and mining, while public health toward the closing years of the period received the special attention of the government.

The Period of Rising Expenditure, 1892/3 to 1902/3

The rapid growth of government expenditure in Natal over the period 1892/3-1902/3 followed very closely the growth of revenue.

In the previous chapter we have shown that changes in revenue were largely dependent on changes in imports. This is not typical of modern African economies, where, as a rule, government expenditure depends on exports, which usually constitute a decisive part of commercialized production. In these economies incomes are largely determined by the world demand for their few primary export products. A considerable proportion of government revenue is then derived from taxes on incomes originating in export earnings; and this, in turn, affects levels of government expenditure. Thus export earnings provide the link between expenditure and revenue.

In Natal, however, the position differed in two important respects. First, total export had a large import content, which consisted of manufactures, capital goods, and industrial raw materials. Second, in the absence of export taxes and direct taxes on the incomes of the commercial and industrial sectors, government revenue had to rely mainly on import taxes and railway earnings. The latter, as we have seen, were also closely related to imports.

Between 1892/3 and 1893/4 the Colony's expenditure followed the downward trend in revenue. The most significant decrease was under the heading of "public services," the decrease of which followed the reduction in the expenditure on railways. Another factor was the reduction in the working costs of the railways due to the substitution of local for imported coal.[1]

In 1894/5 the downward trend was reversed and expenditure continued to rise for the next nine years. The income from the improvement in trade provided the resources for the increased expenditure under the main headings (see Table 1.6). A considerable saving was, however, effected by a reduction in public debt payment from the estimated £514,000 to £331,000, because the 5 per cent debentures issued under Law No. 35 of 1880 were converted into a 3.5 per cent loan instead of being redeemed.[2]

The improvement in imports reflected in the railway traffic was largely responsible for the increase in expenditure by a total of £477,000 during the budget years 1894/5 and 1896/7. In addition, expenditure was increased by such unforeseen events as the Glencoe rail disaster, the worst in the history of the Natal railways,[3] which added over £20,000 to the railway expenses; there was also the cost of rinderpest prevention and locust extermination, amounting to some £108,000.[4] The growing budgetary surpluses caused enhanced spending in most of the major groups of expenditure.

In 1896/7 the Government Laboratory and Government Savings Bank were two new services. The latter was made compulsory by legislation.[5] The Government Laboratory was created to help those engaged in mining, prospecting, and agriculture.[6]

In 1897/8 total expenditure rose by £187,000 to reach £1,812,-000. In the absence of complete audited accounts for that year[7] the details of expenditure were reconstructed from fragmentary

1. *Legislative Assembly Debates*, 1895, p. 131. In 1898 the colonial treasurer stated that in the previous ten years the railways had to use imported coal at £2.3.0 per ton. In 1897/8 the savings amounted to £100,000 per annum (*ibid.*, 1898, p. 74).

2. Auditor-General's *Report*, 1895, and *Legislative Assembly Debates*, 1896, p. 116.

3. E. D. Campbell, *The Birth and Development of the Natal Railways* (Pietermaritzburg: Shuter and Shooter, 1951), p. 133.

4. *Legislative Assembly Debates*, 1896, p. 118, and 1897, p. 149.

5. The Savings Bank was originally established by Law No. 7 of 1868, in order to afford facilities for depositing small savings.

6. *Legislative Assembly Debates*, 1896, p. 120.

7. The auditor-general's report for 1897 was never published because of the loss of the audit records when the Pietermaritzburg City Hall was gutted by fire on July 12, 1898.

sources and are in the nature of estimates. The increases were probably due to the strengthening of the police force and the precautions against rinderpest, both of which were anticipated by the colonial treasurer in his budget speech delivered in 1897.[8] The increased expenditure on the police force was caused by its assuming the responsibility of maintaining order in Zululand after its incorporation into Natal. The administration of that territory was taken over by Natal as from January 1, 1898, and the expenditure of the Province of Zululand was included in the estimates of the Colony of Natal as from July 1, 1898. At that time the annual ordinary expenditure of Zululand amounted to only £40,000.

Between 1898/9 and 1902/3 Natal's ordinary expenditure more than doubled. There was also an extraordinary expenditure of some £1,139,000 incurred during the war year and originally accounted for under the heading of "advances," but later included in the consolidated revenue fund.

A considerable part of the increase of the ordinary expenditure was due to the Railway Department. In 1898/9 the cost of the railways amounted to £905,000; by 1902/3 it rose to £2,088,000. The loss of traffic with the Transvaal was more than offset by the military traffic. Moreover, the occupation of the northern part of Natal by enemy forces cut off the sources of cheap local coal, which then had to be replaced by imported fuel. At that time Natal was becoming increasingly dependent on overseas loans for her finances. In consequence the cost of servicing the public debt rose from £341,-000 in 1898/9 to £522,000 in 1902/3. There were also considerable increases in expenditure to make good the damages caused by the invasion, the extension of postal and telegraph services, and new harbor works.

The equipment of volunteers with new artillery and additional expenses undertaken in the fight against bubonic plague and the rinderpest caused expenditure to rise again in 1901/2. It was also agreed to provide subsidy of £34,000 to the Union Castle Company, whose steamers regularly visited Durban.[9]

Further additions to expenditure of £157,000 spent on railway renewals and betterment works were incurred in 1902/3. These

8. *Legislative Assembly Debates*, 1897, p. 149.
9. *Ibid.*, 1901, p. 47.

became imperative in view of the heavy wear and tear on the engines and rolling stock during the war. There were also increases in salaries of civil servants amounting to £34,000 due to the higher cost of living. The annexation of the Northern Districts accounted for new expenditure on the newly created Border Police. Toward the end of the year, however, the Border Police were disbanded and replaced by the existing Police Administration of Natal.[10] The expenditure for 1902/3 included the extraordinary expenses which had accumulated during the war and Natal's share of the invasion losses, amounting to £1,140,000.

The year 1903 ended a period of short-lived prosperity which Natal enjoyed after the war. It was a peak year with regard to the Colony's imports and public expenditure. The remaining years of the colonial rule were overshadowed by the economic depression which followed.

Expenditure during the Postwar Period, 1903/4 to 1909/10

Natal's expenditure was still running high in 1903/4. It proved difficult to accommodate expenses to the falling revenue in view of the demands imposed upon the colonial government by the aftermath of the war and in view of the growing public services. Repatriation of the refugees had to be completed, railway stores replenished, and the provision of agricultural services involved the government in the purchase of dipping tanks for cattle and the further prevention of cattle diseases. These items alone were responsible for an increase of expenditure amounting to some £92,-000.[11] To this must be added rising costs of "general government," "defense," and "public debt service." On the other hand there were savings under the headings of "law and order" and "miscellaneous expenditure."

Between 1904/5 and 1907/8 budgetary deficits persisted. In 1904/5, efforts to economize were partly frustrated by expenses amounting to some £133,000 caused by the new outbreak of East Coast Fever.

In 1905/6 the principal savings effected were under the head-

10. *Ibid.*, 1902, p. 65.
11. *Ibid.*

ings of "public services"—£107,000, "public works"—£82,000, "law and order"—£42,000, and "defense"—£39,000. These were partly offset by the rising "public debt service," which showed an increase of £109,000, and by an increase of £43,000 attributable to "miscellaneous" items. In his attempts to balance the budget the colonial treasurer advocated reduction in salaries of government employees and the imposition of new taxes.[12] These measures were preferred to a reduction in employment. He indicated that the expenditure on the salaries of the civil services (excluding railways) had risen from £365,000 in 1899/1900 to an estimated figure of £887,000 in 1904/5. The Colony could not meet the rapidly rising costs of administration.[13]

During 1906/7 and 1907/8 the attempts to lower expenditure met with little success. Pressure on the railway facilities caused by the heavy transport of coal, which was carried out at low rates, tended to increase the cost of maintaining the railway services. Added interest charges on new loans increased the payments on the public debt.

Reduction in railway expenses led to the fall in the total expenditure of 1908/9. This in turn was due to the fall in the price of local coal caused by the competition of the lower-priced Welsh coal.[14]

Composition of Expenditure

The analysis of the data of government departmental expenditure in the previous sections will now be further broken down in Table 4.6. A comparison of figures in Tables 1.6 and 4.6 reveals that between 1898/9 and 1904/5 the largest sums expended on salaries, wages, and material purchases coincided in time with those spent on public services and public works. The war effort and the period of postwar prosperity were accompanied by higher prices. These encouraged new investments, as well as expenditure on replacements, which resulted in increased wage payments and the purchases of materials. Transfer payments, which included

12. *Ibid.*, 1905, p. 254.
13. *Ibid.*
14. *Ibid.*, 1909, p. 285.

pensions, grants, and gratuities, were relatively unimportant and ranged from 1.2 to 4.3 per cent of total expenditure.

The data on public debt payments pertain to the funded debt only. Payments connected with short-term debts are included under the heading of "salaries, wages, and material purchases." The figures of public debt payments reflect the growing commitments of the colonial administration in providing interest payments and the redemption of the external debt.

Thus far we have considered the current government revenue and expenditure. In order to complete the picture we must also include an analysis of the loan account.

Table 4.6. Distribution of Government Expenditure, Excluding Loan Funds, by Types of Payment, 1892/3-1909/10

Year	Total expenditure £000	Salaries, wages, and material purchases		Pensions, grants, and gratuities		Public debt payments	
		£000	% of total	£000	% of total	£000	% of total
1892/3	1,099.9	787.4	71.6	14.3	1.3	298.2	27.1
1893/4	1,082.4	746.9	69.0	16.7	1.5	318.8	29.5
1894/5	1,148.1	805.8	70.2	17.4	1.5	324.9	28.3
1895/6	1,282.5	940.5	73.3	19.3	1.5	322.7	25.2
1896/7	1,625.0	1,275.1	78.4	28.6	1.8	321.3	19.8
1897/8	1,812.3	1,473.2	81.3	22.2	1.2	316.9	17.5
1898/9	1,908.3	1,561.0	81.8	27.4	1.4	319.9	16.8
1899/0	1,955.1	1,579.5	80.8	25.9	1.3	349.7	17.9
1900/1	2,499.6	2,112.2	84.5	23.2	0.9	364.2	14.6
1901/2	3,052.6	2,567.0	84.1	89.5	2.9	396.1	13.0
1902/3	5,102.0	4,476.5	87.8	149.2	2.9	476.3	9.3
1903/4	4,071.4	3,496.9	85.9	53.0	1.3	521.5	12.8
1904/5	3,814.6	3,141.6	82.4	52.0	1.4	621.0	16.2
1905/6	3,674.0	2,784.4	75.8	159.5	4.3	730.1	19.9
1906/7	3,681.9	2,797.9	76.0	96.8	2.6	787.2	21.4
1907/8	3,689.8	2,750.6	74.5	99.4	2.7	839.6	22.8
1908/9	3,530.6	2,573.5	72.9	92.9	2.6	864.2	24.5
1909/10	3,530.3	2,630.6	74.7	101.1	2.8	798.6	22.5

Source: Natal, Auditor-General's *Reports.*

Chapter 7. The Public Debt

The Growth and Structure of Natal's Public Debt

The preceding three chapters dealt with the volume and composition of government revenue and expenditure but excluded the receipts originating from loans and expenditure on capital account out of loan funds. The present chapter provides a discussion on the latter aspect of government financial activity.

The public debt of Natal began in 1860 with an amount of £50,000 and rose to £7,170,000 by the end of the budget year 1890/1, at which figure it stood for the next two years. During 1891/2 to 1900/1 the debt increased to £11,409,500, or more than 50 per cent. This meant a considerable slowing down in the rate of growth of the public debt as compared with the previous decade, during which it had increased more than fourfold. In that decade the extension of the railroad to the Natal-Transvaal border necessitated large expenditure from the loan account. The capital invested in the open lines absorbed large parts of loans and increased roughly in the same proportion as the debt of the Colony. After 1892/3 railway building lost its previous impetus. The line connecting the Natal system with the Witwatersrand was built by the Netherlands South Africa Railway Company[1] and remained its property. During the remaining years of the nineteenth century only 114 miles of railroads were opened in the Colony.[2]

Between 1900/1 and 1909/10[3] the debt rose to £22,686,594; during that period railway construction was considerably intensified, and over four hundred miles of new lines were built.[4]

Since our interest lies primarily in the changes in the volume of the funded debt and its management, we therefore present in Table 1.7 the amounts of the funded debt, which were obtained by subtracting the temporary, or short-term debt, from the total

1. The N.Z.A.S. (Nederlandsche Zuid Afrikaansche Spporwegmaatschappij) was formed in 1887 to deal with the Delagoa Bay line. The company was later granted temporary loans from Natal government to carry out the construction of the line connecting Natal with Johannesburg (*Legislative Assembly Debates*, 1896, p. 118).

2. W. J. Busschau, "The Development of the Natal Government Railways: An Economic Survey and Critique" (thesis accepted for the degree of Master of Commerce, University of South Africa, 1932), pp. 199-200.

3. Ending on May 31, 1910.

4. Busschau, *op. cit.*, pp. 199-200.

public debt of the Colony. The figures disclose the position as it was at the end of each budget year. For this reason temporary borrowing during the year paid off before its end is not shown.

Table 1.7. Public Debt of Natal, 1892/3-1909/10

Year	Total public debt (1) (£000)	Temporary debt (2) (£000)	Funded debt (3)=(1)−(2) (£000)
1892/3	7,170.4	—	7,170.4
1893/4	8,319.4	259.0	8,060.4
1894/5	8,054.3	—	8,054.3
1895/6	8,019.1	—	8,019.1
1896/7	8,019.1	—	8,019.1
1897/8	8,019.1	—	8,019.1
1898/9	9,019.1	—	9,019.1
1899/0	9,686.5	667.4	9,019.1
1900/1	11,409.5	835.4	10,574.1
1901/2	12,969.1	450.0	12,519.1
1902/3	14,019.1	—	14,019.1
1903/4	16,019.1	—	16,019.1
1904/5	18,019.1	—	18,019.1
1905/6	19,484.1	465.0	19,019.1
1906/7	20,597.8	923.7	19,674.1
1907/8	21,024.6	1,350.0	19,674.6
1908/9	21,534.9	1,439.0	20,095.9
1909/10	22,686.6	2,590.7	20,095.9

Source: Natal, *Blue Books, Statistical Year Books,* and *Auditor-General's Reports;* Union of South Africa, *Report of the Controller and Auditor General of the Union* (Natal), 1911.

It appears that short-term loans carried from one year to another were never a significant proportion of the total public debt; such loans arose mainly from extraordinary circumstances. The funded debt, which in 1892/3 was identical with the total public debt, rose by 1909/10 to £20.1 millions.

In Table 2.7 the amounts of the net funded debt were obtained by subtracting, for each year, the figure of the accumulated sinking funds from the total of the funded debt. The net funded debt is equivalent to what the community would have to pay if it wanted to redeem the debt, allowing for the existing debt-redemption funds. The sinking funds increased from £221,200 in 1892/3 to £1,004,300 in 1909/10.

Table 2.7. Gross and Net Funded Debt of Natal, 1892/3-1909/10

| Year | Gross funded debt (1) (£000) | Sinking funds (2) (£000) | Net funded debt (3) = (1) − (2) (£000) | Net funded debt per capita | |
				Total population (4) £. s. d.	Europeans (5) £. s. d.
1892/3	7,170.4	221.2	6,949.2	12. 7. 4	158.17. 4
1893/4	8,060.4	243.4	7,817.0	13. 7. 7	167. 1. 6
1894/5	8,054.3	262.3	7,792.0	13. 6. 8	170. 9. 6
1895/6	8,019.1	294.3	7,724.8	12.18. 1	160.11. 8
1896/7	8,019.1	275.1	7,744.0	9. 6.11	154. 2. 9
1897/8	8,019.1	308.7	7,710.4	8.18. 6	141. 3. 2
1898/9	9,019.1	320.2	8,698.9	9.13.11	145. 9.11
1899/0	9,019.1	343.7	8,675.4	9. 6. 7	133.11. 4
1900/1	10,574.1	367.8	10,206.3	11. 0. 8	159.18. 5
1901/2	12,519.1	393.0	12,126.1	12.12. 9	165.17.11
1902/3	14,019.1	418.3	13,600.8	13. 1. 8	164.15. 6
1903/4	16,019.1	443.7	15,575.4	14. 0.11	160. 7.10
1904/5	18,019.1	651.2	17,367.9	15. 7. 2	183.18. 7
1905/6	19,019.1	758.2	18,260.9	15.17. 7	193. 8.10
1906/7	19,674.1	796.1	18,878.0	16. 4. 3	204. 4. 5
1907/8	19,674.6	920.3	18,754.3	15.10.11	205. 1.10
1908/9	20,095.9	981.9	19,114.0	15. 6. 1	206. 6. 7
1909/10	20,095.9	1,004.3	19,091.6	. .	. .

Source: Natal, *Blue Books, Statistical Year Books,* and Auditor-General's *Reports;* Union of South Africa, *Report of the Controller and Auditor General of the Union* (Natal), 1911.

A comparison of the gross debt and net debt shows that during the eighteen years under review the gross funded debt increased by 180 per cent, whereas the net funded debt rose by nearly 175 per cent. This indicates that the provision for sinking funds was slightly more than in proportion to the increase in the gross funded debt. However, apart from other factors, a reduction in the average term of the debt which occurred during those years must be taken into consideration in assessing the sufficiency of the available redemption funds (see Table 6.7).

Net debt per capita of total population of Natal rose from £12.7.4 in 1892/3 to £15.6.1 in 1908/9, or by 24 per cent; if only European population is taken into account, the corresponding rise was from £158.17.4 to £206.6.7, or 30 per cent. The steep rise of per capita burden of the debt, in the case of the Europeans, is explained by the fact that the debt was growing at a faster rate than the European population. Temporary reductions in net debt per capita in some years were due, on the one hand, to an increase in population while debt remained stationary, and on the other, to the uneven rate of increase of the sinking funds.

The Supply of Loanable Funds

The supply of loanable funds may be considered under two headings. The first is the supply of short-term loans to cover a temporary shortage of cash needed for ordinary government expenditure, extraordinary payments, or expenditure from loan account before money from capital issues had been realized. In other words, it is the "floating" debt. The second is concerned with long-term government borrowing.

For the colonies the availability of short-term credit in London depended in general on the overall market conditions, and in particular on the market value of long-term colonial bonds. Thus, for example, in 1890 the proposals of some of the colonies to make large issues of bonds caused a feeling of uneasiness among the holders of colonial stocks; they feared that under depressed market conditions an increase in the colonial indebtedness might result in a further depreciation of the market value of their long-term colonial stock holdings. For that reason new requests for credit on the part of colonies had an unfavorable reception in the financial circles of England.[5] This induced Natal to attempt to raise temporary government loans within the Colony. In 1893 an internal loan not exceeding £50,000 was authorized.[6] The principal and interest were to be charged to the general revenue, and the amount was not to be reborrowed. That is, no new debentures were to be issued in respect of any canceled debentures. But those attempts

5. *Legislative Assembly Debates*, 1892, p. 30.
6. Law No. 11 of 1893.

met with little success. Again in 1895 it was advocated that in the case of an investment in assets which have a short life (e.g., relaying of the rails), the financing should be done out of temporary loans raised locally, or in England.[7] A sinking fund would insure that, within the lifetime of the works on which the money was spent, the Colony would repay the loan.[8] This proposal was never given a trial. Prior to the Anglo-Boer War, however, short-term credit was a minor concern. The colonial treasurer had at his disposal accumulated cash balances, and between 1894/5 and 1898/9 these were supplemented from budgetary surpluses. During that period shortages on the loan account were met by temporary borrowing from the consolidated revenue fund. By 1898/9 total advances from the consolidated revenue fund for works to be financed by loans reached a figure of £1,590,000, and it was decided to treat this amount as permanently expended on capital works and not repayable from loan funds.[9]

The emergency which followed the outbreak of the Anglo-Boer War created a demand for short-term borrowing, and loans amounting to £835,000 were obtained from the Bank of England. They were repaid during the budget year 1901/2.

The economic depression, which became marked in 1904, and the Bambata Rebellion of 1906 led to a series of budgetary deficits and extraordinary military expenditure. This time the required funds, amounting to £900,000, were obtained by means of medium-term bonds issued in London.[10] This method of borrowing was applied in the case of a land and agricultural loan and a public works loan.[11] Finally, in 1910 a temporary loan was advanced by the London County and Westminster Bank, in anticipation of the £300,000 required for the purchase of general stores.[12]

The idea of any large-scale borrowing within the Colony could never have been realistic. In Africa, and Natal was no exception, private investment in agriculture and commerce was mainly out

7. It seems that there was a confusion in the mind of the proposer as to the duration of these loans, and the term "temporary" was applied to what would have really been a medium- or a long-term loan.

8. *Legislative Assembly Debates*, 1895, p. 296.

9. Act No. 9 of 1899.

10. Acts No. 4 and No. 47 of 1906.

11. Act No. 17 of 1908.

12. Act No. 8 of 1910.

of the locally accumulated savings.[13] The demands on the domestic financial resources must have been great. Under the then existing circumstances it did not seem that the private sector of the Colony's economy was willing to supply funds to the government at competitive rates of interest. The market mechanism in the form of a stock exchange, issuing houses, and brokers was also lacking.

As early as 1880 the Natal government was able to float a new long-term loan in London and to carry out a conversion at 4 per cent per annum. After 1888 the rate on Natal loan issues fell to 3.5 per cent and in some cases even to 3 per cent.[14] During the last quarter of the century the British interest rates were generally low, and investment in overseas countries increased at an exceptionally high rate. Between 1875 and 1914 capital invested in Britain increased from £5,000,000,000 to £9,200,000,000, or by over 80 per cent. Overseas investment, on the other hand, rose from £1,100,000,000 to £4,000,000,000, or by some 250 per cent. The price levels in Britain were approximately equal at the beginning and the end of that period.[15] It appears, then, that Natal had little choice with regard to the source of loan funds. It is therefore not surprising that the whole public debt of the Colony was external, and that it was contracted in London.

Natal issues were made either at a fixed price[16] or by setting a minimum price and floating the loan by tender. At times the latter method was successful and the loan was allotted at an average price well above the minimum. But this system involved risks of miscalculation: where applications for a loan were inadequate the borrowers were forced to unload the unallotted portions over a number of years. Some of the issues involved underwriting.

On June 30, 1893, Natal's funded debt was £7.2 millions. This figure is arrived at by subtracting the total of conversions and repayments from the total amount of stock created to that date (Table 3.7). Between 1860 and 1893 conversions reached over £4,000,000. This relatively large amount is explained by the fact that full advantage was taken of the fall in the British rates of interest. Loans

13. S. H. Frankel, *op. cit.*, p. 27.
14. *Statistical Year Book*, 1909, pp. 34-35.
15. A. K. Cairncross, *Home and Foreign Investment, 1870-1913* (*Studies in Capital Accumulation*) (Cambridge: Cambridge University Press, 1953), p. 4.
16. Fixed price issues were applied after 1900.

contracted earlier, at rates ranging from 4.5 to 5 per cent, were gradually converted on terms more favorable to the Colony. After 1893 conversions became relatively unimportant because, on the one hand, amounts available for conversion were already considerably reduced and, on the other, whenever market conditions were propitious, Natal was more anxious to use to the full the existing opportunities to contract new loans rather than to convert the old ones.

Between 1893 and 1910 the Colony created £13.3 millions of new stock, of which only £211,900 were conversions. Repayments of the principal amounted to £183,500. Thus the net increase reached £12.9 millions. The total amount of the funded debt, as of May 31, 1910, was therefore £20.1 millions (see Table 3.7).

Let us now briefly analyze the borrowing activities of the Colony in the light of the changing conditions on the London capital market.

Table 3.7. The Effect of Conversions and Repayments on Funded Debt of Natal, 1893-1910

Date	Stock created (including conversions) (£000)	Conversions (£000)	Repayments (£000)	Funded debt outstanding (£000)
As of June 30, 1893	11,332.1	4,091.7	70.0	7,170.4
June 30, 1893, to May 31, 1910	13,320.9	211.9	183.5	12,925.5
As of May 31, 1910	24,653.0	4,303.6	253.5	20,095.9

Source: Natal, *Statistical Year Book*, 1909, pp. 34-35; Union of South Africa, *Finance Accounts, Appropriation Accounts, Loan Funds, and Miscellaneous Funds, with the Report of the Controller and Auditor General of the Union* (Natal), 1911.

The last loan prior to 1893 was created in 1890 and amounted to £2,000,000.[17] At the end of the budget year 1892/3 the unissued balance of that loan was £890,000. The favorable circumstances which accompanied the creation of the loan of 1890 were largely

17. Law No. 29 of 1890.

the result of the conversion in 1888 of British consols from 3 to 2.75 per cent. This led to an abnormal demand for colonial stocks. For nearly three years applications made by colonies for new issues were oversubscribed. Conditions changed, however, with the advent of a crisis in 1890. They became even less favorable when some of the colonies had to take up over £3,000,000 of expiring debentures within the space of a year.[18] The outstanding balance of £890,000 was floated toward the end of 1893, when conditions on the London market for colonial loans began to improve.[19] The prophets of doom who predicted that the granting of responsible government to Natal would adversely affect the credit of the Colony were proved wrong. The crown agents issued a call for tenders for the above loan at a minimum of £94 per £100 of nominal value. However, the average amount raised was £95.5.0. At the same time an Australian issue realized £85 and other good securities obtained only as much as £93.[20] Natal's high standing on the market reflected the investors' confidence in the future of her economy.

This highly satisfactory position was maintained during the following few years, and by 1896, when the financial results of the railway link with Witwatersrand had become apparent, the market quotations of Natal bonds were extremely favorable. Of all the British colonies, Natal's financial standing was second only to that of the Cape and South Australia. In his 1896 budget speech the colonial treasurer was in a position to remark that "we stand uncommonly well if we wish to go into the market."[21] But, in the meantime, budgetary surpluses were used for expenditure on capital account and the Colony did not "go into the market" until 1899. During the parliamentary session of 1898/9 a £2,000,000 loan was authorized,[22] and one half of that amount was raised early in 1899 at 3 per cent per annum.[23] A further portion of that loan amounting to £555,000, together with a 3 per cent loan of £1,000,000,[24] was floated in 1901. The amount realized was £92.10.0 per

18. *Legislative Assembly Debates*, 1892, p. 30.
19. Auditor-General's *Report*, 1894, p. xix.
20. *Legislative Assembly Debates*, 1894, p. 182.
21. *Ibid.*, 1896, p. 137.
22. Act No. 7 of 1898.
23. *Legislative Assembly Debates*, 1900, p. 21.
24. Act No. 4 of 1900 (Public Works Loan).

£100, and this price compared favorably with a 3 per cent German loan issued at the same time at only £87.10.0.[25]

It should be mentioned that the British Colonial Stock Act of 1900, which authorized the Trustees to invest in colonial government bonds, helped to extend the market for the registered and inscribed stocks of colonial governments.[26]

Early in 1902 the balance of the 1898/9 £2,000,000 loan amounting to £445,000, as well as a sum of £1,500,000, which was the first installment of £3,000,000 at 3 per cent per annum, authorized in 1901,[27] was floated at a fixed price of £93.[28] The remaining half of the £3,000,000 loan was offered at a minimum of £94 and realized £94.1.1. Unlike the first installment, this issue was received without enthusiasm. A general decline in the prices of colonial stocks was a further indication of depressed market conditions.[29] The rate of interest on new loans floated by Natal went up to 3.5 per cent. The general state of confidence was adversely affected by the war in the Far East and by the depression in South Africa. Two further loans were, however, floated by the Colony: one in 1904 of £2,000,000[30] at £95, and another in 1905 of £1,000,000, which realized a relatively high price of £97.10.0.[31] Both these loans bore a rate of 3.5 per cent per annum.

During the remaining period of colonial rule, borrowing by the Natal government was largely in the form of loans carrying a rate of interest at 4 per cent per annum, and having a currency of three or four years. This method of borrowing was applied to the Orange River Colony Railway Loan of £425,000,[32] the two Rebellion Loans, totaling £900,000,[33] and an agricultural and public works loan of £250,000.[34] The latter carried a rate of interest at 3.5 per cent per annum.[35] During 1909/10 another loan of £500,000 was contracted by the Colony.

25. *Legislative Assembly Debates*, 1901, p. 46.
26. Cairncross, *op. cit.*, p. 89.
27. Act No. 29 of 1901.
28. *Legislative Assembly Debates*, 1902, p. 64.
29. *Ibid.*, 1903, p. 319.
30. Act No. 40 of 1903.
31. Act No. 7 of 1905.
32. Act No. 2 of 1905.
33. Acts No. 4 and No. 47 of 1906.
34. Acts No. 27 of 1907 and No. 17 of 1908.
35. *Ibid.*

The supply of loan funds involved expenses which varied considerably. The customary minimum rate for underwriting of colonial loans was 1 to 5 per cent, banker's commission ¼ to 1 per cent, broker's commission ¼ per cent, and the stamp duty amounted to a further ¼ per cent.[36] In the case of Natal the total of those expenses ranged between 1.5 and 3.0 per cent.[37] Underwriting charges reflected the risk involved, and rates much higher than the minimum were quite common.[38] It appears, therefore, that the low rates charged on Natal loans reflected the favorable attitude of lenders toward the credit worthiness of the Colony.

The Expenditure from Loan Funds

Natal records of government capital expenditure are deficient with respect to the origin of sums expended on public works and various other capital projects. Capital works had been financed partly from loan funds and partly from sums obtained from the current revenue of the Colony; but no clear statement exists which would indicate the proportion of a particular capital expenditure covered from borrowed funds.[39] For example, in 1893 the colonial treasurer stated that total government capital expenditure incurred by Natal to December 31, 1892, amounted to £8.1 millions.[40] Of this

36. Cairncross, op. cit., p. 91.

37. Blue Books and Statistical Year Books, 1892/3-1909. Underwriting was not a rule.

38. Cairncross, op. cit., p. 91.

39. From the point of view of public capital formation there is, of course, little merit in distinguishing between the different sources of finance. The prevalent body of opinion maintains that attempts to make such distinctions often stem from the fallacious idea that by analogy with business enterprise, loan receipts have to be used for capital expenditures. Otherwise the funds to service the debt would not be forthcoming. But the ability to pay interest and to repay loans depends on a government's power to raise taxes and not on the returns on the particular expenditure made from the loans. (See A. R. Prest, Public Finance in Underdeveloped Countries, London: Weidenfeld and Nicolson, 1962, p. 125.) However, there are two important reasons why that approach had little application in the case of Natal. First, the entire public debt was external. Second, Natal's taxable capacity was very limited. It seems unlikely, therefore, that the Colony would have been willing to make interest payments on its entirely external debt out of tax revenue. In the light of the above fact, it is important that loan funds were spent on productive investment which provided direct means of payment. The accounting procedure which was followed was certainly not meaningless in the context of the investment policy adopted by the government. This point may be of interest not only to the historians of public finance but also to the administrators in some of the newly developing countries.

40. Sessional Papers of the Legislative Council, 1893, No. 6, p. 34.

amount £1.1 millions was expended on various public works and other items, £5.9 millions on railway construction, and £1.1 millions on harbor works. However, these figures also include expenditure from sources other than loan funds. It is estimated that the total amount of the Colony's expenditure from loan funds was £6.7 millions as of June 30, 1893. A comparison between the latter and the former figure, adjusted to the same date, discloses that capital expenditure incurred from sources other than loan funds amounted to some £1.6 millions. By May 31, 1910, the amount expended from loan funds reached £20.8 millions. Thus total expenditure from loans was nearly trebled during the eighteen years under review.

The history of Natal's capital expenditure during the years under consideration may be divided into four distinct periods. The first, extending from 1892/3 until 1895/6, was characterized by an extremely conservative approach to the expenditure of loan funds, which was confined mainly to works already under construction. The economic position of the Colony during those few years has been previously described (see Chapter 5) and it is, therefore, unnecessary to stress again the element of uncertainty and suspense inherent in the government's financial policy. Moreover, to finance the work in progress, advances were made from the consolidated revenue fund in anticipation of the funds arising from the flotation of the remaining portion of the loan of 1890. After the issue of this loan in 1893, a considerable part of the proceeds was used to reimburse the revenue fund. In the absence of new flotations the policy of borrowing from the revenue fund was continued.

The second period extends from July 1, 1895, to December 31, 1898, and it coincides with a series of surpluses on the revenue account, which together with the previously accumulated credit balances, allowed the government to proceed with many capital projects without the necessity of contracting new loans.

Whereas during the former period the average capital expenditure per annum was £107,000, during the latter period annual expenditure reached an average of half a million. The next nine years covered a period when borrowing activities were revived and public capital formation continued to be intensive. Construction of new railway lines was made possible by the loans raised, while conditions on the capital market were propitious. The role played in the

economic development of Natal by the extension of railway transport will be discussed in Chapter 10. At present it may suffice to
mention that during that period the Umzinto, Richmond, and Buf-
falo-Vryheid lines were completed. The Pietermaritzburg-Grey-
town, Dundee-Buffalo, and several other lines were built. The Port
Shepstone and Natal-Cape lines were begun. Particular attention
was also paid to harbor development.[41]

During the budget years 1898/9 to 1906/7 the average per
annum expenditure from loan funds was £1,200,000; but in the
last period extending from 1907/8 to 1909/10, it dropped to £575,-
000 per annum. The first signs of distress had already appeared in
1905/6. It became necessary to exercise caution with regard to
the Colony's commitments in the face of falling revenue. To this
was added the difficulty of raising loans in London, and also the
fact that £700,000 of the loan funds had to be used for the payment
to the Transvaal for the Northern Districts, incorporated into Natal
after the Anglo-Boer War. This considerably reduced the balance
available for planned loan expenditure.[42] Finally, the outbreak of
the Bambata Rebellion in Zululand in 1906 further strained the
financial position of the Colony. The expenditure from loan funds
caused by the Rebellion reached £885,000 and was spread over
a period of three years.

As regards the distribution of expenditure from loan funds the
most striking feature is the high proportion expended on railway
construction, which by 1910 amounted to 63 per cent of the accumulated total. Next in order of importance are harbor works,
which accounted for 17 per cent, and public works, 8 per cent. The
latter item included sums spent on government buildings, roads,
bridges, and post and telegraph. The share of Natal's contribution
to the Zulu War of 1879 and expenditure incurred after 1906 in
connection with the Bambata rising was 5 per cent. Other expenditure, which included sums spent on Indian immigration during the earlier period, and the payment of £700,000 for the Northern Districts to the Transvaal, amounted to 6 per cent of the total.
The balance of 2 per cent corresponded to the expenditure on agri-

41. *Legislative Assembly Debates*, 1898 to 1906.
42. *Ibid.*, 1895, p. 250.

cultural development of the Colony to which contributions from loan funds began during the budget year 1903/4.

The way in which loan funds were expended gives rise to a distinction between "reproductive" and "deadweight" debt. Using this distinction Table 4.7 provides an analysis of the public debt of Natal in 1892/3 and 1909/10.[43]

It appears from the figures that a satisfactory computation of the "reproductive" and the "deadweight" debt must include unexpended balances under the heading of the "reproductive debt," and must add the cost of raising loans to the "deadweight debt." The logic of this method of accounting is simply that the unexpended part of the loan, if required, could be used for debt redemption or servicing while the portion equal to the cost of raising loans is obviously never available for productive investment. If this principle is followed, totals of the reproductive debt for 1892/3 are £6.2 millions, or 86.4 per cent of the public debt for that year, and £18.9 millions, or 85.4 per cent of the public debt for 1909/10. Thus, between 1892/3 and 1909/10 there was little change in the proportion of the reproductive and the deadweight debt, the former having been maintained at a relatively high level.

Some Aspects of Debt Management

Debt management is concerned with the timing and the choice of the most appropriate type of debt as well as the channels of borrowing, repayment, or refinancing. It can be made to serve both the cause of reducing the budgetary charge of the debt service and the wider interests of fiscal policy.[44] Other aspects of debt management include the influence upon the rate of interest payable on the debt, the duration of the debt, and the provision of funds for debt redemption. The aspects of public debt management and fiscal

43. The arithmetic involved in the calculation of Table 4.7 is as follows:
   Public debt = nominal value of loans contracted − repayment of the principal
   where
   Nominal value of loans contracted = amount realized + cost of raising loans.
   Thus, assuming that borrowing on account of public debt is the only source of loan funds:
   Total expenditure from loan funds = public debt − cost of raising loans − unexpended balance of loan funds + repayment of the principal.

44. U. K. Hicks, *British Public Finances, Their Structure and Development, 1880-1952* (London: Oxford University Press, 1954), pp. 173-174.

policy relating to the existence of an internal debt did not apply in Natal since the whole of the Colony's public debt was external. Natal could exercise little choice in this respect.

The rate of interest on particular loans contracted by the Colony was determined by the London market. Given the Colony's preference for loans of a certain duration, the prevailing rate of interest had to be accepted as a datum. The position was, however, different with regard to the average rate of interest on the total debt, since that rate could have been influenced by conversions. It has been

Table 4.7. **Expenditure from Loan Funds, 1892/3-1909/10** *(thousands)*

	1892/3	1909/10
Productive:		
Railways	5,820.0	12,978.8
Harbors*		3,447.5
Public works		1,579.7
Agriculture		495.6
Other	369.4	300.0
	6,189.4	18,801.6
Non-productive:		
Zulu War	250.0	250.0
Indian immigration†	212.1	212.1
N. Districts†	—	700.0
Bambata Rebellion	—	883.6
	462.1	2,045.7
Cost of raising loans	582.2	1,549.3
Unexpended balance	6.7	543.5
	588.9	2,092.8
Total loans contracted	7,240.4	22,940.1
Less		
Repayment of principal	70.0	253.5
Total public debt	7,170.4	22,686.6

*Part of the investment under this heading was not directly productive, but it was impossible to account for such detailed items due to the lack of information.

†These two items were indirectly productive as the introduction of Indians and the incorporation of the Northern Districts increased the output of the Colony's economy and the revenue from taxation. However, it was decided to adopt a more conservative approach, following the classification used by the colonial treasurer (*Legislative Assembly Debates*, 1908, p. 516).

Source: Union of South Africa, *Finance Accounts, Appropriation Accounts, Loan Funds, and Miscellaneous Funds, with the Report of the Controller and Auditor General of the Union* (Natal), *1911*.

shown that the opportunities for converting debts bearing interest of 5 or 4.5 per cent to 4 or 3.5 per cent per annum were largely exhausted by 1893. The total conversions after that year were insignificant (see Table 3.7). However, as a result of former conversions and new borrowings after 1880 at 4 per cent or less, the average rate was brought down to 4.24 per cent in 1892/3. Table 5.7 shows the average gross and net interest cost of the funded debt between 1892/3 and 1909/10. The gradual lowering of the average rate of interest during that period was mainly the result of the increasing proportion of the debt bearing lower rates. A slight rise in the interest rate since 1905/6 is due to the appearance of

Table 5.7. Gross and Net Interest Cost of Funded Debt, 1892/3-1909/10

Year	Interest paid on gross funded debt (£000)	Interest as per cent of gross funded debt %	Revenue from investments (£000)	Net interest cost (£000)	Net interest as per cent of net funded debt %
1892/3	304.3	4.24	12.7	291.6	4.20
1893/4	312.0	3.87	17.1	294.9	3.77
1894/5	311.1	3.86	19.9	291.2	3.74
1895/6	310.0	3.87	17.7	292.3	3.78
1896/7	307.6	3.84	14.4	293.2	3.79
1897/8	316.0*	3.94*	12.4*	303.6*	3.94*
1898/9	307.3	3.41	16.3	291.0	3.35
1899/0	324.4	3.60	20.0*	304.4	3.51*
1900/1	338.9	3.21	20.5*	318.4*	3.12*
1901/2	370.6	2.96	22.5*	348.1*	2.87*
1902/3	451.1	3.22	24.9	426.2	3.13
1903/4	497.8	3.11	15.5	482.3	3.10
1904/5	590.9	3.28	26.0	564.9	3.25
1905/6	643.8	3.39	14.9	628.9	3.44
1906/7	691.8	3.52	11.4	680.4	3.60
1907/8	724.1	3.68	11.7	712.4	3.80
1908/9	741.2	3.69	25.8	715.4	3.74
1909/10†	797.6	—	25.1	772.5	—

*Estimates.

†Since the 1909/10 amounts are for eleven months only, the rates of interest are omitted as they have little meaning.

Source: Natal, *Blue Books, Statistical Year Books,* and Auditor-General's *Reports;* Union of South Africa, *Report of the Controller and Auditor General* (Natal), 1911.

short- and medium-term loans bearing a higher interest charge of 4 per cent.

As regards the duration of the public debt, colonial debt management preferred long-term borrowing. First, funds borrowed were usually invested in projects the fruition of which extended over a fairly large number of years. Second, long-term borrowing made for simplicity and certainty in debt structure. It protected the Colony against sudden requests for debt retirement. This consideration was particularly important in the case of loans of foreign origin, which were often supplied by a small group of financial houses. Therefore it is not surprising that efforts were later made to convert short- and medium-term debt into a funded debt.

The average term of the public debt during the period under review, as shown in Table 6.7, is computed for each year by multiplying the amount of every loan by the relevant number of years of its tenor and dividing the sum of products thus obtained by the total figure of the public debt. The result is an average number of years weighted by the respective money amounts.

Table 6.7. Average Term of Natal's Public Debt, 1892/3-1909/10

Year	Average term in years	Year	Average term in years
1892/3	41.1	1901/2	37.9
1893/4	40.6	1902/3	37.9
1894/5	40.0	1903/4	37.3
1895/6	39.2	1904/5	36.7
1896/7	38.2	1905/6	35.0
1897/8	37.2	1906/7	33.2
1898/9	37.7	1907/8	31.6
1899/0	36.7	1908/9	30.8
1900/1	36.1	1909/10	29.2

Source: Natal, Auditor-General's Reports; Union of South Africa, Report of the Controller and Auditor General of the Union (Natal), 1911.

The average term of the public debt was reduced from 41.1 years in 1892/3 to 29.2 years in 1909/10. A particularly marked shortening of the average term of the debt began to take place after 1904/5, when the Colony's borrowing was largely in the form of loans maturing within one to three years. The efforts of the government to convert these loans to a long-term basis, thereby lengthening the average term of the public debt, were interrupted by the change in the political position of the country with the creation of the Union of South Africa.

The systematic contribution of funds for debt redemption required the existence and administration of sinking funds. But so far no provision for sinking funds was made in respect to the loans raised from 1886 onwards. In his budget speech delivered in 1902, the colonial treasurer stated that at the then existing level of annual contributions to the sinking funds, they would prove insufficient for the repayment of loans maturing in 1909 and 1919. Recommendations had also been made by the auditor-general and the Public Accounts Committee that the proceeds of land sales should be devoted to paying off the public debt. By bringing these proceeds into general revenue, the Colony had been living on its capital. They also suggested that the surplus earnings of the railways should be utilized for debt redemption.[45] But this advice was never followed.

Between 1892/3 and 1903/4 the average annual contribution to sinking funds was about £25,000 or from 1/6 to 1/3 of 1 per cent of the total debt. To remedy this highly unsatisfactory position and, at the same time, to improve the system of accounts, legislation passed in 1904[46] introduced a consolidated loan fund composed of a capital account and an income account. So far, the existing loan funds account reflected capital transactions only. The addition of an income account created a separate framework for transactions related to the payment of interest on public debt. A provision was introduced that any deficiency appearing upon the income account should be covered from the general revenue of the Colony. A Board of Public Commissioners was set up, whose duty it was to supervise the administration of loan funds. The Board was empowered to devote any sum standing to the credit of the capital account and not required for advances to the redemption or purchase of stock or debentures issued for the loans forming

45. *Legislative Assembly Debates*, 1902, p. 3.
46. Act No. 46 of 1904.

the public debt of the Colony.[47] As a result of these new provisions, there was an improvement in the level of contributions to the sinking funds during the remaining years of the colonial government.

Conclusions

It has been alleged that the mineral discoveries in the interior led to the rise of Natal's public debt, which reached alarming proportions.[48] It is largely true that the mineral discoveries stimulated railway and harbor construction with a view toward increasing the Colony's share in the carrying trade as the growing market in the interior expanded. This, in turn, led to a rapid increase of the public debt in the years 1882 to 1890.[49]

After 1891 the growth of the debt slowed down considerably, and only after 1898 did it begin to grow again rapidly. By then the relation between the increase in the Colony's indebtedness and the "mineral revolution" in the North became much less direct. Only part of the new borrowing became related to investment activities which were stimulated directly by the expansion of the Transvaal market. The most typical of these was the improvement of the main railroad and of the harbor facilities in Durban. The bulk of railway building in that period may, on the other hand, be related to the development of agriculture and of other industries in Natal.

A few comparisons may throw some light upon the significance of the public debt of Natal in relation to its economy. Of the geographical product in 1903/4 the public debt of the Colony amounted to 90 per cent and interest payments on that debt to 2.8 per cent. On the other hand, interest payments were 20 per cent of the ordinary revenue in 1903/4. If similar data are taken for the Union of South Africa in 1910/11, the respective percentages would be 89, 3.5, and 27.[50] A comparison between these two sets of percentages

47. *Ibid.*
48. D. A. Farnie, *op. cit.*, p. 132.
49. See Chapter 2, p. 36.
50. This is the nearest set of data available, since no geographical product estimates were ever made for earlier years for South African territories. It is also of interest that the experience of economically developed countries indicates that annual interest payments amounting to 3 or 4 per cent of the national income can be borne lightly, while 7 or 8 per cent sets up serious repercussions (Hicks, *op. cit.*, p. 177).

shows that Natal was in a better position than South Africa as a whole. But the indebtedness of the Union at its inception was never a source of any serious anxiety.

Far more important, however, than the above comparisons is the proportion between the "reproductive" and the "deadweight" debt. This question has already been discussed and it is unnecessary to return to it. But mention must be made that in only ten of the eighteen years under review did government services show a surplus of revenue over expenditure sufficient to cover net interest on the funded debt. During the whole period total surpluses from government services were in excess of total net interest payment to the extent of nearly £ 1.4 millions. Thus government services and enterprises, which included railways and various public utilities largely financed from loan funds, represented an investment which, on the average, paid for itself.

It may also be of interest to consider the view of the then colonial treasurer with regard to the "burden of the deadweight" debt in 1908.[51] By assessing the burden of the deadweight debt per head of Europeans and non-Europeans, on the basis of the proportions of their respective contributions to the revenue derived from taxation, and taking these as the indicators of the tax-paying capacity of those groups, the treasurer arrived at a figure of £13.8.5 per head of the European population, and 19s.6d. per head of the African, Indian, and Coloured peoples. He considered these amounts as reasonable, and stated that "the Colony's position in relation to its Public Debt compared most favorably with that of any other Colony in the Empire."[52]

The danger was not so much the level of Natal's debt but rather that all of it was external.[53] Hence of more immediate concern was the impact of debt servicing upon the balance of payments position of Natal. Debt servicing involved the transfer of interest and amortization payments to Great Britain. The exchange question was non-existent since British currency was legal tender in Natal. What mattered was the problem of transfer: producing a sufficient

51. A modern approach to the problem of the burden of the public debt would be in terms of the real cost of taxes which must be levied to service it.

52. *Legislative Assembly Debates*, 1908, p. 517.

53. This was typical of South Africa as a whole. The colonial debt which the Union took over in 1910 was, to the extent of 92 per cent, external.

amount of goods and services marketable abroad in order to secure funds for these payments.

Owing to the paucity of data on the financial aspects of the Colony's relations with the outside world, no definite conclusions can be formed with regard to the impact of debt servicing upon the balance of payments of the Colony; it would appear that it never was a source of any serious embarrassment. In an era which eschewed all artificial restrictions on the movements of resources within the Empire, the balance-of-payments position of the Colony was left to the free play of economic forces. It was their task to take care of the problems created by the transfers resulting from the existence of an external debt.

Chapter 8. The Administration of the Fiscal System

Introduction

The administration of a fiscal system is mainly based on its legislative framework. This framework sets definite limits to the fiscal and, indirectly, the general economic policies pursued by government. But it often happens that the administration of a fiscal system brings to light imperfections in the existing legislation, and hence suggestions for improvement. The legislative framework of the fiscal system which obtained in Natal in 1893 has been outlined in Chapter 3. In this chapter it is proposed to deal only with changes which were introduced in the years that followed. It will be seen that most of these changes were suggested by administrative practices.

The subject of budget administration, in spite of its dryness, is one of vital importance. The government's role in economic development depends, *inter alia*, on how efficient the government is. This, in turn, depends largely on the efficiency with which the fiscal system is administered.

The ideal way to measure that efficiency would be in terms of the cost of a given output of public goods and services. Given the prices of factors employed by the government, a reduction of cost per unit of output of an unchanged quality would indicate increased efficiency.[1] The difficulties of comparing efficiency may be considerable if an empirical approach to the problem is adopted. Moreover, a technique which is suitable for an analysis performed on a living economic organism is not always suitable for a post-mortem. However, the concept of efficiency of a fiscal system may be given a somewhat wider connotation by including in it the implementation of budget plans. Such an extended notion of efficiency can be traced to a number of factors which, in most cases, can be assessed on the basis of the existing historical material. Such factors include, among others, the efficiency of tax administration, the accuracy of budget estimates, and the degree of departmental and parliamentary control over expenditure. It is with the help of these three factors that an attempt is made to throw some light on the problem of the efficiency of Natal's fiscal system.

1. The concept of efficiency used here sidesteps the wider issues of the optimum allocation of resources between the public and the private sectors of the economy.

The Efficiency of Tax Administration

The efficiency of tax administration may be considered under the headings of the cost of tax collection and the cost of control over tax evasions. Ideally only the cost of collection proper is unavoidable. If all the taxpayers were honest people and no controls were necessary, the cost of controlling evasions would disappear; but as long as any taxes are levied at all, some cost of collection will always be present.

Net tax revenues are equal to the amount collected less the cost of collection. Assuming the continuity of the functions involved, net tax revenues are maximized at a point where a small increase in the cost of collection yields exactly the same amount of additional revenue. However, since the process of tax collection is discontinuous and it is more appropriate to consider it in terms of two inequalities, the time period implied by annual budgeting should not be disregarded.

In Natal the import and the excise duties were the only taxes to which costs of collection were directly apportioned. In the case of most other taxes expenditure was associated with a whole group of taxes, and the authorities in charge of their collection were also performing a number of other functions. Such was the case of the magistrates, who in addition to levying the hut tax and several other taxes and fees, carried out their functions, supervised the police, and acted as general administrators in their magistracies. It was necessary, therefore, to estimate the cost of collection, as no direct amount could be calculated.

The costs of tax collection display an interesting characteristic; viz., the averages, for all the years included in Table 1.8, show a wide range of cost between the direct taxes, licenses, and other business taxes on the one hand, and import and consumption taxes on the other. The estimated average cost of collection for the first group was 2.42 per cent, and for the second group 4.84 per cent of the totals collected. The cost of collection expressed as a percentage of the total amount of the taxes collected was 3.95 per cent. This over-all average may be considered as a fairly low figure. Nevertheless, a low cost of collection creates suspicion that the administration of some of the taxes might have been inefficient, and

Table 1.8. Cost of Tax Collection, 1892/3-1909/10

Year	Direct taxes, licenses, & other business taxes			Import & consumption taxes			Total taxes collected (£000)	Total cost of collection* (£000)	Cost as per cent of total collected
	Amount collected (£000)	Cost of collection* (£000)	Per cent	Amount collected (£000)	Cost of collection (£000)	Per cent			
1892/3	125.5	3.1	2.47	240.6	14.3	5.94	366.1	17.4	4.75
1893/4	128.6	3.2	2.49	214.3	14.0	6.53	342.9	17.2	5.02
1894/5	134.3	3.3	2.46	213.2	13.7	6.43	347.5	17.0	4.89
1895/6	136.5	3.4	2.49	289.1	14.5	5.02	425.6	17.9	4.21
1896/7	162.8	3.8	2.33	439.1	16.8	3.83	601.9	20.6	3.42
1897/8	201.0	4.8	2.39	410.9	17.6	4.28	611.9	22.4	3.66
1898/9	209.0	4.9	2.34	469.0	16.7	3.56	678.0	21.6	3.19
1899/0	154.8	4.1	2.65	556.7	18.0	3.23	711.5	22.1	3.11
1900/1	250.4	5.3	2.12	701.3	17.9	2.55	951.7	23.2	2.44
1901/2	285.8	5.9	2.06	901.4	23.9	2.65	1,187.2	29.8	2.51
1902/3	301.1	6.1	2.03	1,078.0	31.2	2.89	1,379.1	37.3	2.70
1903/4	284.8	6.9	2.42	830.0	38.0	4.58	1,114.8	44.9	3.91
1904/5	297.0	7.2	2.42	638.7	38.1	5.97	935.7	45.3	4.84
1905/6	381.5	8.1	2.10	635.3	35.9	5.65	1,016.8	44.0	4.33
1906/7	414.9	8.7	2.10	600.4	34.1	5.68	1,015.3	42.8	4.22
1907/8	396.1	8.5	2.15	533.4	33.0	6.19	929.5	41.5	4.46
1908/9	494.5	13.5	2.73	523.7	31.7	6.05	1,018.2	45.2	4.44
1909/10	430.4	16.2	3.76	504.9	31.1	6.16	935.3	47.3	5.06

*Estimates.

Source: Natal, Auditor-General's Reports; Union of South Africa, Finance Accounts, Appropriation Accounts, Loan Funds, and Miscellaneous Funds, with Report of the Controller and Auditor General of the Union (Natal), 1911; Budget Speech, 1909, p. 283.

that an increase in expenditure on the collection of the tax might have resulted in an increase of revenue substantially in excess of cost.

The auditor-general's reports express the opinion that while the payments of the Native hut tax were satisfactory, there were frequent failures to pay the license and stamp duties. Except in abnormal times, very little of the hut tax could be looked upon as lost, because of the efficiency of the simple machinery of collection and infrequency of deliberate evasion.[2] In so far as licenses and stamp duties were concerned, the auditor complained of the inadequacy of inspection. As a result many professions and trades were carried on without the payment of the required license fees. A complaint was also made that the procedure of affixing stamps by private persons instead of by public officers opened the way to the evasion of stamp duties.[3]

In 1898 the Public Accounts Committee recommended an inspection of licenses which was subsequently carried out and which resulted in a number of people being charged with contravening the License and Stamp Act.[4] Another example of tax evasion mentioned by the auditor-general in 1908 was the poll tax. Defection in payment of this tax must have been frequent due to inability of the police to undertake proper inspections.[5]

Complaints were also made with regard to the collection of import duties. Customs authorities had no legal power to search vessels or to seal ships' stores. The authorities were dependent upon the reports of ships' masters as the basis of their control.[6] It was also reported that the proprietors of goods kept in the open bonded warehouses had free access to the stock under bond without any customs supervision. Thus goods may have been withdrawn without payment of duty.[7] These few instances support the previous contention that an increased expenditure on tax collection might have led to improved efficiency, partly by the imposition of stricter control over evasions.

2. Auditor-General's *Report*, 1896.
3. *Ibid.*, 1897.
4. The Public Accounts Committee, *Report of 27th July, 1898*.
5. Auditor-General's *Report*, 1908, p. xiii.
6. *Report upon the System of Keeping the Public Accounts in the Colony of Natal*, 1896, No. 7, p. 2.
7. *Ibid.*, p. 14.

The Accuracy of Budget Estimates

No government can carry out its economic policy satisfactorily if its budget forecasting is extremely inaccurate. Whether economic policy is concerned with the implementation of large-scale development plans, or solely with keeping a country's finances on an even keel, this principle cannot be disregarded. The accuracy of budget estimates also enhances efficiency. It is reasonable to assume that most governments plan for efficient administration, and the degree of accuracy with which their plans are realized determines largely how efficient they are.

It is often difficult to state whether budget estimates are for planning purposes or for forecasting future revenue and expendi-

Table 2.8. Estimated and Actual Revenue, 1892/3-1909/10

Year	Estimated revenue (£000)	Actual revenue (£000)	Difference between estimated and actual revenue (£000)
1892/3	1,241.4	1,069.7	171.7
1893/4	1,067.4	1,011.0	56.4
1894/5	1,126.8	1,169.8	−43.0
1895/6	1,194.4	1,457.3	−262.9
1896/7	1,615.9	2,213.1	−597.2
1897/8	2,088.4	1,964.3	124.1
1898/9	1,882.0	2,081.4	−199.4
1899/0	2,099.9	1,886.7	213.2
1900/1	2,287.7	2,970.7	−683.0
1901/2	2,937.6	3,439.8	−502.2
1902/3	3,302.4	4,334.2	−1,031.8
1903/4	4,075.3	4,160.1	−84.8
1904/5	4,172.4	3,384.8	787.6
1905/6	3,966.0	3,666.0	300.0
1906/7	3,901.7	3,483.6	418.1
1907/8	3,641.5	3,510.4	131.1
1908/9	3,491.4	3,569.3	−77.9
1909/10	3,698.8	4,293.7	−594.9

Source: Natal, Auditor-General's *Reports;* Union of South Africa, *Finance Accounts, Appropriation Accounts, Loan Funds, and Miscellaneous Funds,* with the Report of the Controller and Auditor General of the Union (Natal), 1911; Natal Government Gazette.

ture. The important difference between the two frequently becomes indistinct, particularly when the original budget is adjusted by supplementary estimates.

Table 2.8 presents estimated and actual revenue of Natal during the period 1892/3 to 1909/10. It can be seen that there were eight years when expectations of revenue were disappointed. The remaining years showed an excess of actual over estimated revenue. The last column shows the extent of the variations.

But a far better test of the accuracy of estimation can be found in the concept of the average gross percentage error of estimation, which is calculated by subtracting 100 from the percentage ratio of estimated to actual revenue (expenditure) in each of the years in question and taking the mean of these readings.[8] The inaccuracy of estimation of Natal's revenue measured by means of the average gross percentage error amounts to 12.5 per cent. It should be borne in mind, however, that this is a mean percentage error; errors in individual years are far greater.

If a similar method of statistical analysis is applied to the data of estimated and actual expenditure shown in Table 3.8, an average gross percentage of error of estimation of 8.0 per cent is obtained. Thus over the period under review the mean percentage error of estimation is greater in the case of revenue than in the case of expenditure.[9]

The magnitude of the errors of estimation can be ascribed to various factors. When the annual estimates were being prepared the financial results of the current budget year were only vaguely known. A similar difficulty was encountered when supplementary estimates of expenditure were drawn up.[10] Moreover, the period 1892/3 to 1909/10 was noted for its business fluctuations the violence of which coincided with political events. These had a strong adverse impact on government finance. However that may be, the suspicion still remains, especially with regard to the expenditure of the

8. The average net percentage error of estimation, on the other hand, is the mean of the percentage ratios of estimated to actual revenue (expenditure).

9. It is interesting to note that average gross percentage error of estimation of revenue and expenditure for the thirteen West Indian colonies, for the period 1930-53, calculated by A. R. Prest, was 13.0 and 7.1 per cent respectively (Prest, *op. cit.*, p. 134). The technique of error estimation used in this chapter was similar to that used by Prest.

10. This was the position until 1899, when monthly audits were introduced.

Colony, that errors were also due to acts of deliberate policy. The fact that in all the years under review the estimated expenditure always exceeded the actual expenditure lends support to this idea. Confirmation is also found in the views of the Select Committee on Public Accounts in its report of 1903. The Committee adopted a critical approach toward overestimation and stated that "a feeling of false security is engendered by the idea that sums may be safely inserted in the estimates to meet some remote contingency because they will not be spent if they are not required." In the opinion of the Committee this practice lessened the motive to economize, in so far as saving under one item could be supplied to meet

Table 3.8. Estimated and Actual Expenditure, 1892/3-1909/10

Year	Estimated* expenditure (£000)	Actual expenditure (£000)	Difference between estimated and actual expenditure (£000)
1892/3	1,272.2	1,099.9	172.3
1893/4	1,195.6	1,082.4	113.2
1894/5	1,406.1	1,148.1	258.0
1895/6	1,313.4	1,282.5	30.9
1896/7	1,681.6	1,625.0	56.6
1897/8	1,929.9	1,812.3	117.6
1898/9	2,006.6	1,908.3	98.3
1899/0	2,160.0	1,955.1	204.9
1900/1	2,579.8	2,499.6	80.2
1901/2	3,276.1	3,052.6	223.5
1902/3	5,216.2	5,102.0	114.2
1903/4	4,317.9	4,071.4	246.5
1904/5	4,361.8	3,829.6	532.2
1905/6	4,002.5	3,670.6	331.9
1906/7	3,923.6	3,681.9	241.7
1907/8	3,824.8	3,689.8	135.0
1908/9	3,659.0	3,530.6	128.4
1909/10	3,972.0†	3,530.3‡	441.7

*Including supplementary estimates.
†Full budget year.
‡Eleven months only.
Source: Natal, Auditor-General's *Reports*; Union of South Africa, *Finance Accounts, Appropriation Accounts, Loan Funds, and Miscellaneous Funds, with the Report of the Controller and Auditor General of the Union* (Natal), 1911; Natal Government *Gazette*.

excesses under another, weakened the resistance of the Treasury to overestimating, and deprived Parliament of its control over what should be supplementary estimates.[11]

In order to improve the procedure the Committee recommended that the estimates should be handled by an Estimates Committee specially set up for the purpose. The estimates should be presented to Parliament independently and in advance of the supply bill, and dealt with, vote by vote, in a series of resolutions. These resolutions would form the basis for the supply bill, which would then be voted in a single resolution, and would form an authoritative guide for the treasurer and auditor-general.[12] This recommendation was rejected by the government.[13]

Departmental and Parliamentary Control over Expenditure

The most important stages of the budgetary process, from the point of view of control, are parliamentary authorization of the estimates of revenue and expenditure, implementation of the budget by the executive, and an analysis of the financial results. We shall mainly refer to these stages in this section.

In Natal the new Constitution of 1893 brought no radical change in the system of accounts. A vital change in the accounting procedure and in the system of control over government expenditure was, however, introduced in 1898, as a result of the recommendations of the report of 1896 on the system of keeping the public accounts in Natal.[14]

The report suggested abolition of the existing system of central control over public expenditure, known under the name of the "voucher system," and the introduction in its place of a new system of control exercised by the ministerial heads of departments assisted by the public accounting officers. The voucher system made the treasurer responsible for all issues of money to meet voted expenditure by various accounting departments. Under this system the treasurer had no responsibility as to the propriety of the expendi-

11. The Select Committee on Public Accounts, *Report No. 15*, 1903, par. 26.
12. *Ibid., Report No. 2*, 1904, p. 9.
13. Auditor-General's *Report*, 1906/7, p. 3.
14. This report was the result of investigations carried out by Mr. John Bromley from the British Exchequer and Audit Department (*Documents Presented*, No. 7, 1896).

ture by the respective spending departments. The vouchers were only noted in the Treasury and passed on to the auditor-general for examination. This method compelled the auditor-general to draw up the annual appropriation accounts without their being subjected to second check.

The report recommended an alternative system by which all the issues would be made by the treasurer from the government's account at an approved bank. The requisitions by the public accounting officers concerned would have to bear the signature of the ministerial heads of departments, who would be restricted to the current requirements of a given period of a month. This insured that effective control would be maintained over public balances. The treasurer's duty would be to render a monthly account of all his transactions to the auditor-general.[15]

There was thus an important difference between the existing and the suggested system of accounting. Under the former, accounts were paid by the treasurer without examination, beyond ascertaining that they were within the vote of Parliament or executive authority; the audit of the transaction was delayed until the actual voucher reached the Audit Office. Under the latter system, the accounting officer would have to examine the accounts prior to payment, thus acting as a primary auditor of the accounts under his control.

The recommendations contained in the report of 1896 were received favorably by the government and the Select Committee on Public Accounts of 1896. Their delayed adoption in 1898 was accompanied by the issue of detailed financial instructions.[16]

However, the new system proved to be deficient in several respects, and its enforcement was often unsatisfactory. During the subsequent years complaints were frequently made by the controlling authorities about the transposition of votes from one year to another and from one item to another whereby excess expenditure

15. *Report upon the System of Keeping the Public Accounts in the Colony of Natal,* 1896, No. 7, p. 5.

16. *Financial Instructions Regulating the Mode of Keeping and Rendering the Accounts of Receipts and Expenditure,* 1898. These *Instructions* did not apply to the Natal government railways, since it was recognized that "profit-making" departments must enjoy a greater measure of financial independence (*Colony of Natal Financial Instructions,* 1898, par. 102).

was charged to items on which there were available balances.[17] In 1903 the Select Committee on Public Accounts pointed out that the existing financial instructions were interpreted in too liberal a manner by the Treasury, and that expenditure largely in excess of the amount provided in the estimates was incurred under executive authority.[18] Nevertheless, both the Select Committee on Public Accounts and the Departmental Committee on Financial Instructions of 1903[19] agreed that it would be advisable to secure funds for new and quite unforeseen services. This could be done by means of a contingencies account. An account of this kind had in the past successfully been used in Great Britain and in the Cape. The Treasury would make advances from that account, which would be included in the estimates for the succeeding year and repaid to the account.[20]

The suggested remedy was adopted and a contingencies fund of £200,000 was established during the budget year 1904/5.[21] But this solved only one part of the problem. The laxity of control over the expenditure remained a sore point with the auditor-general.[22] Cases were repeatedly occurring where ministers approved additional expenditure without the treasurer's consent. As a first step it was imperative that all proposals involving increased expenditure should be submitted to the treasurer, as he was responsible for finding the means to meet them. Nevertheless, the treasurer himself was also to blame for financing ordinary expenditure from the moneys placed in the hands of the Public Debt Commissioners for loan and sinking fund purposes.[23] There was nothing in the laws of Natal to prevent him from doing this, but the auditor complained that this facility of borrowing led to slowness on the part of Parliament to provide the treasurer with funds. It also provided the executive with the power of spending which the auditor was unable to control.

These matters were taken up in 1905 and 1906 by the Select

17. Auditor-General's *Report*, 1899, p. 2; Select Committee on Public Accounts, *Report No. 1*, 1900, p. 12; *First Report of the Departmental Committee on Financial Instructions*, 1903.
18. Select Committee on Public Accounts, *Report No. 15*, 1903, par. 7.
19. *Ibid.*, par. 6.
20. *Ibid.*, par. 7.
21. Act No. 21 of 1904.
22. Auditor-General's *Report*, 1904.
23. *Ibid.*, 1907, p. 7.

Committee on Public Accounts. The assumption by the executive of apparently unlimited powers to draw upon the revenues without reference to Parliament was a grave defect in the constitutional machinery of the Colony. This was possible because the vital principle of constitutional government that Parliament is supreme in matters of finance could not be enforced.

In the United Kingdom, a country the colonists were always eager to imitate, treasury drafts were invalid without the approval either of the comptroller and auditor-general, or the Bank of England. The Bank was forbidden to honor unauthorized drafts. The British Parliament had a further check upon the executive in that certain important sources of revenue were granted from year to year only.

In Natal the legislation relating to the contingencies fund lacked completeness, because it placed a limit only on the amount which could be issued by vote of the Executive Council. On the other hand, there was no effective provision which would prevent spending without Parliamentary approval. The Committee urged the introduction of legislation, which would subject the treasurer's power to operate upon the accounts into which revenue and proceeds of public loans were paid, to the approval of an officer independent of the executive, and directly responsible to Parliament.[24]

Moreover, practically the whole of the revenue was collected under standing orders. Thus under the existing arrangements it would have been perfectly possible for the executive of the Colony, by an evasion of the law for which no punishment was provided, to carry on the government for an indefinite period, without calling Parliament.[25]

Similar complaints were repeated by the Select Committee on Public Accounts in 1908, but evidence of any steps to rectify this serious deficiency of control is lacking. It would appear that with the growing prospects of unification of the South African territories under one government, the problems of the local constitutional reforms did not attract much interest.

Another point raised as a result of the investigations of the Select Committee on Public Accounts was the administration of

24. Select Committee on Public Accounts, *Report No. 2*, 1906, par. 1.
25. *Ibid., Report No. 12*, 1905, par. 4.

government stores. The Committee of 1895 paid particular attention to the large stocks of goods accumulated by the store departments, and valued at £ 197,000. The Committee pointed out that
the conditions which, in the past, warranted the maintenance of
such large stocks, no longer existed, since the means of communication with the overseas markets had been considerably improved. One
of the adverse effects of this undue accumulation of materials was
the locking-up of the cash resources of the government. A recommendation was therefore made to bring all the store departments
under one administration, in order to improve the control over the
size of stocks.[26] It was also discovered that the principal storekeep-
ing departments, namely the railways, harbors, and public works,
did not carry out periodical and complete stocktaking.[27]

Further investigations were conducted by the special commission appointed to report on the management of government stores.
Among the various important improvements introduced as a result
of the commission's recommendations was that all the purchases
from the United Kingdom were to be made through the agent-general of the Colony.[28] With regard to the local purchases of goods,
the commission recommended that quotations should be obtained
from all firms dealing in the articles required, and the lowest offer
should be accepted.[29] This was of particular importance, as by far
the greater proportion of miscellaneous stores was purchased from
local merchants. With only a few exceptions, the prices were not
subject to any contract, and the receipts of the articles purchased
were missing. Consequently no control over expenditure could be
exercised and there was a complete absence of a check against
fraud.[30] Furthermore, large sums were lost to the government by
way of discounts, which in many instances were not obtained. In
1901 the Select Committee recommended that tenders should be
called for articles that could be purchased locally, and that men
with practical knowledge of the goods required should be employed
as buyers for the various departments.[31]

26. Ibid., Report No. 2, 1895, par. 18.
27. Ibid., Report No. 17, 1898, par. 13.
28. The Office of the Agent-General of the Colony of Natal in London was
created in 1893.
29. Report of the Colonial Stores Commission, 1899.
30. Letter of the auditor-general to the colonial secretary dated April 27, 1901.
31. Select Committee on Public Accounts, Report No. 1, 1901, par. 5/a.

The problem was largely solved with the appointment of a Standing Committee on Stores in 1902. This was an important step forward in framing the regulations relating to the administration of and control over the government stores.[32]

Conclusions

The subject of the administration of a fiscal system assumes particular importance in young countries, where the standards of financial administration are in the course of being shaped and where there is a tendency to burden governments with increasing responsibilities. The picture sketched in this chapter is one of ill-defined legal framework, deficient administration of the existing financial regulations, and the frailty of human nature of officials and the public alike.

The first stage of the control over the fiscal system of Natal rested in the hands of the ministerial heads of departments, who were responsible for authorizing the expenditure of their respective departments. We have seen that they often stretched the letter of the law beyond the breaking point.

The next stage was the audit and the publication of the auditor's report. The auditor-general's precarious position can be best described in his own words written in 1893:

The raison d'être and rational explanation of the Auditor's existence is that he should act as guardian of the Treasury in the interests of the tax-payer. The inadequacy of his powers in this respect has been felt more than once during the past year, and this weakness must continue until it be declared by law that he is responsible to Parliament, and that his office is held during good behaviour and not merely during pleasure.[33]

The years which followed brought little improvement.

The final stage of control was the parliamentary examination of past expenditure, which was often of little interest and value owing to the delayed presentation of complete accounts.[34] Natal had the advantage of the services of members of the Committee on Public Accounts, who were appointed annually. Their reports were

32. *Ibid., Report No. 15*, 1903, par. 6.
33. Auditor-General's *Report*, 1893, p. xix.
34. Often one year's delay.

of inestimable value, but unfortunately their recommendations were as often ignored as they were heeded.

Thus, in spite of the efforts of some well-meaning officers of the government and members of Parliament, the administration of the fiscal system of the Colony left much to be desired. In this respect Natal was in a position similar to that of many poor countries which are not receiving the more extensive, more efficient administration demanded by their fiscal and economic inadequacies.

Part III

Chapter 9. Some Aspects of Taxation and the Impact of Taxes on the Economic Development of Natal

Introduction

In this chapter we propose to discuss the impact of particular taxes on business and on private incomes. These two aspects of taxation are closely linked to the problem of the economic development of the Colony. In addition, an attempt is made to answer the vital question of how the burden of taxation was distributed among the various racial groups. It must be observed that the analysis suffers from incompleteness of the statistical data, which often have to be supplemented by estimates. However, the conclusions reached at this stage do have an important bearing on the final findings of this investigation.

The Impact of the Tax System upon Business Activity

Taxes affecting business activity may, in the main, be divided into two groups: (a) taxes which fall on all business units of an industry and regularly account for part of tax costs, and (b) those which do not display such characteristics.

The first group includes import and excise taxes, business licenses, property taxes, etc., which are normally added to the average costs of the firms in question. Also included in this category are monopoly profits derived from the railways and other public services. These profits are equivalent to a tax imposed upon the users of these services. As a rule entrepreneurs attempt to pass them on to the buyers of their products by increasing the prices. The degree to which shifting[1] of such taxes actually takes place can be ascertained only on the basis of a detailed study which is often not feasible. Typical of the second group of taxes are business profit taxes, the property transfer taxes, etc. Bearing in mind this division we now consider the effects of particular taxes on the profitability and form of business organizations, as well as the size and direction of business investment.

1. The term "shifting" as used here is related to the concept of "effective incidence" considered by R. A. Musgrave, *The Theory of Public Finance* (New York: McGraw-Hill, 1959), p. 230.

Customs duties. By far the most important in its effects was the tax on imports. We assume here that the price elasticity of demand for imported consumer goods was small, as most of these goods were necessities for which locally produced substitutes were lacking. Because a considerable part of the duty was shiftable, this favored the profitability of the importer's business. The effects of import taxes on investment can be ascertained by an analysis of the tariff policy, which protected local industries and affected the importation of capital goods and raw materials.

In Natal both these approaches began to receive increasing attention in the first years of the twentieth century. Although the protective effects of customs duties lie outside the scope of the tax policy, they are vital from the point of view of Natal's industrial development. It may, therefore, not be irrelevant to treat this problem in some detail.

The first attempts to introduce protection through import taxes were rather disappointing. The framers of the 1903 tariff claimed that it was designed to provide protection to certain industries. In fact, it was ill-designed to stimulate industrial development and did not embody any definite policy. In 1906 a commission was appointed to inquire into the question of the encouragement of manufacturing industries in Natal.[2] The commission reported in favor of protection and leveled strong criticism against the existing tariff. Numerous cases were pointed out where an unreasonably high duty was imposed on raw materials used by local manufacturers. The commission recommended the introduction of a new tariff which was to be based on the following classification of imports:

1. All raw materials—they were to be admitted free of duty if imported from the United Kingdom, or from any reciprocating British possession. A duty of 5 per cent ad valorem was to apply in all other cases.
2. Semi-manufactured articles, which were not likely to be manufactured in Natal, but which were being or were likely to be used by local manufacturers—it was indicated that the rate of duty on this class should be low.

2. *Report of Industries and Tariff Revision Commission*, 1906.

3. Goods manufactured or likely to be manufactured in Natal—
a duty of 25 per cent ad valorem was recommended.

4. Non-enumerated goods, consisting of those never likely to
be produced in Natal—on this class a duty of 15 per cent
ad valorem was to apply.

The commission also recommended that the preference granted
to the British goods should be increased from 2.5 to 5 per cent ad
valorem.

After the publication of this report, Natal in 1906 gave notice
of withdrawal from the Customs Union.[3] A conference was summoned, and as a result of a compromise reached between Natal
and the other members of the Union the ad valorem rate on non-
enumerated goods was increased from 10 to 15 per cent. The preference accorded to Britain and the reciprocating British colonies
was raised to 3 per cent ad valorem in the case of ad valorem duties,
and specific duties were imposed in other cases.[4]

On the basis of the available statistical data it is difficult to
assess the effectiveness of the protective measures introduced in
1906. Total imports fell from £10,337,000 in 1905/6 to £8,577,500
in 1908/9. But these figures reflect also the transit trade of the Colony. During the same period the revenue from import taxes declined from £569,500 to £477,200, but at the same time the number
of industrial firms rose from 811 to 922.[5] However, other industrial
census data are not conclusive in establishing a case for industrial
progress. One may, therefore, be justified in partly agreeing with
the opinions of contemporary critics who ascribed the fall in customs revenue between 1905/6 and 1908/9 to protection, which
enabled Natal to produce an increasing proportion of its requirements.[6]

In 1908 another commission was appointed, and it also reported
in favor of protection.[7] Its findings were based on ample evidence.
The views of the commission on the peculiar position of the "new
countries" are of great interest. The commission pointed out that
a country like the United Kingdom

3. Van der Poel, *op. cit.*, p. 130.
4. Law No. 9 of 1906.
5. See Chapter 1, Table 6.1.
6. Budget speeches and the reports of the collector of customs for 1907 and 1908.
7. *Report of the Customs Tariff Enquiry Commission,* 1908, pp. 9-15.

with its enormous shipping and carrying trade, also vast foreign and colonial investments, and its status as a distributing centre for the whole world, all acting as sources of income, is in an entirely different position . . . to that of any new country.

In contrast, "new countries depend upon their own resources only" and "only to develop those resources is a new country justified in borrowing money." The commission then observed that

apart from machinery and implements, to be used in the development of resources and industries, so long as a new country is importing all, or nearly all, of its necessaries of life and general requirements, it stands to reason that, if it cannot pay for these by its exports, not only must the balance of trade be against it with the result of draining it of its available cash—a process of exhaustion which can only end in ruin—but the process is likely to be hastened owing to the consumers being at the mercy of the importers, who have been known to charge high prices when without that healthy competition which local producers always introduce.[8]

What the members of the commission had in mind was that, owing to the smallness of the local market, the importers would tend to create a monopoly in a particular line, often based on the exclusive right of representation. This phenomenon is not uncommon today in many underdeveloped countries.

From this, two conclusions followed: first, that the South African importers were the main opponents of the policy of protection; and second, that protection was necessary to material progress, particularly in a new country, which like Natal was "not exceptionally favored by Nature." The commission explained that by protective duties they meant duties which were adequate to enable local manufacturers to sell their products in competition with similar imported articles. The commission stated that the objects of protection were:

a. To reduce in time, the cost of living by encouraging industries to be built up in the country, thereby creating competition between local producers and importers.

b. Through encouraging the growth of industries, to provide employment for a bigger population, to increase the country's spending power, and *pro tanto* improve trade generally.

8. *Ibid.*, p. 9.

c. To achieve an export surplus, and thus establish a balance of trade in favor of South Africa.[9]

Thus the establishment of industrial firms, by helping to increase employment, would encourage immigration and thereby enhance the market for other firms. It was also stated that "the establishment of one industry frequently leads to the establishment of others, allied or subsidiary."[10] It may be observed that the latter argument could be advanced by the modern opponents of the "balanced growth" approach—whose reasoning is in terms of the linkage effects.

The report also dealt with two vital questions which attracted much attention at that time: one of them was the popular request that protection should be accorded only to those industries which employed a certain proportion of white labor; the other was concerned with the abolition of the preferential railway rates. But there was a marked lack of sympathy on the part of the commission toward the first proposal. However, the grounds on which it was opposed were economic rather than moral. Too high a proportion of costly white labor would have destroyed the competitiveness of some of the industries.[11]

The preferential railway rates were originally introduced to give local producers an advantage over foreign producers at a time when the coast colonies looked to Witwatersrand as practically their only market for their surplus products. With the growth of agriculture and of other industries, it was recognized that the coast colonies must find overseas markets, and that the reasons for facilitating up-traffic had disappeared. Moreover, the preferential railway rates, being a hidden subsidy, complicated the problem of protection by means of customs duties to such an extent that the implementation of any simplified and scientific customs tariff was impracticable. It was therefore recommended to abolish the preferential railway rates and to grant an equivalent compensation by means

9. *Ibid.*, p. 11.
10. *Ibid.*, p. 12.
11. An illuminating example is cited in the report of the local match industry, which employed 26 whites as against 405 Coloured workers, yet the amount expended in wages per annum was £6,150 on whites and £6,750 on Coloureds (*ibid.*, p. 13).

of increased customs duties to those industries which would be injuriously affected by such abolition.[12]

The report recommended a revision of the customs tariff and the introduction of

1. A "Protection Schedule" in which every article enjoying protection would be placed, and the duty would not be lowered for a term of ten years.
2. A "Reserved Raw Materials Schedule," in which would be placed all raw materials (not procurable from South African production) employed in the manufacture of articles named in the "Protection Schedule." The duty applicable to the "Reserved Raw Materials Schedule," if any, would not be raised for a period of ten years.[13]

The formation of the Union of South Africa prevented the adoption by Natal of the recommendations of the commission. Together with the preceding report of 1906 these recommendations represent the first attempt to formulate some definite policy of economic development.

Unfortunately the report of 1908 had serious weaknesses. It was vague on the point of selection of industries to be protected. It seemed to imply that the protection of infant industries could be considered a panacea for most economic ills in an underdeveloped country. One of these ills was the problem of capital supply, and the report implicitly assumed that the artificial atmosphere of protection would automatically help to attract foreign funds. But general experience has been that tariff protection of infant industries had failed because it had done little or nothing to create the capital needed for industrial development. Generally, private capitalists were reluctant to invest in low-income countries for the purpose of producing for the domestic market.[14]

In mitigation one might add that not only were the framers of the report limited by their terms of reference, but they also lived in an epoch when a systematic approach by administrators to the prob-

12. *Ibid.*, pp. 16-18.
13. *Ibid.*, p. 26.
14. Ragnar Nurkse, *Problems of Capital Formation in Underdeveloped Countries* (Oxford: Basil Blackwell, 1962), pp. 105-106.

lems of economic development was an exception rather than the rule.

Excise duty. The impact of this tax on the profitability of the firms producing local spirits was complicated by the fact that rum, the main product of the distilling industry, was at the same time a by-product of the sugar industry. Changes in the supply of rum would, therefore, depend on the changes in the output of sugar, and would be in the same direction. The supply of cane sugar tends to be inelastic. Assuming that the supply of cane sugar were inelastic, the incidence of the excise duty on rum would be wholly on the distillers. In the case of total profits from the sugar milling and the production of spirits falling below the level of the "normal profits," the supply of both these products might have eventually been reduced and their prices would have risen. Then the incidence of the duty would have, at least partly, fallen upon the consumers. However, the duty was relatively low and the profits from the production and sale of rum were said to be considerable.[15] In the absence of more precise information about the elasticities of the demand for and the supply of rum, it is impossible to arrive at any clear-cut conclusions regarding the incidence of the excise duty on that product.

Taxes Originating from Monopoly Profits of Public Utilities

In the case of business units, taxes imposed in the form of monopoly profits derived from public utilities and services are normally added to the average costs. It is therefore natural to expect that, whenever possible, they would be passed on to the buyer of the products of the firms concerned. The government of Natal enjoyed practically a monopoly in the railway, harbor, postal, telegraphic, and several other public utilities and services. The services could, therefore, be used to earn monopoly profits, equivalent to a tax on the users of these services. By the same token, any net loss covered from the general revenue of the Colony would have amounted to a subsidy from the general body of taxpayers to the user of the above services.

15. C. E. Axelson, *op. cit.*, p. 96.

However, the railway traffic to the inland territories did not enjoy a monopolistic position, for it was subject to the competition of the railroads run by other maritime colonies.[16] Therefore a little more ought to be said about the role played by Natal's public utilities as a source of taxation.

It is impossible to arrive at any exact tax figure derived from that source. In the first place, the computation of net profits or losses would have to take into account the proportion of the total interest payments on the funds invested in those services. As no such figures are available it is only possible to make a rough estimate of interest payments pertaining to the capital invested in the railway and harbor services. In the second place, it is difficult to establish to what extent the Natalians or the foreigners contributed to the estimated profits or losses of the Colony's public utilities. Unfortunately no satisfactory data exist which could throw light on the subject.

The whole question of taxation of public utilities is to some extent simplified by the fact that the services, other than railway and harbor services, were relatively unimportant. Profits pertaining to them were an insignificant proportion of the total revenue from taxation. They will, therefore, be omitted from the ensuing discussion. Railway and harbor services, on the other hand, made considerable profits at times.

Table 1.9 shows that with the exception of 1892/3, 1893/4, 1894/5, and 1899/1900, in which losses were incurred, net profits of these two public utilities ranged from over £84,000 in 1906/7 to £538,600 in 1909/10. Thus railway and harbor services were in some years used as an important source of taxation.

With regard to the proportion of these profits made at the expense of the foreign users, the only information we have refers to the railways. Thus the reports of the general manager of the railways state that in 1897 through traffic contributed 60 per cent of the receipts. According to the same source, foreign traffic with overberg stations contributed 54 per cent to railway receipts in 1904, 56 per cent in 1905, and 50 per cent in 1906. It should not be inferred, however, that between 50 and 60 per cent of railway profits were made on through traffic, unless one assumes that the same proportion

16. This was a case of "competition among few" which in later years was reduced by mutual agreements affecting rating policy.

of the expenditure was incurred in carrying it. Since this traffic involved a long haul and little handling, it is likely that it was less costly to carry than local traffic.[17] This view is confirmed by the data contained in the general manager's report for 1908. It can therefore be assumed that more than 50 to 60 per cent of profit was due to transit trade.

Let us consider briefly the official views on the running of the public utilities in Natal. An authoritative statement was made in this connection by the colonial treasurer in his budget speech of 1907.

Our Railways and Harbour . . . should not be "taxing machines" but the Colony must be sure that its commercial undertakings are run upon principles as sound as those which govern the business of a sound commercial man, and that they yield a fair margin of profit on the capital invested.

He then remarked:

17. Axelson, *op. cit.*, p. 125.

Table 1.9. Estimated Net Profits and Losses of Railways and Harbor, 1892/3-1909/10

Year	Revenue (£000)	Expenditure* (£000)	Net profit (£000)	Net loss (£000)
1892/3	524.7	603.5	—	78.8
1893/4	494.0	586.7	—	92.7
1894/5	581.9	590.4	—	8.5
1895/6	811.1	674.6	136.5	—
1896/7	1,374.5	852.2	522.3	—
1897/8	1,078.7	824.9	253.8	—
1898/9	1,128.0	949.2	178.8	—
1899/0	877.1	1,050.8	—	173.7
1900/1	1,679.0	1,436.7	242.3	—
1901/2	1,833.5	1,651.6	181.9	—
1902/3	2,409.9	2,003.2	406.7	—
1903/4	2,615.2	2,148.9	466.3	—
1904/5	1,995.1	1,807.6	187.5	—
1905/6	2,200.6	1,837.3	363.3	—
1906/7	1,990.2	1,906.0	84.2	—
1907/8	2,140.4	1,943.5	196.9	—
1908/9	2,147.1	1,872.9	274.2	—
1909/10	2,613.9	2,075.3	538.6	—

*Expenditure includes estimated interest on capital invested.
Source: Natal, *Blue Books, Statistical Year Books,* and Auditor-General's *Reports.*

If the people of this Colony provided more than sufficient money to meet the cost of the Administration of Government for the benefit of the Colony, there would be reasonable ground for the reduction of railway rates . . . .[18]

The treasurer's allusion to a "fair margin of profit" and the desirability of reducing the railway rates embodies by implication the modern principle of public utility pricing based on the equation of price and marginal cost. His idea of "fair profit" would approximate the normal profit earned under competitive conditions.

In the light of modern views on the problem of public utility pricing, the case of Natal appears to be of considerable interest. In our time the impasse created by the debate on the refinements of the marginal cost pricing approach led practical-minded economists to adopt a more down-to-earth procedure of pricing. This can, perhaps, best be expressed by stating that the accounts of the trading or fee-charging bodies should be as nearly as possible on a commercial basis, and should roughly try to cover costs. The latter should be defined so as to include interest and depreciation.[19] The treasurer's view that the Colony's public utilities must be run upon "principles as sound as those which govern the business of a sound commercial man" are largely in keeping with the present opinion on the matter. It can only be regretted that the financial needs of the government and the interterritorial agreements made it impossible to apply the ideals enunciated by the colonial treasurer with regard to the question of pricing. Moreover, the separation of the commercial activities from the main accounts of the central government would have brought to light the extent to which taxes or subsidies were taking place.

Land tax.[20] By introducing in 1908 a tax based on a flat rate of ½*d.* for every pound sterling of assessed unimproved value of the "beneficially" occupied land, the authorities imposed a proportional tax. It may be presumed that the valuations reflected the income derived from the land. But since the valuation for tax purposes

18. *Legislative Assembly Debates,* 1907, p. 295.
19. Prest, *op. cit.,* p. 78.
20. It is convenient to treat the land tax as a business tax. Whether the purpose of acquiring land was farming or speculation, it could broadly be considered as a business activity. That the land tax had an impact on private incomes is another matter, and this aspect will receive attention in the latter part of this chapter.

excluded the value of the improvements, the tax had no disincentive effects with regard to investment by the farmers and planters which aimed at increased productivity.[21] It may be objected that in the case of the above tax the principle of equity was far from being satisfied. This, however, cannot be considered as a serious drawback, as land taxation is not expected to be a refined instrument from an equity standpoint.[22]

On the other hand, the higher rate of the special land tax levied on land not "beneficially" occupied had the explicit purpose of penalizing uneconomic land use. The legislators might have had in mind the practice of holding large tracts of good farm land idle or leasing it to Africans and Indians and thus depriving the prospective European farmer of the possibility of making use of it. Striking inequalities in the distribution of land holdings and large-scale absentee ownership affected Natal's agriculture throughout the period of its colonial history.

Licenses. License taxes levied at rates varying with the nature of the business or profession but not with its actual size or income may be considered regressive, and excessive license rates may prevent the establishment of new businesses. The impact of license taxes in Natal, which were far from being moderate, might have reacted adversely on the investment in new firms. However, those liable for licenses must sooner or later have succeeded in shifting the tax forward on the buyers or backward on the producers of the traded commodities.

Company tax. So far we have been discussing those taxes which fall on all competing business units in an industry and regularly account for part of tax costs. We shall now have to consider taxes which do not display these characteristics. Thus the joint-stock company tax, being a tax on net profits, would not form part of shiftable tax costs.

In 1908 Natal recognized that the income of joint-stock com-

21. A special provision of the Income Tax Act of 1908 introduced progressive taxation of the income from land in those exceptional cases when the income tax assessed on such income exceeded the land tax. Only then were increases in productivity subject to taxation.

22. Haskell P. Wald, *Taxation of Agricultural Land in Underdeveloped Economies* (Cambridge, Mass.: Harvard University Press, 1959), p. 212.

panies could not be left untaxed. At the same time it was felt that moderation should be applied in fixing the rates of company taxation. This seems to have been the correct approach, as high company tax rates may retard the growth of joint-stock enterprise. Moreover, the absence of fear of competition from new companies might tend to intensify tendencies to monopoly or oligopoly among existing companies.[23] The legislators were also aware of the advantage of a flat rate tax which, unlike a graduated tax on net business income, did not penalize more efficient producers. But the company tax introduced in 1908 did not survive another budget year; its impact on profitability was therefore of short duration and its influence on the form of business organization negligible.

On the whole, it was rather the absence of company taxation that had a more lasting influence on economic growth. Self-financing was stimulated by company profits unaffected by taxation. In addition, the Colony's attractiveness for prospective investors was also enhanced, as compared with those countries which might have been better endowed by nature, but which levied company taxes.

Transfer duty. Transfer duty on the transfer of landed property belongs to a category of taxes which do not regularly form part of the business costs. Under competitive conditions, a firm attempting to shift that tax may lose part of its market, since the competing firms do not necessarily pay it. This conclusion must, of course, be modified once competition becomes imperfect.

In Natal transfer duty exerted a marked influence on the size and direction of business investment. A heavy tax of this nature tends to restrict the acquisition of land by those who may be capable of the most productive utilization of the soil. In Natal this was particularly true of the immigrants who were short of capital, as opposed to speculative land companies with considerable financial resources. Speculation in land was encouraged by the expectation of large capital gains based on the hopes of a large future immigration. A contributory factor was the absence of a land tax, and as a result large tracts of uncultivated land were held by such companies.[24] C. W. de Kiewiet tells us that

23. Prest, *op. cit.*, p. 41.
24. Axelson, *op. cit.*, p. 30.

between 1857 and 1860 less than three hundred immigrants entered the country. Yet by a system of almost promiscuous largesse more than 1,360,000 acres were alienated. Before the colony had been in existence a quarter of a century, it had not land left sufficiently attractive to encourage immigration on a scale commensurate with its needs and ambitions.[25]

The same writer states that after 1864

out of an area of 12,000,000 acres two-thirds had been alienated, of these 2,000,000 acres had been set aside for native locations. Since fully one-half of the European population lived in the two towns of Durban and Pietermaritzburg, 6,000,000 acres were in the possession of a population of 8,000 individuals including women and children. That nearly a million acres of the best land in the colony had become the property of a single company still more conspicuously revealed the nature of Natal's land distribution.[26]

In order to facilitate the acquisition of farms by new settlers, the transfer duty on land purchased from the Crown by immigrants was reduced to £1,[27] but this measure proved of little avail. It can thus be seen that in the absence of other taxes which would have discouraged speculation, the low transfer duty on Crown land sales favored speculative rather than productive investment in land.

The Impact of the Tax System upon Private Income

This section deals with the effects of taxes on individuals and households in their dual capacity as income recipients and consumers. Under this heading we shall investigate a variety of ways in which a tax may have a civilizing effect, influence consumption habits, or affect incentive to work and save. Furthermore, we shall try to determine the incidence of a given tax and its burden in relation to income. In the main, two groups of taxes may be distinguished: (a) those paid directly by income recipients such as property owners, (b) those paid indirectly in the form of increased prices. In Natal the first group included such taxes as the hut tax, poll tax, income tax, succession duty, and the land tax. The most important taxes classified under the second heading were customs tariffs and excise duties.

25. C. W. de Kiewiet, *The Imperial Factor in South Africa*, pp. 189-190.
26. *Ibid.*, p. 190.
27. Ordinance No. 5 of 1849.

Hut tax. Apart from the main aim of providing revenue, the hut tax was originally intended to have a civilizing influence on the Africans and to help indirectly the economic development of the Colony. This was to be achieved by encouraging the Natives to cultivate export crops which were accepted in payment of the tax, by enlarging the scope of money economy, and last but not least by increasing the supply of African labor (see Chapter 2).

It can easily be seen that the first of these three measures was in conflict with the remaining two. It was illogical to encourage the Natives to pay taxes in kind, and at the same time to expect them to become acquainted with the use of money. The method of tax collection also proved that payments in kind could only have been accepted below market price in order to compensate the government for the extra costs involved in these transactions. As a consequence this arrangement tended to discourage payments in kind and to promote the use of money. Furthermore, the encouragement of African crop farming for export was in direct conflict with the burning need for eliciting a greater supply of wage labor required by Europeans. Thus it is not surprising that the original intention soon gave way to the requests of the white colonists for more African labor. But even if payments in kind never became significant, Natives living in the proximity of markets obtained the money to pay their hut tax by selling cattle or the products of their cultivation. As cultivation was customarily carried on by the women, and each wife was entitled to a separate hut, hut tax payments as well as the income derived from cultivation were in direct proportion to the number of wives.[28] Hence, the hut tax was roughly proportional to income, but its burden was undoubtedly heavier in places where the marketability of agricultural products was reduced by the greater distance from the markets.[29] Another source from which the tax money was obtained was working for money wages. As years went by, the gradual increase in the amount of Native wage labor supplied was the result of population growth and the scarcity of cultivable land. Since, due to the tax, the supply of African labor

28. This was one of the reasons why a hut tax was introduced in preference to a uniform head tax upon all adult males. In a polygynous society where cultivation and wealth were in exact proportion to the number of wives possessed by individuals, the latter tax would have been more inequitable.

29. Axelson, *op. cit.*, p. 50.

and produce rose, the prices paid for them by the Europeans were probably lower than they would otherwise have been.[30] It appears then, that the incidence of the hut tax was largely on Africans.[31]

The only concession granted to the Natives who showed a higher degree of civilization was the exemption from the hut tax. This particularly applied to those Natives who had one wife only and who occupied European-style houses, instead of the traditional Native round huts. Nevertheless, the number of such exemptions was insignificant, being 1,451 in 1883 and 777 in 1898.[32]

The adverse effects of the tax upon the conditions of living were probably considerable. The raising of the hut tax in 1875 led to overcrowding.[33] A similar phenomenon was observed nearly a quarter of a century later, when it was pointed out that "a tax of a fixed amount on each hut tends to prevent the building of huts by unmarried men, and so produces in certain districts an amount of overcrowding which is unhealthy and demoralizing." It was suggested from the same source "that the evil might be avoided, the revenue supplemented, and the labor supply increased by imposing a poll tax, either on unmarried male adults only, or generally in substitution for hut tax."[34]

Taxation derived from forced labor. In addition to the tax on huts, a form of taxation exclusively applicable to Africans included the obligation to supply personal services in the form of labor. This kind of taxation was not uncommon in the colonies. In Natal, under the Native Code, the governor, as Supreme Chief, was empowered to call upon all Africans living in locations to supply labor for public works or for the general needs of the Colony, and to fine and imprison them in case of disobedience.[35] The use of compulsory Native

30. *Ibid.*, p. 49.
31. The relation between the hut tax and African wage earnings was roughly as follows: when the hut tax of 7s. per annum was first imposed in 1849 African wages were 5s. to 10s. per month; when it was increased to 14s. per annum, wages stood at 10s. to 15s. per month. No further increases in this tax were introduced in spite of the fact that, during the first years of the twentieth century, African wages rose to between 20s. and 40s. per month. But then Africans had to pay other taxes in addition to the hut tax.
32. Axelson, *op. cit.*, p. 105.
33. Reports of resident magistrates, *Blue Books.*
34. *The Natives of South Africa, Their Economic and Social Condition,* ed. the South African Native Races Committee (London: John Murray, 1901), p. 246.
35. *Code of Native Law,* Part 1, Chap. 1, sections 36, 38, and 39.

labor during the later years of colonial administration in Natal is illustrated in Table 3.9.

This table shows that the power to call upon Natives to supply labor for public works was used a great deal. The system led to the

Table 2.9. The Hut Tax Collected from the Africans, 1892/3-1909/10

Year	Amount collected (£000)	Year	Amount collected (£000)
1892/3	79.5	1901/2	142.2
1893/4	82.4	1902/3	149.3
1894/5	84.9	1903/4	156.2
1895/6	76.8	1904/5	173.5
1896/7	94.0	1905/6	144.1
1897/8	129.6	1906/7	194.6
1898/9	135.4	1907/8	181.8
1899/0	102.0	1908/9	187.6
1900/1	168.1	1909/10	183.4

Source: Natal, *Blue Books* and *Statistical Year Books.*

Table 3.9. Number of Natives Supplied to the Public Works Department, 1894-1905

Year	Number of Natives supplied	Number of Natives convicted for disregarding labor orders
1894	3,471	65
1895	3,514	81
1896	3,612	119
1897	3,798	128
1898	4,105	151
1899	3,568	127
1900	3,298	134
1901	3,929	138
1902	4,227	148
1903	4,599	165
1904	4,527	217
1905	4,710	190

Source: *Native Affairs Commission,* 1907, p. 1008.

restriction of the individual's freedom to work for whom he pleased; there was always a possibility that the government would fix the rate of wages at a low level since the supply of laborers was assured. The existing evidence indicates that the actual wages paid were less than the Natives could have earned had they been freely employed.[36] According to the information provided by the Native Affairs Commission of 1906/7, prior to 1899 compulsory labor's wages amounted to 12s.6d. per month plus meal rations and 2s.6d. in lieu of meat rations. By 1899 the wages rose to between 15s. and 20s. per month plus meal rations; even then they were still considerably short of the wage rates paid to Native laborers in other avenues of employment.[37] The difference between free and compulsory labor's wage rates could thus be considered as a tax.

The reports of the magistrates indicated that this system of labor was greatly disliked by the Africans, and at times it had to be enforced by severe measures. It caused many Natives to leave the reserves and to live on private lands where they were exempt from such obligations, although they had to pay high rents. A large proportion of labor for public works was, however, recruited in the ordinary way in free competition with other employers.[38]

Poll tax. A poll tax equal in amount for each taxpayer is the simplest of all taxes. Inequality of incomes makes such a tax regressive. If the condition of equity were to be satisfied its effect would have to be more than offset by progressive taxes. For this reason the legislators in Natal intended to rectify the impact of this regressive tax by the introduction of other taxes. The new proposal included a progressive income tax.[39]

Table 4.9 shows that the amount of poll tax collected from other races was fairly stable throughout the years under review, whereas the Native contribution steadily declined. Initially many Natives failed to apply for exemption, and later some of them became liable for the hut tax.

The poll tax imposed in 1905 fell heavily on non-Europeans; such a tax would normally make a man work harder, since it would

36. Axelson, *op. cit.*, p. 44.
37. *Report* of the Native Affairs Commission, 1906/7, p. 1008.
38. Axelson, *op. cit.*, p. 45.
39. *Legislative Assembly Debates*, 1905, p. 253.

have a strong income effect. The poll tax tended to increase the supply of non-European labor and helped to keep wages down. This was particularly true of those Africans who were exempted from hut tax, and of the unindentured Indians. In the absence of sufficient data it is not possible to assess the real burden of this tax; since most of the Africans worked for wages for part of the year only, the poll tax formed a considerable proportion of their income. The burden was made heavier by the economic depression, which tended to lessen employment opportunities, and by great losses of cattle due to an outbreak of East Coast Fever. There is also ample evidence that for some years the Natives had not found it altogether easy to pay existing taxes and rents, particularly since the latter had increased considerably. Complaints were also made that the reciprocity of assistance, which had been very real within the African family, was disappearing. The payment of the poll tax made the unmarried sons less willing to assist their fathers than formerly.[40]

Personal income tax. The primary object of introducing an income tax in 1908 was to augment public revenue. Once the reason for this disappeared, the tax was abolished. It is doubtful, therefore, whether its secondary object was to equalize the burden of taxation, even if this had been the original intention of the legislators. Table

40. *The South African Natives, Their Progress and Present Condition*, p. 92.

Table 4.9. The Poll Tax Collected from Natives and Other Races, 1905/6-1908/9

Year	Total poll tax collected £	Poll tax collected from	
		Natives £	other races £
1905/6	125,143	76,490	48,653
1906/7	103,832	53,905	49,927
1907/8	99,792	49,090	50,702
1908/9	94,537	45,018	49,519

Source: J. Stuart, *A History of the Zulu Rebellion, 1906, and of Dinizulu's Arrest, Trial, and Expatriation* (London: Macmillan, 1913), p. 131.

5.9 shows the extent to which income tax was progressive. In the examples used it is assumed that no deductions are allowed.

Table 5.9. Income Tax Rates in Percentages

Taxable income £	Married %	Single %
150	Nil	Nil
240	Nil	0.94
300	0.50	1.25
400	1.00	1.56
500	1.30	1.75
600	1.50	1.88
700	1.64	1.96
800	1.83	2.11
900	2.04	2.24
1,000	2.21	2.44
1,100	2.46	2.67
1,200	2.68	2.86

Note: Based on income tax rates as stated in Chapter 5.

Generally the impact of an income tax is analyzed in terms of its income and substitution effects. Incentives to work are usually considered in terms of a choice between work and leisure. However, less developed economies have their own peculiarities, and thus in addition we may have to consider the problem of choice between non-taxed work and taxed work.[41] It may be a choice between un-taxed or partially taxed subsistence production and output for sale in the money sector. A tax which is considered too burdensome, by forcing people back into the subsistence sector, may retard the growth of the cash sector. This tendency was probably mitigated in Natal by a fairly high exemption limit, which in the case of personal income tax applied to incomes up to £150 per annum for un-married and £240 per annum for married men.

This brings us to another peculiarity of the less developed economies: the marked unequal income distribution results in a large number of persons earning incomes which would prove too costly to assess for tax collection. Consequently the assessment limit is bound to be relatively high and the total tax yield rather low.

41. Prest, *op. cit.*, pp. 34-35.

Land tax. Insofar as the incidence of the ordinary land tax was concerned it can be assumed that it fell upon the landlords. This is based on the assumption that the amount of land available for rental was unaffected by the tax and that rental rates were largely determined by well-established local custom, rather than by competitive bidding. They thus responded slowly, if at all, to the introduction of the tax on land, which was, moreover, of short duration. Under the circumstances the whole of the tax would then have been paid from the rent.

The situation created by the introduction of the special land tax was a little more complicated. This tax applied in the case of Africans and Indians occupying land owned by Europeans and considered to be suitable for European use. In such a case the Africans and the Indians were regarded by the legislators as incapable of "beneficial" occupation. It appears, then, that if the occupation of such land by non-Europeans were to continue, they had to be able to compete for the hire of land on equal terms with Europeans. Were the non-Europeans to pay higher rents than before, the incidence of the special land tax would, at least partly, have been on them. In fact, the position of African tenants remained practically unaltered, since it was considerably more profitable to let land to them rather than to the Europeans, as the former were able to pay generally higher rents than the latter. This was due to the ability of Native young men to earn money in wage employment.[42]

Import and excise duties. The second group of taxes which had an impact upon private income includes primarily import and excise taxes. With regard to the excise taxes little can be added to what had been said in the previous section. Unlike the excise duty, which largely affected a limited group of Indians and African consumers of locally produced spirits, customs duties exercised a varying influence upon the income and consumption of all the population groups in the Colony.

In Natal the over-all impact of customs duties on the cost of living was probably high, particularly if we consider the limiting case when they are entirely shifted upon the consumer of imported goods. Moreover, import duties, like most shifted taxes, tend to be

42. Goodfellow, *op. cit.*, p. 164.

regressive because low-income families as a rule consume a higher proportion of their income than high income families. For a long time a very large proportion of manufactures used in the Colony was of foreign origin. Many foodstuffs consumed by Europeans were also imported. Also several increases in customs duties followed Natal's accession to the Customs Union (see Chapter 5). In the absence of other taxes on Europeans, customs duties were largely responsible for the high cost of white labor. In a country where skilled labor was in short supply, and the little that was available tended to drift to the Transvaal, it was the average workingman who bore the brunt of taxation, and not the well-to-do. Thus it is not surprising that demands were sometimes heard for a highly progressive income tax.[43]

It may also be observed that the reliance on the taxation of consumer goods imports, for which income elasticity of demand was high, might have been largely responsible for more than proportionate reductions in public revenue when incomes were falling. This was particularly important in a world subject to intense business fluctuations.

The Distribution of the Burden of Taxation According to Races

This section deals with two problems. First, what proportion of the revenue from taxes was contributed by Europeans and what by non-Europeans? Second, how did the per capita tax compare with the average incomes of either group?

The "racial" approach to Natal's system of taxation suggests a twofold division into (a) taxes which were payable exclusively by non-Europeans, and (b) taxes which applied to all races.[44] Thus the hut tax payable exclusively by Africans provides an example of tax discrimination on the racial basis. Taxes imposed irrespective of race were the poll tax, income tax, customs duties, etc. Unfortunately the official data never indicated, in any reliable way, what proportions of the taxes which applied to all races were contributed by the various racial groups. The 1904 census provides data on the contribution to the total public revenue of the Colony by the

43. *Legislative Assembly Debates*, 1905, p. 696.
44. The principle applied here is that of the "statutory" taxpayer and not the "ultimate taxpayer."

various races for the period 1895-1904. After careful analysis we cannot accept them as entirely reliable. Some of the data contained there appear to be either grossly overestimated or underestimated. This applies particularly to the revenue from customs duties and from the several public utilities which included the revenue contributed by the other South African territories.

Table 6.9 provides an estimate of the distribution of the tax revenue according to the two major racial groups and is based (a) on that part of the information provided in the 1904 census which appears to be acceptable; (b) on the statements of the colonial treasurer concerning the proportions of taxes paid by Europeans and non-Europeans;[45] (c) on the statements made by the Native Affairs Commission of 1903,[46] and on evidence of the witnesses regarding the annual payment of indirect taxes per head of African population.[47]

The revenue from taxation computed in Table 6.9 excludes the taxes derived by way of net profits on public utilities. Moreover, allowance must be made for the fact that prior to 1903 a proportion of the revenue from import taxes was contributed by other territories. The error resulting from this was probably smaller in 1892/3 and 1893/4 than in later years, because of a drastic reduction in the transit trade. It appears, therefore, that owing to errors which could not be eliminated, the estimates were less accurate for the period 1894/5 to 1902/3 than for the other years given in Table 6.9.

It is convenient to analyze the relation between per capita taxes and incomes by first considering the position in 1903/4, for which we have an estimate of the gross geographical product.[48] In that year the average annual income per head for Europeans and non-Europeans was £124.9.10 and £5.10.2 and taxation £7.9.9 and 7s.8d., respectively. It follows that the European taxes amounted to 6 per cent of income, whereas the corresponding figure for the non-Europeans was nearly 7 per cent. If one assumes for the two racial groups a somewhat similar proportion of per capita income in 1893/4 and in 1903/4,[49] it appears that in

45. *Legislative Assembly Debates*, 1908, p. 517.
46. *Report of the S. A. Native Affairs Commission*, 1903-5.
47. *Ibid.*
48. See Appendix A.
49. There are no valid reasons to suppose that there was any marked change in

1893/4 non-Europeans must have paid in taxes a higher proportion of their per capita earnings than Europeans. This arises because the difference between the per capita taxes paid in 1893/4 by the two racial groups was larger than in 1903/4 and it was in favor of the Europeans.

On the same assumption of an unchanged proportion of per capita income between the races a similar conclusion can be drawn if we compare 1903/4 and 1908/9. Thus the percentage of income paid in taxes by the non-European population was higher, and that of the European population lower in 1908/9 than in 1903/4. This arose because non-European taxes per head rose and those of the European fell between the two dates.

The significant fact that non-Europeans were forced to pay a

the distribution of income between the two racial groups during the whole period under consideration. The change, if any, was in favor of the Europeans, which tends to strengthen our conclusions with regard to the disparity of the burden of taxation.

Table 6.9. Estimated Contribution to Revenue from Taxes by Europeans and Non-Europeans, 1892/3-1908/9

Year	Europeans		Non-Europeans	
	Total (£000)	Per capita £ s. d.	Total (£000)	Per capita £ s. d.
1892/3	202.9	4. 12. 9	163.2	6. 4
1893/4	174.7	3. 14. 8	168.2	6. 3
1894/5	176.0	3. 17. 0	171.5	6. 4
1895/6	246.1	5. 2. 3	179.5	6. 6
1896/7	360.5	7. 3. 6	241.4	6. 3
1897/8	361.6	6. 12. 5	250.3	6. 6
1898/9	438.3	7. 6. 8	239.7	6. 4
1899/0	394.1	6. 1. 4	317.4	7. 4
1900/1	644.6	10. 2. 0	307.1	7. 1
1901/2	860.7	11. 15. 6	326.5	7. 4
1902/3	1,032.4	12. 10. 0	346.7	7. 3
1903/4	727.1	7. 9. 9	387.7	7. 8
1904/5	527.7	5. 11. 9	408.0	7.11
1905/6	476.3	5. 0. 11	540.5	10. 3
1906/7	512.5	5. 10. 10	508.3	9. 6
1907/8	432.3	4.1 4. 7	502.7	9. 0
1908/9	523.9	5.1 3. 1	494.3	8. 6

higher percentage of their incomes in taxes than Europeans reveals only one-half of the story. The other half takes into account the tremendous disparity in the marginal utility of incomes. We also have to decide whether the benefits that non-Europeans received were in proportion to their tax contribution to the public revenue.[50] This consideration, however, has to be postponed until the next chapter. At this stage we merely conclude that in Natal, apart from the possible benefits to be derived from the public expenditure, a heavier relative burden of taxation was borne by the non-European than by the European, and that in the last years of colonial rule it tended to grow heavier.

Conclusions

In Natal taxation formed a small proportion of the national income as compared with many backward countries today. In 1903/4, for which we have estimated the gross geographical product, total taxes amounted to only 6 per cent of the latter. Direct taxes did not even reach 1 per cent. The Colony had to rely to a large extent on indirect rather than on direct taxation, owing to the low average level of incomes which would have made the collection of taxes based on income extremely expensive. Originally, the only direct tax which could be imposed upon the African population under the then existing conditions was the hut tax. It was also the only practicable way of taxing the output of the large subsistence sector. Later on a poll tax was added.

For a long time the only taxes that applied to Europeans were the indirect taxes. This form of taxation suited particularly a community of traders who took advantage of the geographical position of their country to "tax the foreigner." This reliance on indirect taxation introduced an element of serious instability into public finances. The volume of transit trade on which so much depended was itself largely determined by the extent of gold-mining development, which varied considerably with changing conditions. To this we must add the importance of the earnings from the railway and harbor services.

---

50. No modern system of taxation is based on an equivalence of payment and benefit, but in Natal this principle applied to the white population as a whole.

The tax system of Natal was devised so as to have the most favorable effect on the profitability of the business activities of the white community. The absence until 1908 of a personal and company income tax and a tax on land aimed at obtaining this result. The hut tax and the poll tax had the subsidiary aim of eliciting an increased supply of cheap non-European labor. High taxes on the Africans were possible because they had no way of escaping them. Low taxes on white immigrants were designed to encourage them to settle in the Colony and to persuade them to remain. Thus the guiding principle of the authorities was to keep the taxes on Europeans down to a minimum, and to see to it that the African paid his "due share" of taxation. The determination of these tax levels was in the hands of the legislature, which reflected the vested interests of the European minority.

In order to obviate the possibility of a Crown veto, taxes introduced after 1905 applied to the whole population. The poll tax, which did not eliminate the old hut tax, scarcely contributed to the modernization of the system of native taxation; it only increased its burden. With regard to the European community the poll tax was out of date and highly regressive. This raises the question whether the state of economic development attained after the Anglo-Boer war justified the introduction of the more advanced form of direct taxation. If an income tax is to be imposed, people engaged in economic activities must be able to account for their incomes. Moreover, a sufficient number of people must earn incomes above the assessment limit. The taxation of private and company incomes introduced in 1908 produced mediocre results. The land tax was still less successful. Both these taxes were introduced half-heartedly.

In view of the relative importance of the import taxes and the highly uneven distribution of incomes, the entire tax system appeared regressive, and it favored a small upper income group. Furthermore, this over-all inequitability had assumed a distinctly racial aspect.

Chapter 10. Public Finance and Capital Investment

Introduction

The problem of capital investment in Natal was related to public finance in two different ways. First, government directly invested in the social overhead capital. Second, it provided incentives to private investment by means of fiscal measures and institutional arrangements.

The most outstanding role played by the government of the Colony in the field of capital investment was the provision of the social overhead capital. This included the creation of infrastructure facilities such as transport and communication, investment in agriculture and mining, and expenditure on social services like education and health. The building up of an infrastructure, besides supplying basic services, provides the necessary economic environment which makes private investment more attractive. Improvements in health, education, and training are equivalent to the formation of human capital.[1]

These introductory remarks suggest the broad pattern which will be followed in this chapter. Government development expenditure will be discussed under the headings of expenditure on "fixed capital investment" and "other development expenditure." In addition, mention will be made of the various incentives and measures introduced in order to foster economic growth. Similarly, as in the preceding chapter, factors affecting the different races will also be introduced, this time with reference to the distribution of expenditure on certain kinds of the social overhead capital between the various races of the Colony.

Public Expenditure on Fixed Capital Investment

Fixed capital investment was financed both from ordinary and capital expenditure of the government, and the proportions between the amounts originating from either of these two sources varied considerably from year to year. The figures supplied in this section indicate gross investment, since it was not possible to calculate exactly the amounts spent on replacement. There are several ways

1. *Taxes and Fiscal Policy in Underdeveloped Countries*, p. 4.

of appreciating the annual amounts contributed to public fixed capital investment. However, in the case of Natal, the only practicable manner was to relate the public expenditure on fixed capital formation to the total amount of public expenditure.

Government expenditure on gross fixed capital formation depended on the availability of investment funds originating either from overseas borrowing or from the ordinary revenue of the Colony. Public fixed capital investment rose steeply after 1894/5, reaching a peak figure of £2,840,200 in 1902/3; it subsequently declined owing to the depressed conditions of the economy and the reduced supply of overseas loans for development purposes. Expressed as percentage of total public expenditure it fluctuated between a minimum of 7.1 per cent in 1893/4 and a maximum of 44.1 per cent in 1901/2. Yet for six of the eighteen years covered in Table 1.10, it exceeded 27 per cent. These data suggest that at that time Natal expended on fixed capital investment a proportion of its public expenditure which does not compare unfavorably with the proportions of expenditure on the entire development programs of many African countries in recent years.[2] In 1958 these proportions ranged from one-tenth to over one-third of total public expenditure. Natal's public expenditure on gross fixed capital investment is shown under various headings in Table 1.10.

Roads, bridges, and buildings. A large proportion of the expenditure under this heading was on maintaining the road system in a good state of repair and the construction of new roads and bridges. This was an essential part of the infrastructure in a country where the railroads provided only the bare framework of transportation. The remainder of the expenditure was on the construction of administrative buildings.

Railways and harbor works. It is convenient to consider under one heading the expenditure on the gross fixed capital investment pertaining to the railways and harbor works because of the close connection between these two public utilities. The extension of the railway system and the growth of tonnage conveyed required the provision of adequate harbor services. Thus it is obvious that the

2. See United Nations, Economic Commission for Africa, *Economic Bulletin for Africa* (Addis Ababa), I (June, 1961), 22.

Table 1.10. Gross Public Fixed Capital Investment at Current Prices, 1892/3-1909/10

Year	Expenditure on Gross Fixed Capital Investment					Total govt. expenditure* (6) (£000)	(5) as per- cent of (6) (7) %
	Roads, bridges, & buildings (1) (£000)	Railways (2) (£000)	Harbor works (3) (£000)	Other works (4) (£000)	Total (5) (£000)		
1892/3	102.3	85.7	59.5	18.7	266.2	1,715.2	15.5
1893/4	65.5	0.8	48.0	6.6	120.9	1,703.1	7.1
1894/5	220.3	—	—	24.4	244.7	1,295.6	18.9
1895/6	233.9	—	2.4	60.3	296.6	1,515.2	19.6
1896/7	140.6	539.0	93.2	6.2	779.0	2,397.4	32.5
1897/8†	...			...		3,182.1	...
1898/9	213.0	261.8	134.1	8.3	617.2	2,289.3	27.0
1899/0	166.5	684.5	133.2	27.5	1,011.7	2,771.3	36.5
1900/1	184.5	624.9	188.5	15.2	1,013.1	3,241.4	31.3
1901/2	253.5	1,283.0	336.6	21.9	1,895.0	4,293.3	44.1
1902/3	516.2	1,921.7	329.7	72.6	2,840.2	6,785.2	41.9
1903/4	378.3	1,360.6	287.4	108.4	2,134.7	5,363.8	39.8
1904/5	289.5	641.0	439.3	32.0	1,401.8	6,214.9	22.6
1905/6	231.5	537.1	294.2	18.3	1,081.1	5,675.5	19.0
1906/7	185.2	669.0	234.5	13.1	1,101.8	6,054.5	18.2
1907/8	98.5	492.1	52.2	11.9	654.7	5,503.9	11.9
1908/9	68.2	341.3	13.8	3.0	426.3	4,110.4	10.3
1909/10	153.8	538.6	83.9	47.6	823.9	4,780.8‡	17.2‡

*Column 6 is adapted from Table 1.4.
†The data for 1897/8 are not available (see Chapter 4).
‡Estimate.
Source: Natal, Auditor-General's Reports.

latter would lose its *raison d'être* without the former. This point is illustrated by the relationship between the expenditure on the railways and the harbor works (see Table 1.10).

The Harbor Board, established in 1880, played an important part in the development of the Durban harbor. With the advent of responsible government this body was replaced by the Harbor Department. It continued to supervise harbor works, which included the maintenance of the existing services in a working order. A marked increase in the expenditure on harbor works took place after 1897/8, reaching a maximum figure of £439,300 in 1904/5. In 1903 an important step forward was made with the provision of cold-storage facilities.[3] Moreover, the budget year 1905/6 marked a new effort to develop the harbor at Port Shepstone. After a few years' interval the development of Natal railways was resumed in 1896/7 and the expenditure on gross fixed capital investment in that area reached its highest level of £1,360,600 in 1903/4 (Table 1.10). Whereas the last two decades of the nineteenth century were marked by the extension of the main line joining Durban and Johannesburg, the first decade of the twentieth century saw the construction of the branch lines.[4]

The railway system of the Colony was built so that it favored more imports from overseas than local production in general, or agricultural development in particular.[5] To remedy this weakness the extension of the railway network was undertaken for the benefit of the farming community. Government views on that problem were clearly expressed by Prime Minister Sir Harry Escombe during the budget debate in 1897:

Is the great agricultural wealth of our land never to be properly developed? Because some of those who have already received huge benefits by railway communication in the past stand shivering for fear they may, in return, be called to pay something towards railway communication for those who for years have been taxed for the benefit of the main line and those living along it.

Referring to the Greytown Railway Bill, then under consideration, he added:

3. Auditor-General's *Report*, 1904/5.
4. See Chapter 1, Table 13.1.
5. Goodfellow, *op. cit.*, p. 137.

This railway will pay from the beginning; and even were it not so, experience has proved in America and elsewhere that the building of railways in undeveloped country pays. How much more will it pay in a country like ours, of which it may be truly said not one acre is desert? These railways will pay from firstly the immense impetus they will give to the development of our land, and, secondly, by a fair interest on the capital invested.[6]

Did the future fulfil these hopes? The railway statistics for 1907-9[7] show that even the old branch lines, which should have been well established, were run at a loss. Profits derived from the main line were used to cover losses on the other lines. Thus branch lines continued to exist only because of the profitability of the main line. It may therefore be stated that consumers in the inland states helped to develop backward Natal areas. The high rates paid by those consumers made it possible to maintain the branch lines, and the farmers served by these lines obtained transport at a price lower than the actual cost.[8]

Thus in some cases it may happen that the benefits conferred upon the direct recipients of the service may be supplemented by indirect benefits to the community. Objections may arise only when a certain form of subsidization results in a net loss to the society as a whole. Dealing with the construction of branch lines in South Africa, Professor R. A. Lehfeldt points out that the question really is one of how far to go, since "it should be remembered that the immediate loss has to be paid for by higher rates on the rest of the railway system, and these obstruct the development of wealth and population in centres already inhabited."[9] It may be concluded that if branch-line construction is overdone, the development of the country may easily be retarded rather than accelerated. The fact that after a number of years Natal branch lines still had to be subsidized also seems to indicate that agricultural development had disappointed expectations.

Undoubtedly railway construction played the most important part in the provision of the infrastructure. The railways made it

6. *Legislative Assembly Debates*, 1897, p. 257.
7. Comparable data are not available for earlier years.
8. W. J. Busschau, *op. cit.*, p. 124.
9. R. A. Lehfeldt, "Railway Policy in South Africa" (*Proceedings of the Economic Society of South Africa*, July, 1925), quoted in Busschau, *ibid.*

possible to maintain an extensive transit trade and to develop such Natal industries as coal, sugar, etc. However, had the branch lines been built at a slower rate, greater efficiency, resulting in lower costs and consequently lower rates, would have possibly led to a higher rate of economic growth.[10]

Other works. This heading covers relatively small amounts expended on gross fixed capital investment pertaining to the telegraph services and agricultural development. The first of these formed an essential part of the infrastructure concerned with communications, whereas the second item represented fixed investment in the government agricultural extension program, including experimental farm buildings, irrigation, and various other works.

Some Macroeconomic Aspects of Public Works

The purpose of this section is to investigate the connection between public works programs and business fluctuations. In particular, we shall consider the impact of the expenditure on public capital investment on employment, incomes, and the price level.

Underdeveloped countries are frequently faced with violent short-term fluctuations in income and output as a result of internal or external factors. Natal was no exception in this respect, and under the circumstances the only realistic policy which could have been followed by the government was to accumulate surpluses in the years of prosperity to be used to cover the deficits arising in the years of depression. This is the advice given today to the less developed countries, where it is recognized that the fluctuations in income affecting them are of a basically different character than those in the industrial countries.[11] But whenever such policy was followed in Natal, as during the early 1890's, it was accidental rather than intentional. The traditional ideal of a balanced budget was held in high esteem by the framers of the Colony's fiscal policy, and other approaches were not recognized. The only remedy for the dwindling revenue that they recognized was retrenchment.[12]

10. *Ibid.*
11. Prest, *op. cit.*, p. 110.
12. *Legislative Council Debates*, 1892, p. 49, and *Legislative Assembly Debates*, 1905, p. 254.

In contrast to these views, the opinions pronounced by some of the members of the legislature seemed to be well ahead of their times. In criticizing the colonial treasurer's policy of economy and retrenchment during the budget debate in 1892, Mr. H. Binns, a member of the Council, remarked:

. . . it is to be regretted that all the public works of the Colony have to be stopped. . . . I do think that a mistake has been made in that we have not kept back to a certain extent some of these public works to meet an occasion as we shall probably have to deal with for some little time from the present.

He then expressed the opinion that

the sooner we can raise some money . . . and start some of the most urgently required public works, so as to find work for some of those men who are out of employment, the better will it be for the Colony.[13]

During the same debate another member of the council, a Mr. King, had reminded his colleagues that

it is by means of spending . . . that Natal is enabled to go on. It is not all lost that you give to a man. You give it to him and he gives it to another man and the money is still in the community. We do not impoverish the community by putting men on public works.[14]

Unfortunately, it took nearly half a century before such views became generally accepted.[15]

Another vital aspect of public works was their impact on the level of prices in the Colony and on the cost of works. This point was fully realized but not always observed. Regarding the stoppage of public works in the Colony Mr. Binns pointed out in 1893 that "you would have been enabled to construct those works far away more cheaply than you can do in times of prosperity and inflation."[16] This vital problem found even more general expression in the words of the colonial treasurer, who stated:

13. *Legislative Council Debates*, 1892, p. 40.
14. *Ibid.*, p. 46.
15. A fair account of the views on the problem of employment should also include the rather different opinion expressed during the same debate by a member of the Council, Dr. Sutherland: ". . . it is a great evil, it is the rankest socialism which can exist to ask a government to borrow money for the purpose of giving employment. We must avoid that" (*ibid.*, p. 44). This statement requires no comment except that it reflected the principles behind the official policy.
16. *Ibid.*, 1893, p. 28.

The policy of expending large sums on public works is one that has many attractions, but the experience of other Colonies shows that it has its drawbacks. The effect of incurring large expenditure of this kind in an unduly short period is to raise the standard of wages and the cost of living generally. The cost of construction is thereby generally enhanced . . . .[17]

In practice the public works program seldom followed the policy advocated during the debates. Instead of having been spaced so as to even out business fluctuations and reduce unemployment and costs, the bulk of Natal's public capital formation had taken place during the periods of prosperity when labor was scarce, incomes rising, and prices far from declining.

Other Development Expenditure and Measures

We now come to expenditure which had a definite impact on the economic development of Natal, but was not in the nature of fixed capital investment. The related public measures and institutional arrangements which influenced economic growth will also be discussed.

Expenditure on education and health contributed most to the formation of "human capital." It is superfluous to stress that investment in education, health, and sanitation does pay rich social and economic dividends, "yet it does not result in the creation of the depreciable assets which are admissible to government capital accounts."[18] Table 2.10 analyzes the ordinary government expenditures on the educational and health services, agricultural extension, and the development of mining. During the period under review these expenditures fluctuated from about 4 to 8 per cent of the total ordinary expenditure. In terms of absolute figures, by far the largest increase took place in the development expenditure on agriculture, to which particular attention began to be paid in the first years of the twentieth century.

Education. The attitude toward government expenditure on education was one of restraint,[19] and it was not uncommon to hear

17. *Ibid.,* 1894.
18. *Taxes and Fiscal Policy in Underdeveloped Countries,* p. 5.
19. *Legislative Council Debates,* 1892, p. 41.

opinions that the education of children is more the responsibility of the parents than the state.[20] With regard to non-European education the recommendations contained in the report of the Native Affairs Commission of 1846 remained a dead letter. The suggestion of that commission that in each location a "model mechanical school" was to be instituted where "the useful arts should be taught and practically illustrated," and where "systematic agricultural instruction was to be given" was turned down on the miserable pretext of economy.[21] During the years which followed little was done to provide education for non-Europeans. What had been accomplished was

20. *Ibid.*, p. 44.
21. Edgar H. Brookes, *The History of Native Policy in South Africa from 1830 to the Present Day* (Cape Town: Nasionale Pers, 1924), p. 29.

Table 2.10. Ordinary Expenditure on Education, Health, Agriculture, and Mining, 1892/3-1909/10

Year	Expenditure on					Total ordinary expenditure (6) (£000)	(5) as per cent of (6) (7) %
	Education (1) (£000)	Health (2) (£000)	Agriculture (3) (£000)	Mining (4) (£000)	Total (5) (£000)		
1892/3	37.1	9.9	3.6	2.3	52.9	1,099.9	4.8
1893/4	37.4	9.2	3.5	2.5	52.6	1,082.4	4.9
1894/5	35.5	10.0	3.7	2.8	52.0	1,148.1	4.5
1895/6	40.4	10.4	3.7	3.5	58.0	1,282.5	4.5
1896/7	39.9	12.5	10.6	..	63.0	1,625.0	3.9
1897/8	..	..	..	..	..	1,812.3	..
1898/9	51.2	21.3	25.0	4.7	102.2	1,908.3	5.4
1899/0	53.2	19.6	20.4	3.6	96.8	1,955.1	5.0
1900/1	56.1	23.4	24.5	4.4	108.4	2,499.6	4.3
1901/2	69.4	26.2	66.0	7.7	169.3	3,052.6	5.5
1902/3	82.9	67.6	61.3	15.2	227.0	5,102.0	4.4
1903/4	98.7	62.9	102.4	11.7	275.7	4,071.4	6.8
1904/5	107.4	74.3	97.3	10.2	289.2	4,029.6	7.2
1905/6	99.1	41.5	76.7	8.0	225.3	3,670.6	6.1
1906/7	102.0	39.9	122.7	7.8	272.4	3,681.9	7.4
1907/8	105.5	36.0	130.3	6.8	278.6	3,689.8	7.6
1908/9	108.0	35.7	83.9	7.1	234.7	3,530.6	6.6
1909/10	112.6	37.0	115.0	12.9	277.5	3,530.3	7.9

Source: Natal, Auditor-General's *Reports.*

largely due to missionary effort. In 1897 the annual government expenditure on Native education was about 11s.10d. per child as against £3.19.5 for a European child—a remarkable difference.[22]

The indifference of Africans toward education could not possibly be blamed for such a low level of government support. In 1899 the Inspector of Native Education publicly admitted an increased interest in education throughout the Colony among the Natives.[23] By 1906 the rate of the government grant on African schools increased to 17s.11d. per child, but it was still extremely low as compared with the £6.8.7 granted per European child. The total government expenditure on Native education in that year (excluding the upkeep of the education office) amounted to only £8,227, a sum which by no means reflected the educational needs of the Africans, or their contributions to the revenue. Moreover, in 1906 only 165 Native schools were receiving government grants, as compared with 188 such schools in 1899. The official explanation for this reduction was the lack of suitably qualified teachers. The 165 Native schools receiving government grants had a total average enrolment of 4,256 boys and 6,815 girls.[24] This was the way in which the colonial authorities catered to the educational needs of a population of nearly one million Africans. The European attitude toward Native education was one of widespread prejudice and was influenced by a feeling of anxiety arising from the overwhelming number of Africans.[25]

Health. The level of expenditure on health services was rather erratic and showed sharp increases with the outbreak of various epidemics. It was particularly high during the war and the postwar years, and in 1904/5 it reached the highest figure of £74,300 (Table 2.10), of which £27,000 was spent on vaccination alone. Apart from the general preventive health measures, the government bore part of the cost of maintaining the Colony's hospitals.

Agriculture. Agriculture progressed slowly in the early 1890's, and at that time the government was not infrequently criticized

22. *The Natives of South Africa: Their Economic and Social Condition,* p. 175.
23. *Ibid.*
24. *The South African Natives, Their Progress and Present Condition,* p. 151.
25. *Ibid.,* p. 149.

for not giving it adequate support.[26] By joining the Customs Union in 1898 Natal began to participate in the free trade in South African produce, which stimulated the Colony's agricultural output. But the postwar depression and the dwindling earnings from the transit trade helped most to direct attention to the development of agriculture and forestry. The recorded increases in the tonnage of agricultural products carried over the railways were an indication of the rapid growth of output.[27] The most progressive branches of agriculture were sugar and the black wattle. Whereas in 1895 412,000 cwts. of sugar were produced, the 1909 output reached 1,550,000 cwts. During the same period exports of wattle bark rose from 68,000 cwts. to 706,000 cwts.[28] Another promising crop was maize, the exports of which reached nearly 40,000 tons in 1907.

In the first years of the twentieth century the policy of the government was to assist agricultural development by Europeans within the limits of its power.[29] This it had done by providing various agricultural extension services including expert advice, laboratory services, seeds, fertilizers, extermination of locusts, etc.[30] Experiments were also made by the government in the export of frozen meat and fruit, with satisfactory results.[31] The attempts to promote agriculture were also expressed in such legislative measures as the Agricultural Development Act of 1904[32] and the Land and Agricultural Loan Fund Act of 1907.[33] The Act of 1904, administered by the Land Board, aimed at the development of rural settlements by surveying and making available agricultural land. During the three years of its operation, 1905 to 1908, 672 settlers were placed on the land made available to them, and in spite of the cattle-fever epidemics the demand for land persisted.[34] The Land and Agricultural Loan Fund Act of 1907 established a fund for promoting the occupation, cultivation, and improvement of the agricultural and

26. *Legislative Assembly Debates*, 1908, p. 514.
27. *Ibid.*
28. W. B. Worsfold, *The Union of South Africa* (Boston: Little, Brown & Co., 1913), p. 348.
29. *Legislative Assembly Debates*, 1909, p. 287.
30. *Ibid.*, 1900, pp. 21 and 24.
31. *Ibid.*, 1908, p. 514.
32. Act. No. 44 of 1904, "To aid and encourage the Agricultural Development of Natal."
33. Act. No. 27 of 1907.
34. *Legislative Assembly Debates*, 1909, p. 287.

pastoral lands of the Colony. It provided for the granting of advances to farmers to pay off existing liabilities, to effect improvements, and to purchase livestock and plants. Loans were granted on the security of the land. During the first year of operation of the act, 152 loans amounting to a total of £86,000 were approved.[35] The introduction of the credit facilities created by the Act of 1907 was undoubtedly induced by the fact that generally small farmers are unable to borrow cheaply from private lenders because of the risks of this kind of lending, and because of the cost of administering it.

Mining. With the exception of coal, mining was of little importance in Natal (see Chapter 1). However, research in this field was supported by the government, and reports on the mining industry and the results of geological surveys were published from time to time by the Mines Department. The latter was in charge of boring for minerals and water, prospecting, and the administration of mining laws.

The Government Savings Bank

In primitive countries government can play an important role in encouraging both saving and the provision of institutions lending accumulated savings to investors. Thus one of the several measures to stimulate economic growth in Natal was the introduction of savings bank facilities in 1869,[36] provided by the creation of the Government Savings Bank. The original regulations empowered the colonial treasurer and resident magistrates to receive deposits of money which were to earn interest at 4 per cent per annum. A statutory proportion of 7/8 of the total deposits had to be invested in gilt-edged securities which as a rule yielded a rate of return insufficient to cover interest payments to the depositors. The difference was paid from the general revenue of the Colony, which procedure was regarded "as justified by the public duty to encourage thrift among the community, for whose benefit the institution is intended."[37] Deposits by Africans could not be retained for

35. *Ibid.*
36. Law No. 7 of 1868.
37. *Report of the Select Committee on Public Accounts*, 1896, par. 3.

fines or liabilities incurred by the tribe or kraal. This exemption did not apply to any liability incurred by an African depositor himself.[38]

Between 1893 and 1909 the total number of depositors increased from 5,630 to 23,212, and the balance to their credit from £146,000 to £505,000. The statistics show, however, that in 1909 there were only 590 African and 2,298 Indian depositors, and the balances to their credit were £11,700 and £46,200 respectively.[39]

The Savings Bank was possibly instrumental in encouraging saving habits, but it failed to elicit adequate response from the non-European community. Moreover, the fact that the deposits were invested by the agent-general in London[40] prevented the Natal investors from availing themselves of local savings which thus could not contribute to the development of the Colony.

The Development Expenditure on Non-Europeans

So far no mention has been made of the proportion of development funds expended on the non-European races inhabiting Natal.[41] The purpose of Table 3.10 is to fill this gap.

Several difficulties were encountered in estimating the proportion of ordinary revenue expended on the formation of the non-European "human capital." Of necessity the data had to be limited to the period 1900/1 to 1908/9, since no detailed information for the previous years is available. It was decided to include amounts spent on general welfare; undoubtedly such expenditure, by improving living standards, must have had a civilizing impact. The amounts included in this category were those statutorily "reserved for native purposes."[42] But since some "not reserved" expenditure was sometimes incurred, a compromise solution was adopted by accepting the total expenditure shown in the colonial accounts under the heading of the "Native Affairs Department." It was also felt

38. Law No. 7 of 1868.
39. See Appendix E.
40. *Ibid.*
41. For obvious reasons expenditure on fixed capital investment had to be omitted from our analysis because of the lack of sufficient data. This, however, should not affect our conclusions, as the services involved were those for which, as a rule, fees were charged.
42. Originally £5,000 and after 1894/5 £10,000 per annum was reserved for the welfare and the education of the Natives; however, these amounts were not always expended.

that any overestimation resulting from such a procedure might be offset by the omission of small sums spent on non-Europeans, particularly on Indians under other headings. On the other hand, expenditure on education and health for all non-Europeans is largely self-explanatory.

It appears that total expenditure per head of non-European population shown in Table 3.10 ranged between 9d. and 1s.6d. per annum. These amounts cover all expenditure which directly or indirectly benefited the non-Europeans. Other expenditure not related to development was either used to control and rule those people, to enforce the legal system imposed on them, or to provide services for which fees were charged.

A comparison between the per capita rates of non-European taxation indicated in Table 6.9 and the per capita expenditure on non-Europeans discloses that the latter formed from 7 to 20 per cent of the former. It follows then that the use of a large part of revenue from non-European taxation for the benefit of the European community tended to increase the already immense inequality of incomes and wealth.

A contemporary source reported the complaints by Africans:

Table 3.10. Contribution from Ordinary Revenue to the Development Expenditure on Non-Europeans, 1900/1-1908/9

| Year | Expenditure on | | | | Per head of non-European population s. d. |
	General welfare (£000)	Education (£000)	Health (£000)	Total (£000)	
1900/1	23.9	10.9	3.0	37.8	11
1901/2	23.0	11.2	3.3	37.5	10
1902/3	25.0	10.0	33.4	68.4	1. 5
1903/4	23.7	14.1	29.0	66.8	1. 4
1904/5	18.8	15.6	45.5	79.9	1. 6
1905/6	12.1	15.8	13.3	41.2	9
1906/7	16.3	15.3	11.9	43.5	10
1907/8	16.7	16.3	8.6	41.6	9
1908/9	16.9	17.3	9.5	43.7	9

Source: Natal, Auditor-General's *Reports.*

"The government takes little interest in us, except with regard to the payment of taxes, and that it gives money grudgingly for our benefit."[43] No modern system of taxation is really based on an equivalence of payment and benefit. This makes it possible for high incomes to be progressively taxed in order to provide for the welfare of the poorer classes, who benefit in excess of their contribution by taxation to the public revenue. The conclusion we are forced to draw, however, is that in Natal the opposite was true.

43. *The South African Natives, Their Progress and Present Condition*, p. 149.

Part IV

Chapter 11. Conclusions

At the turn of the nineteenth century Natal displayed some of the basic characteristics of an underdeveloped country. Income per head of population was low; and about 85 per cent of the Colony's inhabitants lived in rural areas and were engaged in agriculture, an activity which contributed less than 20 per cent of the gross geographical product. There was also a fairly sharp dividing line between the subsistence and the exchange sectors of the economy. Overcrowding of Africans in the rural reserves was the result of an unequal distribution of land, the bulk of which was owned by the Europeans, who often rented it to the native tenants or left it uncultivated. The African agriculture lacked cash crops of any importance. For a long time, European farming was handicapped by the absence of a sufficiently large local market for its products and its inability to produce exportable staples. Later on, this handicap was partly removed by the growing markets for sugar, maize, and wattle bark. But agriculture by itself was incapable of imparting momentum to the rest of the economy.

Because of Natal's exceptional geographical position on the route to the Witwatersrand goldfields, economic growth obtained its main stimulus from the activity of carrying goods. This activity required the creation of the necessary infrastructure. Nevertheless the transit trade, in spite of being an important source of income, had a limited impact: it benefited a small section of the community and was only loosely related to the rest of the economy.

As a consequence the European population derived its income primarily from the secondary and tertiary industries, whereas the Africans had to rely on their "subsistence" agriculture and on low-wage employment provided by Europeans. Most members of the Indian working population were employed on the sugar plantations or in manufacturing and mining, or earned their livelihood as small landholders.

The pattern of income distribution displayed a high degree of inequality between the European and non-European population. Income per capita accruing to the Europeans was nearly twenty-four times higher than that earned by non-Europeans. This disparity could be maintained in the long run only by artificial measures.

Between 1893 and 1910 government expenditure more than trebled, while the population of the Colony roughly doubled.[1] A marked increase in the proportion spent on public services largely reflected the growing importance of the government railway system.

On the revenue side, indirect taxes in general, and import taxes in particular, formed the largest proportion of government income. The economy did not lend itself to a system of taxation based on direct taxes. The reliance on indirect taxation was responsible for a strong element of instability of revenue. The volume of imports depended largely on the extent of gold mining development in the Transvaal, which varied considerably with changing economic and political conditions.

Two distinct periods may be discerned in the history of the fiscal policy of Natal. The first of them lasted until the Colony joined the South African Customs Union in 1898. During that period Natal relied on low customs duties, which enabled her to compete with the Cape and Delagoa Bay for the transit trade with the interior. At the same time care was taken to avoid the direct taxation of Europeans and not to increase the existing burden of indirect taxes. There was also a tendency to impose what appears to have been an undue share of taxation on the African population.

The main features of the second period of the history of Natal's fiscal policy were the evolution of the tariff system and the growing reliance on the revenue derived from the net earnings of the railway and harbor services. The reliance of the colonial authorities on indirect taxes was characteristic, at that time, of the colonial type of economy. This is still typical of primitive economies because of the ease with which such taxes can be administered and the fact that these economies supply a large part of their requirements from imports. The movement away from the reliance on import duties was slow. Natal followed the usual pattern of underdeveloped countries where basic changes in the tax structure often reflect the degree to which locally produced goods are substituted for imports. The extension of the South African free trade area was responsible for the broadening of the market for locally produced goods.[2] Dur-

1. Current expenditure per head of population rose from £1.19.2 to £2.16.6.
2. Apart from the smallness of the market the other important reasons for the

ing the twentieth century changes in the tariff system were also largely dictated by the desire to provide a measure of protection to the local manufacturers. Undoubtedly Natal's tariff system was partly responsible for the high cost of living and tended to magnify the inequality of income distribution.[3]

The plausibility of the various forms of direct taxation applicable to the African population has previously been discussed. It might be asked, however, why a tax based on the number of cattle owned by the taxpayer had never been contemplated. This would have provided a stimulus to Native agriculture, since a tax of this nature would have tended to prevent overgrazing, and consequently soil erosion. Probably it would have helped to increase the area under cultivation, as well as the productivity of cattle raising.[4] However, in view of the traditional tribal approach of the African toward his cattle, the imposition of such a tax would have probably had serious political consequences, even more serious than those which followed the imposition of the poll tax in 1906. Also, the administration of this form of taxation might have encountered insurmountable technical difficulties.

A serious drag on the economic development of Natal was the lack of a properly designed land tax. That such a tax could have been a practical proposition was proved during the short period of its application. An early and vigorously applied land tax, penalizing the inefficient use of agricultural land and preventing the concentration of large tracts of cultivable land in the hands of speculators might have altered the course of agricultural development. However, for a long time the vested interests in the legislature were too strong to allow that step to be taken. Speculation in land, as has

slow growth of Natal's economy were the low productivity of African labor, the absence of sources of cheap power, and the dearness of white labor, which was attracted by the rapidly developing Transvaal market; a similar tendency was also noticeable in the case of capital.

3. An important contributory factor of a non-fiscal nature which should also be mentioned was the fact that importers, merchants, entrepreneurs, etc., were accustomed to a high mark-up on goods supplied by them. But, of course, it was not a matter of preference of a high mark-up on a small turnover to a lower mark-up on a large turnover, simply because the market was too small to provide them with such an alternative.

4. In present-day Northern Nigeria a tax called *jangali* imposed on the Fulani herdsmen is applied to achieve similar results (J. F. Due, *Taxation and Economic Development in Tropical Africa*, Cambridge, Mass.: M. I. T. Press, 1963, p. 151).

been shown, was based on the expectation of a large future immigration; but paradoxically it was mainly the speculative price increases that prevented mass immigration.

Insofar as the other forms of direct taxation are concerned, the introduction of a short-lived progressive personal income tax was dictated by short-run revenue considerations rather than by any long-run considerations of equity. Its insignificant contribution to the Colony's revenue reflected the difficulty of its application on a wider basis. The company tax, based on a low rate, also produced mediocre results.

We have seen that the government of Natal played a decisive part in the extension of the railroads and other means of communication: it was the public sector of the economy which contributed significantly to the formation of the Colony's capital. At the beginning of the twentieth century its accumulated stock of capital, excluding land, was presumably far greater than the national income.[5]

Nevertheless the development of railroads and other public utilities and services led to the creation of a large external debt. Natal's policy was to obtain funds for the building of the infrastructure from overseas sources rather than through internal borrowing and higher taxation of its own people. The public debt was to a large extent "reproductive" and represented an investment which, on the average, paid for itself. Furthermore, a substantial part of the returns on that investment came from the foreigners to whom the transport services supplied by Natal were of great importance.

There were also other ways in which fiscal policy aimed at stimulating the economic development of the Colony. Various measures were applied to develop agriculture. Unfortunately, the authorities were not only late in the introduction of these measures, but also little was done to improve African agriculture. The liberal principle of laissez-faire prevailed in the Colony, but it was applied in such a way as to favor those who were already a privileged minority.

In a country the size of Ireland, with a white population not exceeding that of a small European town and a non-European popu-

5. W. A. Lewis maintains that in the poorest countries the stock of capital, excluding land, is smaller or not much greater than national income (*The Theory of Economic Growth*, London: George Allen and Unwin Ltd., 1961, p. 210).

lation ten times larger, the Legislative Council visualized itself rather as a "Board of Directors, than men having to do the work of statesmen."[6] Thus the way in which the public finance was used to develop the economy of Natal was dominated by the interests of the ruling race, and one of the problems which the Home Government had to consider when granting responsible government to Natal was the attitude of the colonists toward the Africans, whose well-being was likely to be disregarded.

The colonial system which existed in Natal may be viewed in terms of its impact on the entire social system, comprising both economic and non-economic elements. In reality, the role of the colonial administration went far beyond that of a company ruled by the "board of directors." The administrators had reshaped the ways of living of the native peoples; they had penetrated every corner of the country and could always rely on the support of the white troops.

The conflict between the goals and actions of the Europeans and non-Europeans was easily visible. The Europeans had to rely on African and Indian labor, and there must have been a certain optimum size of white population which would have maximized the income per head of the European community, given the natural resources of the country, the supply of non-European labor, and the state of technology. It is difficult to say whether such an optimum level was actually ever reached during Natal's colonial history. But the idea must have been present in the minds of those who ruled the country. On the other hand the growth of the numbers of non-Europeans helped to produce the required supply of labor and to keep wages close to the subsistence level.

Of the two alternatives, the first of which was to develop the non-European sector of the economy in order to enlarge the internal market and to realize the economies of large-scale production, the colonists had chosen the second: that of keeping the non-European backward and far removed from exercising any measure of political influence. Legal restrictions secured the latter aim, but they had to be supported by a fiscal system which taxed the African heavily and offered him in exchange only a fraction of what he was contributing to the colonial Treasury. What mattered was not that the

6. *Legislative Council Debates*, 1893, p. 30.

taxes imposed on Africans were heavy and that the proceeds were used for purposes which did not benefit them directly, but that taxation served the purpose of keeping them poor. It weakened their power to buy the very essentials of life and lowered their efficiency as laborers. On the other hand, it helped to maintain the supply of cheap labor on which the European sector thrived and without which its industrial structure was inconceivable.

The dictum that "the interests of the Colony demand that the control of its destinies should continue in the hands of men of European descent and race"[7] implied that any attempt to improve the economic lot of the non-European would have been followed by his increased power to exert political pressure and threaten the privileged position of the small European minority. Europeans felt safer and more satisfied with the standards they could secure in the shallow waters of their artificially restricted environment. They were afraid of a flood that would engulf them if full economic potentials were released.

It thus appears that the rationale of the colonial system peculiar to Natal is in terms of a sectoral division of the economy based on race with no significant class distinctions cutting across the racial structure. In this set-up public finance has a special role assigned to it: besides its usual functions it is instrumental in maintaining the wide inequality of income and wealth. In the absence of social mobility between the races, the system tends to perpetuate itself, so that its fundamental features continue to survive.

7. *Legislative Assembly Debates*, 1896, p. 166.

Appendices

Appendices

Appendix A. Gross Geographical Product of Natal, 1903/4[1]

Introduction

The purpose of this appendix is to provide a geographical product estimate of the economy of Natal for the year ended June 30, 1904. The decision not to attempt similar estimates for earlier years was due to the paucity of statistical information. Moreover, territorial changes in 1897 and 1902 would have frustrated the comparability of estimates. Two considerations influenced the choice of the year. First, the colonial census taken in April, 1904, considerably amplified the statistical information given annually in the *Statistical Year Books*. Unlike the census of 1891, which provided basic population and occupational data only, the census of 1904 included information on agriculture, manufacturing, buildings and dwellings, etc., as well as detailed occupational data. Second, the second half of 1903 and the first half of 1904 was a transitional period between the postwar boom and the severe depression which followed. Thus the selection of such a year, devoid of sudden crisis, eliminated the extremes of the business cycle. The level of imports and exports was still high and government expenditure, though falling, was well above the level of the years which followed. Apart from the statistical information given by the 1904 census, the period between July 1, 1903, and June 30, 1904, corresponded to the budget year of the Colony.

Since we are concerned with the total value of goods and services produced within the geographical boundaries of Natal's territory, the concept of gross geographical product is used. It differs from the gross domestic product, which is the product of all resident producers, in that it includes the product of non-resident producers located within the geographical territory, but excludes the product of resident producers located abroad.

National product aggregate, in turn, differs from the domestic product in that it includes the product of resident producers attributable to factors of production supplied by non-residents, but ex-

1. I am indebted for the basic framework of this appendix to the pioneer work by G. Eisner, *Jamaica, 1830-1930: A Study in Economic Growth* (Manchester: Manchester University Press, 1961). Some of the concepts used there were modified because of differences in the economic structure, the data available, and some recent improvements in the methods of national income accounting.

cludes the product of non-resident producers attributable to factors of production supplied by residents.[2] From the practical point of view the difference between the value of the geographical and the domestic product of Natal in 1903/4 was probably so small that it can be neglected, and the two values may be assumed to be roughly the same. Gross national product cannot be estimated because no sufficient data of the net product attributable to the rest of the world are available.

Care was taken to insure that the output of the various sectors and the incomes of the various factors of production and classes of occupations were correlated. This was made possible by the existence of occupational data. As a by-product of this approach an income distribution by races was obtained.

It was decided to preserve consistently the dichotomy between the private and public sectors. As a consequence, under the heading of "building and construction" only private firms were included, whereas public expenditure on building and construction was allocated to the central or local government. The same principle was applied to transport, including railways, and all other activities shared by private enterprise and public agencies.

In view of what had already been said of the GGP, the treatment of exports and of the import content of output is largely self-explanatory. The GGP includes value of output produced for export as well as the value of output for local consumption. By including "value added" we exclude the import content of output and the materials supplied by other productive units, in order to eliminate double counting.

Agriculture, Forestry, and Fishing

Agricultural crops are valued at market prices. This information is given in the *Statistical Year Books* for 1903 and 1904. Imported materials, mainly fertilizers and bags, were deducted. The amount of locally produced materials used could not be ascertained; these are assumed to have been negligible. To arrive at the farm value of the crops produced, the cost of delivering goods to the markets

2. G. C. Billington, "A Minimum System of National Accounts for Use by African Countries and Some Related Problems," in *African Studies in Income and Wealth*, ed. L. H. Samuels (London: Bowes and Bowes, 1963), p. 50.

and the distribution costs of producers were deducted. Transport and distribution costs are included under their respective headings.

The total net value[3] of the crops produced by Europeans is estimated at £1,452,000. It is assumed that European crops were grown with the help of African and Indian labor; African and Indian crops are assumed to have been cultivated without European aid. European incomes from agricultural activities are reduced by the wages paid to non-European labor. Available data show that the majority of the Indians employed on the European plantations were indentured labor. The 1904 census shows that 32,786 Indians were engaged in agriculture. Some of them carried on agricultural activities as small landholders on their own account. Of the 31,000 indentured Indians in the Colony,[4] 901 were employed by the Natal Government Railways.[5] Their wages ranged between 10s. and 14s. per month for adult males, and from 5s. to 7s. per month for women and children. In addition to the money wages they were provided with rations, lodging, and medical attention. The value of wages in kind was conservatively estimated at 6d. per day per head. After five years' service the indentured Indians could re-indenture at a wage ranging from 16s. to 20s. per month for men and 8s. to 10s. for women.[6] Indian employment on European farms probably did not exceed 16,200 persons;[7] their estimated earnings are £249,800 including earnings in kind.

An estimation of the number of African laborers on European farms presented a much more difficult problem. The bulk of African farm labor was supplied by tenants living on European farms. The total income of an agricultural laborer consisted of an average cash wage of 10s. per month, rations, and squatting rights.[8] Because of the lack of reliable statistical data, the earnings of African labor in terms of money wages and payments in kind are estimated at £410,000, which is a measurement of their productivity.

A distinction is made between the production of sugar cane and sugar, as well as by-products such as molasses. Thus, under

3. "Net" is used here to signify the value from which materials produced by other economic units are excluded in order to eliminate double counting.
4. *Report of the Protector of Indian Immigration*, 1904, p. 11.
5. *Reports of the General Manager of Railways*, 1903 and 1904.
6. *Statistical Year Books*, 1903 and 1904.
7. *Census for 1904*, "Occupations."
8. *The Natives of South Africa, Their Economic and Social Condition*, p. 62.

the heading of "agriculture," only the net value of cane produced was included, whereas the value added in the course of sugar manufacture is accounted for under the heading of "manufacturing." The same principle is followed in the case of all crops which were used as raw materials in food processing and other manufacturing industries. Fruit and vegetable production data are adjusted, as the value of output officially given appears to be far too low. The secretary for the minister of agriculture stated in his annual report[9] that information on fruit production was "absurdly inadequate." In 1904 the output of fruit was valued at £30,000 whereas the customs returns showed that more than £80,000 worth of colonial fruit was exported. A considerable quantity of fruit was also sold for local consumption. He suggested a total value of at least £100,000.

European agriculture formed part of the Colony's exchange economy in contrast with the African subsistence agricultural economy. Out of the total African population of 904,000 roughly 820,000 lived within the subsistence sector. The value of African crops is estimated on the basis of farm prices ruling in the neighboring markets.[10] The value thus obtained is £868,000, which represents the average of the 1903 and 1904 values. Crops in 1903 were rather poor, but 1904 was a normal year. The bulk of crops produced was maize and Kaffir corn, which formed the staple diet of the Africans. The average output per head available for consumption was 4.75 lbs. per week—equivalent to 5,849 calories. The required daily calorific intake for a moderately active adult male is 3,000 and for a female 2,400 calories; therefore, food crops available fell far below the required minima. The composition of the weekly supply of food is shown in Table 1.A.

This starchy diet is inadequate to maintain minimum health standards. Meat consumption, estimated at 13 lbs. per man per annum, was too insignificant to affect the pattern of food consumption.[11] Were it not for the earnings of the migrant laborer working

9. *Report of Secretary, Minister of Agriculture,* 1905.

10. Prest, *op. cit.,* Appendix I: "Valuation of Subsistence Output."

11. Dr. A. Richards (*Land, Labour and Diet in Northern Rhodesia,* published for the International Institute of African Languages and Culture, London: Oxford University Press, 1939) mentions a survey in Northern Province which found an average village meat consumption of less than 6 lbs. per man value per annum

for European employers, the rural population could not have maintained itself.

The net value of crops grown by the Indians is estimated at £347,500. Besides general agricultural crops they produced fruit and vegetables. The above figure includes tobacco, which played a prominent part in Indian production and is valued at £190,000.

Animal products produced on European farms included meat, skins and horns, milk, butter, eggs, wool, and mohair. The only important item, however, was meat. The figures of meat production shown in the *Statistical Year Books* seem unrealistic when related to livestock numbers and estimated meat consumption by Europeans. Meat production is estimated on a daily consumption of beef and mutton meat of the order of four ounces per head of European population per day. This amount does not take into account the consumption of pork and poultry. The annual estimated meat requirements of the existing population of 97,100 is, therefore, 8,860,-000 lbs., which represents 6.49 per cent of the dressed meat equivalent to existing numbers of livestock.[12] On the basis of this percent-

Table 1.A. **Weekly Supply of Food Produced by Africans**

Product	Quantity (lbs.)	Calories
Maize	2.36	3,986
Kaffir corn	1.33	1,504
Potatoes	0.44	140
Tubers (amadumbi)	0.11	12
Beans	0.11	169
Pumpkins	0.40	38
	4.75	5,849

(quoted in P. Deane, *Colonial Social Accounting*, Cambridge: Cambridge University Press, 1953, p. 163).

12. The dressed meat equivalents are assumed to be the same as those used by P. Deane in her work *The Measurement of Colonial National Incomes* (National Institute of Economic and Social Research, *Occasional Papers*, XII, 109); i.e., 400 lbs. per head of cattle and 50 lbs. for sheep. If the numbers of animals are converted into cattle units (one cattle unit is assumed to be equal to 400 lbs. dressed

age the total value of meat produced for consumption is calculated as shown in Table 2.A.

Table 2.A. European Output of Beef and Mutton

	Number of animals slaughtered	Total weight (lbs.)	Price per lb.	Total value £
Cattle	17,567	7,026,800	10d.	292,783
Sheep	36,925	1,846,250	6d.	46,156
				338,939

The value of pork consumed is estimated at £9,485. This is based on estimated market price of 6d. per lb., and the official weight of 389,541 lbs. of dressed pork. We assume that half of the poultry numbers was consumed per annum. Valued at 2s. per fowl the total value of meat consumed will now increase by £12,590 to £361,014. The remaining animal products account for an additional £140,228. The final value of the European animal agricultural output of £496,875 includes an amount of £149,400 paid to African farm labor.

There were no official data available for African meat production because African livestock holdings were kept in the form of wealth for prestige reasons and to meet "lobola" (bride price) obligations. This led to overstocking and the attendant evils of soil erosion and veld destruction.[13] Generally the Zulu slaughtered his cattle for ceremonial purposes rather than for food.

African consumption of beef and mutton is estimated on a conservative basis at 6 per cent of the total number of cattle and 11 per cent of sheep slaughtered annually.[14] Average dressed weight

meat; eight sheep equal one cattle unit) the following result is obtained:

	Number	Cattle Units
Cattle	270,671	270,671
Sheep	568,946	71,118
		341,789 x 400 lbs. = 136,715,600 lbs. of dressed meat.

13. Brookes and Hurwitz, *op. cit.*, p. 111.

14. These are the lowest percentages applied by Deane for the Tonga area. The

of African cattle is assumed 300 lbs. and of sheep 40 lbs.[15] The total thus obtained is valued at £320,521.

The number of animals owned by the Indians was comparatively small. Slaughterings were carried out only by Moslems, who formed a small proportion of the Indian population. Hence we can assume that the number of Indian cattle slaughtered was insignificant. There is strong evidence that meat consumption among these two groups was negligible. It is, however, assumed that in addition to the consumption of beef and mutton an allowance of £42,000 could be made for pork consumption by Africans, this being the value of the dressed-meat equivalent to half of the stock of 34,200 pigs owned by them.

Table 3.A. **African Output of Beef and Mutton**

	Number of animals slaughtered	Total weight (lbs.)	Price per lb.	Total value £
Cattle	30,381	9,114,300	8d.	303,810
Sheep	20,053	802,120	5d.	16,711
				320,521

The output of milk and eggs by the non-Europeans is also unimportant. The latter, owing to taboos among the Africans, were largely bartered or sold. Poultry was kept for consumption as well as for barter and sale to European traders.[16] The consumption and sales of poultry are estimated at £22,455 in the case of Africans, and at £1,268 in the case of Indians.

The products of forestry consist of wattle bark and timber valued at £68,556. Fish production is based on the data provided for deep sea fishing, and is valued at £21,000.[17] No data are avail-

---

Tonga people, like the Zulus, are traditionally cattle owners (Deane, *Colonial Social Accounting*, p. 163).

15. *Ibid.*, p. 162.

16. Brookes and Hurwitz, *op. cit.*, p. 119.

17. *Report of the Secretary, Natal Harbor Department*, 1904. The number of deep sea fish brought to Scottsburg was not recorded, but it is allowed for in the above figure of £21,000.

able which could indicate the value of other catches. The value of Indian fish production is estimated at £6,514, which is based on the earnings of the 228 fishermen enumerated in the 1904 census.

Mining

Collieries were the only mining activities of any importance. The value of the output of coal is calculated on the basis of the industrial census returns for 1904, and valued at the price charged at the pit's mouth. Hence it excludes transport and distribution costs. Out of the estimated total of £332,000 the European share is £190,-665. This amount consists of salaries and wages earned by 283 European employees, declared dividends of £92,600 paid by the fourteen companies operating in 1904, as well as other undisclosed earnings.[18] The earnings of the 5,627 non-European workers are estimated at £141,338, of which £114,573 are allocated to Africans and £26,762 to Indians.

Manufacturing

The figures shown under this heading are based on the industrial census of 1904. They are estimates for "value added" but exclude the cost of transport as well as the manufacturers' distribution costs. This census covered manufacturing establishments where goods worth £100 and more were produced per annum. The large number of independent workers such as bakers and confectioners, boot and shoemakers, dressmakers, mechanics, electricians, farriers, etc., who were not covered by the industrial census were enumerated in the occupational census. Thus it is convenient to differentiate between factory workers and independent ones. The value of the output of the latter is assumed to correspond to their approximate annual net earnings. The number of establishments included as factories was 693, and their total net output is estimated at £2,215,678. A striking feature was the importance of establishments engaged in the processing of agricultural products: sugar factories; breweries and distilleries; corn mills; bakeries and creamery establishments; tobacco, cigar, and snuff factories; tanneries;

18. *Report of the Mining Industry of Natal*, 1904.

wattle-bark processing plants; etc. The net output of all these processing plants is valued at £1,055,643, or 47.6 per cent of the total
output of all the factories. The earnings of the European-owned
factors of production are calculated at £1,614,673, the wages of
Africans at £269,828, and the wages of Indians at £331,177.

Under the heading of "independent workers" 4,170 European
and 1,013 Indian workers are included. The earnings of the former
are estimated at £655,304, and those of the latter at £48,407. No
data for African independent handicraft were available, but their
absence cannot materially influence the final total.

Building and Construction

As in the case of "Manufacturing," the data pertaining to "Building and Construction" were obtained from the industrial census
returns for 1904. In addition, account was also taken of the earnings of the ninety-two architects and their assistants who were not
accounted for in the industrial census, but were enumerated in the
occupational census. Allowance was made for transport costs incurred in the case of the building materials handled by building
firms. These costs are included under the heading "Transport."
Building and construction by the government are excluded.

The European share of the total "value added" of £975,527 thus
calculated is £888,857, of which salaries and wages of the 1,141
persons employed amount to £776,618. The earnings of the 1,620
non-Europeans are estimated at £86,670; of this total the Africans'
share is £54,960 and that of the Indians £31,710.

Distribution

"Value added" of the wholesale and retail trade is based on the
estimated earnings of persons engaged in the distributive services
which are enumerated in the 1904 occupational census. Allowance
was also made for business profits. The earnings of the 5,138
Europeans engaged in commercial enterprises are estimated at
£994,596 and those of the 5,058 Indians, who played a prominent
part in the retail trade, at £473,641. These estimates are supplemented by the distribution costs of producers on the assumption

that they could have acted as retail and wholesale distributors of their products. An amount of £217,599 as distribution costs is thus transferred from "Agriculture" and "Manufacturing" to "Distribution."

Transport

It has been mentioned previously that some producers used their own transport within their productive units. The value of these services is now deducted from the totals of the particular branches of the industries; they are accounted for under the above heading, which includes the following transfers:

Agriculture	£133,623
Building and construction	£ 30,000
Manufacturing	£105,936
	£269,559

Other private transport services employed 1,680 Europeans, who account for £279,605; 135 Africans, £4,806; and 602 Indians, £32,848. Whereas the numbers of Europeans and Indians were based on the occupational census, the number of Africans employed in private transport services was difficult to ascertain, and hence the above number is a very rough estimate. It is likely, therefore, that the amount of £586,818 contributed by transport to the GGP is slightly underestimated. The contribution by general and local government to transport services is accounted for under the heading of "Government."

Ownership of Houses

Estimates of the income derived from private dwellings and from rentals are based on the 1904 census, which gives data on buildings and dwellings. Newspaper advertisements also provided information on rentals charged.[19] The amount of rentals charged for African dwellings is assessed on the basis of a return compiled in 1888.[20] It is assumed that African rentals did not change significantly between 1888 and 1904; similar values were quoted by the

19. *The Natal Advertiser* for 1903 and 1904, and other Natal newspapers.
20. *Sessional Papers* of the Legislative Council, No. 5, 1888, p. 17.

South African Native Races Committee in 1908.[21] The latter source supplied the information on rentals charged in the Native Trust and Mission Reserves.

The 1904 census enumerated 37,768 dwellings occupied by Europeans and Indians, classified on a room basis. Indian rentals reflect their low incomes, as well as the fact that the Indians occupied most of the inferior types of dwellings.

Table 4.A. **Rental Value of Dwellings**

	Number of rooms	Number of houses	Rent per annum £	Total rental value £
Europeans	1–2	1,445	24	34,680
	3–4	3,159	48	151,632
	5–6	7,632	72	549,504
	7–8	4,299	96	412,704
	9 and over	2,468	120	296,160
	Not specified	60	—	—
		19,063		1,444,680
Indians	1–2	11,031	3	33,093
	3–4	4,943	9	44,487
	5–6	1,592	12	19,104
	7–8	487	18	8,766
	9 and over	599	24	14,376
	Not specified	53	—	—
		18,705		119,826

It is assumed that the rental value of the dwellings inhabited by Europeans accrued to them as income. This also applies to Indian dwellings.

In order to estimate the rental value of African-occupied dwellings the first step was to classify the rural Africans according to the nature of their tenancy; thereafter the number of huts was calculated and multiplied by the appropriate average annual rental.[22] The total African population of the Colony in 1904 numbered 904,-

21. *The South African Natives, Their Progress and Present Condition,* p. 62.
22. *Ibid.*

ooo; about 80,000 Africans were in "service" and temporarily resident in quarters provided by their employers. There were also some 421,000 Africans who lived as tenants on land belonging to private and often absentee European owners. The average annual rentals paid by them was £2.10.0 per hut. Those who lived on Crown lands paid £2 per hut to the government,[23] while Africans on Native Trust and Mission Reserves paid annually £1.10.0 per hut. Approximately 824,000 Africans were domiciled in the 230,963 huts enumerated in the 1904 census, or approximately 3.6 persons per hut. The estimated values of African rentals are given below:

Rental of 42 1,000 Africans living on the European-owned land, and occupying 118,000 huts at £2.10.0 per annum   295,000

Rental value of 109,963 huts occupied by 392,290 Africans living in Native Trust and Mission Reserves, on the freehold land owned by them, and the communal lands in Zululand at £1.10.0 per annum   164,945[24]

                                                                         £459,945

The total rental value of African dwellings is thus estimated at £459,945, of which £295,000 accrued to the European owners of land, and only £164,945 to the African population.

Government

The value of services rendered is calculated from the report of the auditor-general, which gives details of salaries and wages paid by the administrative section of the central government. Railway accounts, on the other hand, do not show details of the earnings of each race. This is remedied by taking into account the racial distribution of employment supplied in the reports of the general manager of railways. Thus the total earnings of Africans and Indians are found by multiplying the respective numbers by standard wage rates for non-Europeans. The average number of salaried

23. There were 10,710 Africans living on Crown lands and occupying 3,000 huts. Total land revenue received by the central government in 1903/4 was £18,778, of which African rents are assumed to have been £6,000. The above amount is included under the heading of "government."

24. *The South African Natives, Their Progress and Present Condition*, pp. 64-65.

staff and laborers employed by the railways in 1903/4 was 4,981 Europeans, 4,866 Africans, and 2,808 Indians, of whom 901 were indentured. European earnings were estimated at £1,718,800, and those of Africans and Indians at £225,500 and £97,100 respectively.

Finances of the local government were dominated by the municipalities of Durban and Pietermaritzburg, whose expenditure in 1903/4 accounted for 95 per cent of a total expenditure estimated at £391,600. In many cases the accounts of Durban and Pietermaritzburg did not differentiate between salaries, wages, and materials. Therefore, estimates were made to fill in the gap. Only total expenditures by the remaining municipalities were available. Interest payments on the public debt are treated as a payment for factor service.[25]

Other Services

Finance and banking. The *Statistical Year Books* supply only scanty information on commercial banks and building societies. The information on other financial services was obtained from the occupational censuses and local newspapers. In 1903 and 1904 five commercial banks were in operation in Natal, of which only the Natal Bank, Ltd., had its head office in the Colony. It was therefore possible to ascertain the amount of its paid-up capital and the dividends paid out in 1903-4. The remaining four banks had their head offices elsewhere. On the basis of existing statistics neither the amount of their capital in Natal nor the dividends paid by them could be ascertained. In view of the above difficulties, estimates of the gross earnings of commercial banks are based on the volume of deposits and interest payments, as well as their assets and approximate profitability. The results were checked by allowing for verifiable expenses, estimated dividend payments, and transfers to reserve funds. A similar procedure was adopted in the case of the eight building societies then operating in Natal.

It is estimated that the "value added" by these tertiary services of the commercial banks and the building societies amounted to £406,891. In addition, the annual earnings of the 68 insurance

25. Billington, *op. cit.*, p. 16.

agents in the Colony are estimated at £20,400. The total for "finance and banking" is therefore £427,291.

Professions. The professional group included the legal, medical, educational, and religious services. It also covered artists, journalists, independent surveyors, accountants, etc., whose activities are not included under any other heading. There were 171 European and 2 Indian lawyers in private practice. Their average earnings are estimated at £650 per annum.[26] The medical profession consisted of 150 European and 7 Indian medical practitioners in private practice, with average earnings estimated at £650 per annum.[27] The other members of the medical profession consisted of 27 dentists, whose earnings are assumed to be the same as those of the medical practitioners. In addition there were a number of midwives, medical assistants, receptionists, etc., whose total earnings are estimated at £45,520.

The contribution of education to total output is partly covered by educational services provided by government and partly by private schools. The former are included under the heading of "government." Private educational establishments employed 89 European male teachers, whose total annual earnings are estimated at £16,020; the earnings of the 529 female teachers are estimated at £63,480. Salaries of the 55 Indian teachers are £2,915 and those of the four female teachers £192.[28]

The religious services were performed by 265 European ministers and priests. In the absence of reliable information their income is conservatively estimated at £31,800. This is based on the assumption that each European paid 6s. per annum toward the upkeep of this group. There were also 118 European male missionaries and 103 female missionaries whose incomes are assessed at £13,560. We assume that the 79 Indian priests earned £4,740.

Services provided by the 1,556 European members of other professions enumerated in the 1904 census are estimated at £358,058. There were also 307 Indians in this category with earnings of £20,131. The grand total of all these earnings amounts to £772,300.

26. This was the average salary paid to legal officers in government service.

27. This was the average salary paid to senior medical officers in government service.

28. Teachers' salaries in private schools are assumed to be the same as the average teachers' salaries paid in government service.

Domestic services. The 1904 census enumerated 240 male and 1,346 female Europeans employed as domestic servants, governesses, housekeepers, etc. Their total annual earnings are assumed to be £171,156. There were also 2,057 male and 608 female Indian domestic servants, with earnings of £85,351. By far the largest proportion of domestic servants were Africans, numbering 30,050 males and 10,230 females;[29] together their wages are valued at £806,600. We assume that the wages of all people engaged in domestic services included board and lodging. In addition, there were 654 dhobis[30] earning £23,088.

29. *Census Report*, 1904, p. 678.
30. Indian washermen.

Table 5.A. **Estimate of Gross Geographical Product of Natal, 1903/4**

Source		Amount £000
1. Agriculture, forestry, and fishing		
a. Agricultural crops	2,667.5	
b. Animal products	887.5	
c. Forestry and fishing	96.1	3,651.1
2. Mining		332.0
3. Manufacturing		
a. Factories	2,215.7	
b. Independent workers	703.7	2,919.4
4. Building and construction		975.5
5. Distribution		1,685.9
6. Transport		586.8
7. Ownership of houses		2,018.4
8. Government		
a. Central	2,582.2	
b. Local	391.6	2,973.8
9. Other services		
a. Finance and banking	427.3	
b. Professions	772.3	
c. Domestic	1,316.9	2,516.5
Total gross geographical product at factor cost		17,659.4

Catering is also classified as a domestic service. The wages of the 790 male and 345 female Europeans enumerated in the 1904 census are estimated at £178,980, and those of the 1,404 Indians at £51,724.

Table 6.A. Estimate of Gross Geographical Income of Natal, 1903/4

	Total	Europeans	Africans	Indians
Incomes from agriculture, forestry, and fishing				
(a) Wages and salaries	1,139.2	330.0	559.4	249.8
(b) Planters' profits	903.7	903.7	—	—
(c) Small-holders' profits	1,608.3	—	1,253.0	355.3
Other wages and salaries				
(a) Mining	240.0	98.6	114.6	26.8
(b) Building and construction	863.2	776.5	55.0	31.7
(c) Manufacturing	1,579.3	978.3	269.8	331.2
(d) Distribution	293.3	220.1	32.9	40.3
(e) Transport	500.5	350.0	71.8	78.7
(f) Government	2,038.4	1,718.8	225.5	94.1
(g) Other services	1,807.1	826.2	806.6	174.3
Profits and other incomes				
(a) Trade	2,936.8	2,434.8	—	502.0
(b) Professions	709.2	689.6	—	19.6
(c) Government	935.4	935.4	—	—
(d) Other	2,105.0	1,826.3	158.9	119.8
Total gross geographical income at factor cost	17,659.4	12,088.3	3,547.5	2,023.6

Conclusions

The discussion on the compilation of the GGP highlights the gaps in the published data and the difficulties encountered. The most comprehensive data were found in the 1904 census, the *Statistical Year Books*, and the *Public Accounts*. Use was also made of contemporary literature on Natal and newspapers. These sources made it possible to use the output method and to provide an estimate of income distribution on both sectoral and racial bases. Unfortunately the lack of expenditure statistics precluded checks on the output method by means of an analysis of expenditure.

In the racial distribution of the product the 6,686 Coloured persons were included under the heading of "Indians." It was felt that the Coloureds represented too small a group to be treated separately. Economically they were perhaps closer to Indians than to any other racial group.

The sectoral analysis suffers from various gaps which are particularly pronounced in the case of the subsistence sector. For example it was impossible to estimate accurately the quantities of agricultural products consumed on the farms or crops fed to stock, since these were never enumerated. On the other hand, the industrial census figures appear to be reliable; the colonial authorities reported very few refusals when collecting the data.

Wherever reliable data were absent approximations were made. This was often the case with prices and wages. In many instances, however, individual items or their totals could be checked by comparing employment figures from the industrial census with the details from the occupational census.

Finally it should be admitted that it was not possible to calculate, with any degree of accuracy, the margins of error involved in the computation of the subtotals of the GGP, and hence to provide a satisfactory measure of the reliability of the estimates.

Appendix B. Colony of Natal: Consolidated Revenue Fund, 1892/3-1909/10

Year	Amount credited or debited at the beginning of the year (1) (£000)	Revenue for the year (2) (£000)	Consolidated revenue fund (3) = (1)+(2) (£000)	Expenditure for the year (4) (£000)	Balance at the end of the year (5) = (3)-(4) (£000)
1892/3	719.7	1,069.7	1,789.4	1,099.9	689.5
1893/4	689.5	1,011.0	1,700.5	1,082.4	618.1
1894/5	618.1	1,169.8	1,787.9	1,148.1	639.8
1895/6	639.8	1,457.4	2,097.2	1,282.5	814.7
1896/7	814.7	2,213.1	3,027.8	1,625.0	1,402.8
1897/8	1,402.8	1,964.3	3,367.1	1,812.3	1,554.8
1898/9	1,554.8	2,137.3*	3,692.1	3,511.3†	180.8
1899/0	180.8	2,554.2‡	2,735.0	1,990.5	744.5
1900/1	744.5	3,138.7§	3,883.2	2,480.9	1,402.3
1901/2	1,402.3	3,439.8	4,842.1	3,933.0‖	909.1
1902/3	909.1	4,334.2	5,243.3	5,039.0	204.3
1903/4	204.3	4,160.1	4,364.4	4,071.4	293.0
1904/5	293.0	3,384.8	3,677.8	4,029.6#	-351.8
1905/6	-351.8	3,666.0	3,314.2	3,670.6	-356.4
1906/7	-356.4	3,483.6**	3,127.2	3,681.9	-554.7
1907/8	-554.7	3,510.4	2,955.7	3,689.8	-734.1
1908/9	-734.1	3,569.3	2,835.2	3,530.6	695.4
1909/10	-695.4	4,293.7	3,598.3	3,530.4	67.9

*Revenue for 1898/9 includes the following items: (£000)

Current revenue	2,081.3
Indian Immigration Trust Board Account not previously included	56.0
	2,137.3

†From this year onward the "Expenditure" represents issues from the consolidated revenue fund, and not current expenditure as in the previous budget years. The total includes: (£000)

Issues for 1898/9	1,914.7
Advances for works under loans	1,596.6
	3,511.3

‡Revenue for 1899/1900 includes the following items: (£000)

Current revenue	1,886.7
Bank of England advance	667.5
	2,554.2

§Revenue for 1900/1 includes the following items: (£000)

Current revenue	2,970.8
Bank of England advance	167.9
	3,138.7

‖Expenditure for 1901/2 includes the following items: (£000)

Issues for 1901/2	3,097.6
Repayment of Bank of England loan	835.4
	3,933.0

#Expenditure for 1904/5 includes the following items: (£000)

Current expenditure	3,814.6
Additional issues	15.0
Contingencies fund	200.0
	4,029.6

**Revenue for 1906/7 includes the following items: (£000)

Current revenue	3,471.9
Accounting Officers' cash surrenders	11.7
	3,483.6

Source: Natal, *Blue Books, Statistical Year Books,* and Auditor-General's *Reports.*

Appendix C. Colony of Natal: Loan Fund, 1892/3-1909/10

Year	Credited or debited at beginning of year (1) (£000)	Receipts during the year (2) (£000)	Total loan funds (3) = (1)+(2) (£000)	Expenditure for the year (4) (£000)	Balance at the end of the year (5) = (3)-(4) (£000)
1892/3	61.6	560.4	622.0	615.3	6.7
1893/4	6.7	856.6	863.3	620.7*	242.6
1894/5	242.6	17.7	260.3	147.5	112.8
1895/6	112.8	125.0†	237.8	232.7	5.1
1896/7	5.1	770.4‡	775.5	772.4§	3.1
1897/8	3.1	1,366.7‖	1,369.8	1,369.8#	Nil
1898/9**	Nil	941.5	941.5	381.0	560.5
1899/0	560.5	10.7	571.2	816.2	−245.0
1900/1	−245.0	1,038.2	793.2	741.8	51.4
1901/2	51.4	2,122.4	2,173.8	1,240.7	933.1
1902/3	933.1	1,374.7	2,307.8	1,683.2	624.6
1903/4	624.6	1,491.0	2,115.6	1,292.4	823.2
1904/5	823.2	3,031.6	3,854.8	2,836.4	1,018.4
1905/6	1,018.4	2,168.2	3,186.6	2,678.8	507.8
1906/7	507.8	3,164.2	3,672.0	3,162.2	509.8
1907/8	509.8	2,794.6	3,304.4	2,636.9	667.5
1908/9	667.5	1,849.7	2,517.2	1,515.2	1,002.0
1909/10	1,002.0	1,517.8	2,519.8	1,976.3	543.5

*Expenditure in 1893/4 included the fol-owing items: (£000)

Expenditure on public works	79.7
Repayment of advances	541.0
	620.7

†Receipts in 1895/6 included the following items: (£000)

Receipts on account of loans	2.2
Advances from revenue	122.8
	125.0

‡Receipts in 1896/7 included the following items: (£000)

Receipts on account of loan	7.9
Advances from revenue	762.5
	770.4

§Expenditure in 1896/7 included the following items: (£000)

Expenditure on public works	649.6
Repayment of advances	122.8
	772.4

‖Receipts in 1897/8 included the following items: (£000)

Receipts on account of loans	3.0
Advances from revenue	1,363.7
	1,366.7

Expenditure in 1897/8 included the following items: (£000)

Expenditure on public works	607.4
Repayments of advances	762.4
	1,369.8

**From this year on, the "Expenditure" represents issues from the Loan Fund and not the actual expenditure on works under loans. In the later years changes in the system of accounting affected the comparability of the data, a drawback which cannot be overcome on the basis of existing information.

Source: Natal, *Blue Books, Statistical Year Books,* and Auditor-General's *Reports.*

Appendix D. Colony of Natal: Municipal Finance, 1892/3-1909/10

Year	Revenue (£000)	Expenditure (£000)	Municipal debt (£000)	Sinking funds (£000)
1892/3	171.6	182.7	411.0*	—
1893/4	179.2	225.9	612.3	104.9
1894/5	237.5	229.3	680.7	116.1
1895/6	298.4	190.3	683.8	130.3
1896/7	234.5	245.2	761.7	143.6
1897/8	225.2	290.4	838.7	157.9
1898/9	177.5	187.3	1,488.2	163.2
1899/0	253.3	269.7	1,763.2	154.4
1900/1	321.1	317.5	2,369.6	180.2
1901/2	390.9	446.8	2,332.4	195.6
1902/3	527.6	634.1	2,638.7	240.8
1903/4	827.8	720.1	2,953.3	250.9
1904/5	567.0	701.8	3,530.5	269.8
1905/6	565.5	624.6	3,582.8	316.1
1906/7	541.2	603.0	3,548.2	267.3
1907/8	523.0	540.8	3,733.4	290.2
1908/9	530.7	518.2	3,822.0	317.2

*Net amount.
Source: Natal, *Blue Books* and *Statistical Yearbooks*.

Appendix E. Natal Government Savings Bank, 1893-1909

| Year | Deposits on December 31 | | | | N.G. Savings Bank deposits as percentage of total bank deposits | Number of depositors on December 31 | | | |
	European (£000)	African (£000)	Indian (£000)	Total (£000)	%	Europeans No.	Africans No.	Indians No.	Total No.
1893	..	..	..	146.1	7.5	..	..	..	5,630
1894	..	..	..	155.4	7.4	..	..	..	6,285
1895	..	..	..	172.3	6.5	..	..	..	6,963
1896	204.5	2.0	16.9	223.4	7.6	7,531	111	618	8,260
1897	240.4	1.7	19.7	261.8	10.3	8,945	158	760	9,863
1898	250.9	4.4	17.7	273.0	9.9	9,595	209	1,128	10,932
1899	281.0	4.9	15.4	301.3	7.9	10,675	251	655	11,581
1900	396.7	6.1	23.4	426.2	8.7	13,267	303	936	14,506
1901	481.5	7.6	34.1	523.2	9.6	16,003	353	1,310	17,666
1902	534.8	11.4	46.3	592.5	10.7	17,936	455	1,787	20,178
1903	562.2	10.0	45.1	617.3	12.3	20,115	416	1,712	22,243
1904	508.6	8.7	43.3	560.6	11.4	19,499	371	1,763	21,633
1905	475.7	8.1	41.3	525.1	10.7	19,193	404	1,753	21,350
1906	461.1	7.9	40.2	509.2	11.7	18,996	382	1,806	21,184
1907	457.5	8.3	36.9	502.7	12.1	19,246	432	1,847	21,525
1908	437.8	9.4	41.8	489.0	12.0	19,643	504	2,043	22,190
1909	447.3	11.7	46.2	505.2	11.7	20,324	590	2,298	23,212

Source: Natal, Blue Books and Statistical Year Books.

Appendix F. South Africa: Index of Retail Prices of Food, Fuel, and Light, 1895-1910 *(1910=1000)*

Year	Retail price index	Year	Retail price index
1895	1,044	1903	1,188
1896	1,120	1904	1,108
1897	1,128	1905	1,071
1898	1,159	1906	1,002
1899	1,178	1907	993
1900	1,165	1908	1,016
1901	1,314	1909	1,003
1902	1,275	1910	1,000

Source: Official Year Book of the Union of South Africa, No. 6, 1910-1922.

Appendix G. Colony of Natal: The Sequence of Prime Ministers and Colonial Treasurers under Responsible Government

First Parliament (1893-7)

1893-6   Prime minister: Sir J. Robinson
           Colonial treasurer: G. M. Sutton
1897   Prime minister: H. Escombe
           Colonial treasurer: G. M. Sutton

Second Parliament (1897-1901)

1897-9   Prime minister: Sir Henry Binns
           Colonial treasurer: W. Arbuckle
1900-1   Prime minister: Lt. Col. Sir A. H. Hime
           Colonial treasurer: W. Arbuckle

Third Parliament (1902-3)

1902-3   Prime minister: Lt. Col. Sir A. H. Hime
           Colonial treasurer: G. Payne

Fourth Parliament (1903-6)

1903   Prime minister: Lt. Col. Sir A. H. Hime
           Colonial treasurer: T. Hyslop
1903-5   Prime minister: G. M. Sutton
           Colonial treasurer: G. M. Sutton
1905-6   Prime minister: C. J. Smythe
           Colonial treasurer: T. Hyslop

Fifth Parliament (1906-10)

1906   Prime minister: C. J. Smythe
           Colonial treasurer: T. Hyslop
1906-7   Prime minister: F. R. Moor
           Colonial treasurer: E. A. Brunner
1908-10 Prime minister: F. R. Moor
           Colonial treasurer: E. A. Brunner;
           after July 13, 1908, A. T. Oliff

Bibliography

Books

Arndt, E. H. D. *Banking and Currency Development in South Africa* (*1652-1927*). Cape Town: Juta & Co., Ltd., 1928.

Brookes, E. H. *The History of Native Policy in South Africa from 1830 to the Present Day*. Cape Town: Nasionale Pers, 1924.

Brookes, E. H., and N. Hurwitz. *The Native Reserves of Natal* (*Natal Regional Survey*, Vol. VII). Cape Town, London, New York: Oxford University Press, 1957.

Bruwer, A. J. *Protection in South Africa*. Stellenbosch: Ecclesia Printing Works, 1923.

Cairncross, A. K. *Home and Foreign Investment, 1870-1913* (*Studies in Capital Accumulation*). Cambridge: Cambridge University Press, 1953.

Cambridge History of the British Empire, Vol. VIII, 2nd ed. Cambridge: Cambridge University Press, 1963.

Campbell, E. D. *The Birth and Development of the Natal Railways*. Pietermaritzburg: Shuter and Shooter, 1951.

Cana, F. K. *South Africa from the Great Trek to the Union*. London: Chapman & Hall, 1909.

Deane, P. *The Measurement of Colonial National Incomes* (National Institute of Economic and Social Research, *Occasional Papers*, XII). Cambridge: Cambridge University Press, 1948.

———. *Colonial Social Accounting*. Cambridge: Cambridge University Press, 1953.

Due, J. F. *Taxation and Economic Development in Tropical Africa*. Cambridge, Mass.: M. I. T. Press, 1963.

Egerton, H. E. *A Short History of British Colonial Policy*. London: Methuen & Co., Ltd., 1932.

Eisner, G. *Jamaica, 1830-1930: A Study in Economic Growth*. Manchester: Manchester University Press, 1961.

Emden, P. H. *Randlords*. London: Hodder & Stoughton, 1935.

Evans, M. S. *Black and White in South East Africa*. London: Longmans, Green & Co., 1916.

Eybers, G. W. *Select Constitutional Documents Illustrating South African History, 1795 to 1910*. London: George Routledge and Sons, Ltd., 1918.

Frankel, S. H. *Capital Investment in Africa*. London: Oxford University Press, 1938.

Goodfellow, D. M. *A Modern Economic History of South Africa*. London: George Routledge and Sons, Ltd., 1931.

Hattersley, A. F. *Natalians: Further Annals of Natal*. Pietermaritzburg: Shuter and Shooter, 1940.

——. *The British Settlement of Natal: A Study in Imperial Migration.* Cambridge: Cambridge University Press, 1950.

——. *Portrait of a Colony: The Story of Natal.* Cambridge: Cambridge University Press, 1940.

Hicks, U. K. *British Public Finances, Their Structure and Development, 1880-1952.* London: Oxford University Press, 1954.

Higgins, B. *Economic Development: Problems, Principles, and Policies.* London: Constable and Company, 1959.

Hurwitz, N. *Agriculture in Natal 1860 to 1950 (Natal Regional Survey, Vol. XII).* Cape Town: Oxford University Press, 1957.

Kiewiet, C. W. de. *A History of South Africa, Social and Economic.* Oxford: The Clarendon Press, 1941.

——. *The Imperial Factor in South Africa: A Study in Politics and Economics.* Cambridge: Cambridge University Press, 1937.

Knight, E. F. *South Africa after the War.* London: Longmans, Green and Co., 1903.

Knowles, L. C. A., and C. M. Knowles. *The Economic Development of the British Overseas Empire,* Vol. III. London: George Routledge and Sons, Ltd., 1936.

Kock, M. H. de. *Economic History of South Africa.* Cape Town: Juta & Co., 1924.

Krige, E. J. *The Social System of the Zulus.* Pietermaritzburg: Shuter and Shooter, 1950.

Kuper, H. *Indian People in Natal.* Pietermaritzburg: University of Natal Press, 1960.

Lovell, R. I. *The Struggle for South Africa.* New York: Macmillan, 1934.

Lucas, Sir Charles. *A Historical Geography of the British Colonies.* Oxford: The Clarendon Press, 1918.

Mann, R. J. *The Colony of Natal.* London: Jarrold & Son, 1860.

Natal Chamber of Industries. *Fifty Years of Progress: The Development of Industry in Natal, 1905-1955.* 1956.

The Natal Almanac and Yearly Register. Pietermaritzburg: P. Davis & Sons, 1862-1905.

Palmer, M. *The History of the Indians in Natal (Natal Regional Survey).* Cape Town, London, and New York: Oxford University Press, 1957.

Peace, W. *Our Colony of Natal.* London: E. Stanford, 1883.

Perham, M. *The Colonial Reckoning.* London: Collins, 1963.

Prest, A. R. *Public Finance in Underdeveloped Countries.* London: Weidenfeld and Nicolson, 1962.

Robertson, H. M. *South Africa, Political and Economic Aspects.* Durham, N. C.: Duke University Press, 1957.

Robinson, Sir John. *A Lifetime in South Africa.* London: Smith, Elder and Co., 1900.

Schumann, C. G. W. *Structural Changes and Business Cycles in South Africa 1806-1936.* London: P. S. King & Son, Ltd., 1938.

South African Native Races Committee, ed. *The Natives of South Africa: Their Economic and Social Condition.* London: John Murray, 1901.

———. *The South African Natives, Their Progress and Present Condition.* London: John Murray, 1908.

Stuart, J. *A History of the Zulu Rebellion, 1906, and of Dinizulu's Arrest, Trial, and Expatriation.* London: Macmillan and Co., Ltd., 1913.

Taxes and Fiscal Policy in Underdeveloped Countries. New York: United Nations, 1954.

Theal, G. McCall. *History and Ethnography of Africa South of the Zambezi.* London: Swan, Sonnenschein & Co., 1910.

Twentieth Century Impressions of Natal: Its People, Commerce, Industries, and Resources. Natal: Lloyd's Greater Britain Publishing Company, 1906.

United Nations, Economic Commission for Africa. *Economic Bulletin for Africa* (Addis Ababa), I (June, 1961).

Van der Poel, J. *Railway and Customs Policies in South Africa 1885-1910 (Royal Empire Society Imperial Studies, No. 8).* London: Longmans, Green and Co., 1933.

Wald, H. P. *Taxation of Agricultural Land in Underdeveloped Economies.* Cambridge, Mass.: Harvard University Press, 1959.

Walker, E. A. *A History of Southern Africa.* London: Longmans, Green and Co., 1959.

Wilmot, A. *The History of Our Own Times in South Africa.* London: Juta & Co., 1897-1899.

Worsfold, W. B. *South Africa: A Study in Colonial Administration and Development.* London: Methuen & Co., 1895.

———. *The Union of South Africa.* Boston: Little, Brown & Co., 1913.

Articles

Billington, G. C. "A Minimum System of National Accounts for Use by African Countries and Some Related Problems," in L. H. Samuels, ed., *African Studies in Income and Wealth*, published for the International Association for Research in Income and Wealth. London: Bowes and Bowes, 1963, pp. 1-51.

Botha, C. G. "The Early History of Mining in South Africa," in *Official Year Book of the Union of South Africa*, 1932-3, No. 15, pp. 28-30.

Busschau, W. J. "Some Aspects of Railway Development in Natal," *South African Journal of Economics*, I (Dec., 1933), 405-420.

Farnie, D. A. "The Mineral Revolution in South Africa," *South African Journal of Economics*, XXIV (June, 1956), 125-134.

Gilbert, D. W. "The Economic Effects of the Gold Discoveries upon South Africa 1886-1910," *The Quarterly Journal of Economics*, XLVII (Aug., 1933), 553-597.

Lehfeldt, R. A. "Railway Policy in South Africa," *Proceedings of the Economic Society of South Africa,* July, 1925.

Leverton, B. J. T. "The Natal Cotton Industry: A Study in Failure, 1845-1875," *Communications of the University of South Africa.* Pretoria, 1963.

Robertson, H. M. "150 Years of Economic Contact between White and Black," *South Africa Journal of Economics,* II (Dec., 1934), 403-425; III (March, 1935), 3-25.

Shannon, H. A. "Evolution of the Colonial Sterling Exchange Standard," *International Monetary Fund Staff Papers,* I (April, 1951), 334-354.

Verburgh, C. "The Competition of South African Harbours and Lourenço Marques for the Ocean-borne Imports of the Transvaal: 'Competitive Areas,'" *The South African Journal of Economics,* XXV (Dec., 1957), 264-274.

Public Records

Colony of Natal
    Acts of the Parliament of the Colony of Natal
    Annual Reports of Auditor-General
    Annual Reports of Collector of Customs
    Annual Reports of Colonial Treasurer's Department
    Annual Reports of Controller of Natal Government Savings Bank
    Annual Reports of General Manager of Natal Government Railways
    Annual Reports of Protector of Indian Immigrants
    Annual Reports of Public Accounts Committees
    Annual Reports of Resident Magistrates
    Annual Reports of the Secretary, Minister of Agriculture
    Annual Reports of the Secretary, Natal Harbor Department
    Blue Books, 1850-1892/3
    Census Report, 1891
    Census Report, 1904
    Financial Instructions Regulating the Mode of Keeping and Rendering the Accounts of Receipts and Expenditure, 1898
    First Report of the Departmental Committee on Financial Instructions, 1903
    Government Gazette
    Government House Records
    Laws of the Colony of Natal
    Legislative Assembly Debates
    Legislative Council Debates
    Native Affairs Department Records
    Ordinances, Proclamations, etc., relating to the Colony of Natal,

1836-1855, compiled by W. J. D. Moodie, Pietermaritzburg, 1856

Ordinances, Laws and Proclamations of Natal, 1843-1889, compiled and edited by C. F. Cadiz, R. Lyon, and W. Broome, Pietermaritzburg, 1879-1890

Report of the Colonial Stores Commission, 1899

Report of Customs Tariff Enquiry Commission, 1908

Report and Evidence of the Native Affairs Commission, 1907

Report of Industries and Tariff Revision Commission, 1906

Report of the Mining Industry of Natal, 1906

Report upon the System of Keeping the Public Accounts in the Colony of Natal, No. 7, 1896

Sessional Papers of the Legislative Council

Sessional Papers of the Legislative Assembly

Statistical Year Books, 1893/4-1909

Statutes of Natal, 1845-1899, compiled by R. L. Hitchins and G. W. Sweeney, Pietermaritzburg, 1900-1902

Colony of the Cape of Good Hope

Government Gazette

Blue Books

Union of South Africa

Official Year Book of the Union of South Africa, No. 6, 1923, No. 29, 1956-7

Finance Accounts, Appropriation Accounts, Loan Funds and Miscellaneous Funds, with the Report of the Controller and Auditor General of the Union (Natal), 1911

Reports of the Controller and Auditor-General on the Balances Brought into the Union by the colonies of the Cape of Good Hope, Transvaal, Natal, and the Orange Free State, Union Government, No. 4, 1912

Other

Report of the South African Native Affairs Commission, 1903-5

Statistical Bureau, South African Customs Union (Cape Town)

Annual Statements of the Trade and Shipping of the Colonies Forming the South African Customs Union, 1906-9

Unpublished Materials

Axelson, C. E. "The History of Taxation in Natal Prior to Union." Master's thesis, University of South Africa, 1936.

Breanach, J. J. "The Development of the Public Finances of the South African Republic to 1877, and of the Antecedent Voortrekker Communities of Natal, Potchefstroom and Ohrigstad." Master's thesis, University of South Africa, 1929.

Busschau, W. J. "The Development of the Natal Government Railways: An Economic Survey and Critique." Master's thesis, University of South Africa, 1932.

Emanuelson, O. E. "A History of Native Education in Natal between 1833 and 1927." Master's thesis, University of South Africa, 1932.

Newspapers

The Natal Advertiser
The Natal Mercury
The Natal Witness

Index

accounts: public, 49; system of, 123, 124
administration, costs of, 94
administration of fiscal system, *see* fiscal system
advances, 92
African Banking Corporation, 24
Africans, 4, 4t, 6, 28n, 32, 34, 150; attitude toward education, 167; colonists' attitude toward, 179; complaints by, 171; and forced labor, 147-149, 148t; high taxes on, 157; hut tax on, 77, 79; land cultivated by, 8t; land occupation by, 81n, 143; overcrowding of, 175; per capita income, 27; poll tax on, 76; and responsible government, 43; restrictions on, 39; special land tax on, 152; taxpaying capacity of, 114; tribal, 31; urbanized, 5; voting rights of, 40; welfare of, 43
agent-general, 85, 103, 127, 127n, 170
agricultural development, *see* economic development
Agricultural Development Act (1904), 168
agricultural extension, 163, 165, 168
agriculture, 5t, 6, 7-9, 12, 26, 72, 85, 167-169, 175, 183, 184-189; African, 175, 177, 178; development of, 161, 163, 168; European, 186; expenditure on, 89t, 109t; and Government Laboratory, 91; and gross geographical product, 197t; growth of, 137; incomes from, 198t; measures to develop, 113, 178; and transport, 192
Alfred County, 3
Anglo-Boer war, 10, 13, 58, 63, 100, 107, 157; economic effects of, 54; expenditure caused by, 86
animal husbandry, 8
animal products, 187-189
appropriation accounts, 124
Arbuckle, W., 205
arms and ammunitions sales, 34n
Arndt, E. H. D., 24n
attorney-general, 85
auction duties, 32
auditor-general, 34, 85, 91n, 112, 119, 123, 124, 128
average gross percentage error of estimation, 121
average net percentage error of estimation, 121n
Axelson, C. E., 32n, 33n, 139n, 144n, 146n, 147, 149n

balance of payments, 17, 114, 115
balance of trade, 17, 136, 137
balanced growth, 137
Bambata Rebellion (1906), 56n, 77-78, 79, 100, 107, 109t
Bank of Africa, 24
Bank of England, 54, 100, 126
banking, 23-25, 26
Bantu, 29
Basutoland, 68
Billington, G. C., 184n, 195n
Binns, Henry, member of Legislative Council, 164, 205
Bloemfontein, 68, 73
Board of Public Commissioners, *see* public debt, commissioners
Boers, 5
bonds, *see* colonial bonds
borrowing powers, 45, 49
bounty: on imports of flour, 69, 74; on imports of sugar, 74; *see also* subsidies and subsidization